D0479547

FRIDA KAHLO

ALSO BY HAYDEN HERRERA

————————✖————————

Frida: A Biography of Frida Kahlo

Mary Frank

Matisse

FRIDA KAHLO

THE PAINTINGS

Hayden Herrera

HarperPerennial

A Division of HarperCollins*Publishers*

A hardcover edition of this book was published in 1991 by
HarperCollins Publishers.

FRIDA KAHLO: THE PAINTINGS. Copyright © 1991 by Hayden Herrera. All
rights reserved. Printed in Japan by Dai Nippon. No part of this book
may be used or reproduced in any manner whatsoever without written
permission except in the case of brief quotations embodied in critical
articles and reviews. For information address HarperCollins Publishers,
Inc., 10 East 53rd Street, New York, NY 10022.

HarperCollins books may be purchased for educational, business, or
sales promotional use. For information please write: Special Markets
Department, HarperCollins Publishers, Inc., 10 East 53rd Street,
New York, NY 10022.

First HarperPerennial edition published 1993.

DESIGNED BY JOEL AVIROM
TITLE PAGE PATTERN BY JIM COZZA

The Library of Congress has catalogued the hardcover edition as follows:

Herrera, Hayden.
Frida Kahlo : the paintings / by Hayden Herrera. — 1st ed.
p.   cm.
Includes index.
ISBN 0-06-016699-1
1. Kahlo, Frida—Self-portraits.   2. Kahlo, Frida—Criticism and
interpretation.   I. Title.
ND1329.K33H4   1991
759.972—dc20   90-56348

ISBN 0-06-092319-9 (pbk.)
93 94 95 96 97 CG/DN 10 9 8 7 6 5 4 3 2 1

TO MY MOTHER

CONTENTS

Frida Kahlo:
The Paintings
3

Notes
229

List of Illustrations
237

Selected Bibliography
251

Index
253

FRIDA KAHLO

The intensity of Frida Kahlo's paintings prompted a London critic to warn that her exhibition's walls should be covered with asbestos. The Surrealist poet and essayist André Breton called her art "a ribbon around a bomb."[1] The palpable energy that radiates from Kahlo's small, meticulously observed self-portraits comes from the ferocity of her dialogue with herself and the directness with which she told her story. She painted herself cracked open, weeping beside her extracted heart, hemorrhaging during a miscarriage, anesthetized on a hospital trolley, sleeping with a skeleton, and always—even when she appears beside her pets or her husband, the muralist Diego Rivera—she looks fearfully alone.

With her carnal lips, surmounted by a slight mustache, and her obsidian-dark eyes slanted upward beneath eyebrows that join like outstretched bird's wings, Frida Kahlo was bewitching, almost beautiful. Her gaze bores into us from portrait after portrait. It is disconcerting: she seems to want something from us. There is a peculiar urgency about her desire to be seen and known.

"I paint self-portraits because I am so often alone," Frida Kahlo once said, "because I am the person I know best."[2] She had time to know herself: in 1925, when she was eighteen, a trolley plowed into the bus she was riding home from school, leaving her a partial invalid for life. While recuperating she began to paint. Her first *Self-Portrait,* 1926, reveals that, from the beginning, painting the image she saw in the mirror was both a self-exploration and a plea for attention. This double dialogue continued for the next twenty-eight

OPPOSITE:
**Self-Portrait
as a Tehuana,**
1943.

years, during which time Kahlo produced some of the most extraordinarily personal and original imagery of the twentieth century.

In her own direct and typically self-debunking manner, Frida Kahlo explained: "I paint my own reality. The only thing that I know is that I paint because I need to, and I paint whatever passes through my head without any other consideration."[3] Because she pierced through events and appearances to seize the deepest layers of that reality, each of us feels directly and specifically addressed by her self-portraits. The fierce candor with which she recorded her loves, losses, illnesses, her childlessness, and her abiding passion for her husband was recognized by Rivera. "Frida," he said, "is the only example in the history of art of an artist who tore open her chest and heart to reveal the biological truth of her feelings . . . a superior painter and the greatest proof of the renaissance of the art of Mexico."[4]

Frida Kahlo's paintings are filled with contradictions. There is the tension created by Kahlo's festive, becostumed exterior and her anguished interior. There is the split between her mask of control and the turmoil that thrashed inside her head. Even as she presented herself as a heroine, she insisted that we know her vulnerability. And while she was compelled to see herself and to be truly seen, she hid behind the mythic creature she invented to help her withstand life's blows. For Kahlo, painting self-portraits was a form of both psychological surgery and denial. By projecting her pain out onto an alternate Frida, she not only confronted and confirmed her embattled reality, she also exorcised pain. Giving and withholding, Kahlo imploded emotion into her self-portraits: they were not just a means to communicate feeling, but a device to keep feeling in check. Thus, while her paintings draw us into her power, they also frustrate. They are steely in their distance and obdurate in their silence. The some two hundred works that she produced between 1926, when she began painting, and her death in 1954, at the age of forty-seven, force us to come face to face with Frida, both the legend and the reality, and through her to come face to face with unexplored parts of ourselves.

Frida Kahlo's art revolved around her life, and her life revolved around one place. She was born and died in the "Blue House" at 247 Londres Street in Coyoacán. Letters written during sojourns in the United States and Paris always speak of her longing to return to her barrio of Coyoacán, once a residential suburb, now part of greater

FRIDA
KAHLO
—◾—
4

OPPOSITE:
**Self-Portrait
with Monkey,**
1938.

ABOVE: **The Blue House in Coyoacán, where Frida Kahlo was born and died; now the Frida Kahlo Museum.**

RIGHT: **Frida and her younger sister, Cristina, at the Blue House, seated on the patio wall, c. 1911. Family members include Frida's mother (second from the right) and her grandmother (fourth from the left).**

Mexico City. On her house's cobalt blue facade the words "Museo Frida Kahlo" are now inscribed in large red letters. The entrance is guarded by a pair of giant papier-mâché Judas figures, designed to be exploded on the Saturday before Easter. Passing them, one enters one of the most fascinating places in Mexico—a woman's home with all her paintings and possessions turned into a museum.

Frida Kahlo's palette and brushes lie on her worktable as if she had just put them down. There, near Diego Rivera's bed, are his Stetson hat, his voluminous overalls, and his huge black miner's shoes. The house is full of pre-Columbian and popular art, which the Riveras avidly collected. Grotesque masks, folkloric paintings, pottery, and small, primitive ex-voto paintings called *retablos* line the walls. Glass cases display Tlatilco idols and Kahlo's exotic jewelry. Frida's enormous collection of toys, dolls, and other curios crowds her bedroom shelves.

One case contains a ruffled skirt and embroidered blouse from the Isthmus of Tehuantepec. This was the costume that she habitually wore to please her husband, to assert her Mexican identity, and to hide the slight limp caused by her injured right leg. When Frida Kahlo walked through the streets of San Francisco and Detroit, her floor-length skirts and her beribboned head held high at the end of an elegant neck stopped passersby in their tracks. In New York, schoolboys followed her, shouting "Where's the circus?"[5] And in Paris, Elsa Schiaparelli was so taken with her indigenous costumes that she designed a *robe Madame Rivera*.[6] Frida loved the attention. Her self-creation as a colorful personality made her the perfect foil for her elephantine husband, whom she called "frog-toad" and who loved the attention as well.

Painted on the walls of the Blue House's corner bedroom are the words "Here Frida Kahlo was born on July 7, 1910." Outside, a patio wall declares, "Frida and Diego lived in this house, 1929–1954." Neither statement is true. Frida's birth certificate reveals that she was born on July 6, 1907 at eight-thirty in the morning and that she was named Magdalena Carmen Frida Kahlo y Calderón. Around 1922, when she entered the National Preparatory School, she changed her age, probably because she did not want her classmates and her boyfriend to know that she was older than they were. (A bout with polio at the age of seven may have held her back in school.) Perhaps she chose 1910 as her birth date because that was the year of the outbreak of the Mexican Revolution. Outspoken in her commitment to the ideals of that long and bloody struggle, Frida expressed her ties to what she called *la raza,* or the people, not only in her art but in her dress, her behavior, and the decoration of her home.

Nor did Frida and Diego live in the Coyoacán house during all the years stated on the patio wall. When they were first married, they lived in Rivera's apartment in the center of Mexico City, then in Cuernavaca, and then in the United States, where Rivera was commissioned to paint murals between 1930 and 1933. After returning to Mexico they took up residence in two International Style houses built for them in San Angel—a large pink cube for Rivera and a small blue one for Frida, the two houses linked by a bridge. Friends remember that when Frida was angry, she would simply lock her doors, and Rivera would lumber back and forth from the bridge to the front door until she relented and let him in. In 1939, when Rivera divorced her, Frida returned to her childhood home, which Rivera had bought from her parents years before. After their remarriage in 1940, she continued to live in Coyoacán, and he lived with her when he wanted to, keeping the San Angel houses as his studio.

My Birth, *1932.*

In 1932, when Frida embarked on the project of making a painting of every year of her life, she began at the beginning, depicting, as she put it, "how I imagined I was born."[7] *My Birth* is an odd nativity: none of the three figures in it is alive. A frighteningly large head, identified by its joined eyebrows as Frida, emerges from the mother's womb. The half-born baby drooping into a puddle of blood refers to the child that Frida had just lost in a miscarriage, which made her wish she too were dead.[8] A sheet that shrouds the mother from the waist up makes her spread legs seem all the more naked. "My head is covered," Frida told a friend, "because, coincidentally with the painting of the picture, my mother died."[9]

"My head," Frida said, indicating that the dead woman is herself as well as her mother. Thus, in *My Birth* Frida not only is born but gives birth to herself. A close friend, the photographer Lola Alvarez Bravo, remarked, "Frida is the only person I know who, by their own will, created their own life. She is the only person who gave birth to herself."[10] Years later, Frida wrote in her diary next to several small self-portraits: "The one who gave birth to herself . . . who wrote the most wonderful poem of her life."[11] And it is true that Frida's own, shockingly unsqueamish artistic vision was born when the pain of miscarriage made art more central than ever to her battle for survival.

In the place of the dead mother's hidden head, Frida painted an icon that does not bode well for the child's future: the weeping Virgin of Sorrows pierced by daggers. Frida recalled that she included the Virgin as "part of a memory image, not for symbolic reasons."[12] Indeed, this image is precisely the kind of painting her devoutly Catholic mother might well have hung on her bedroom wall. The bed, said Frida, was the actual bed in which she and her younger sister, Cristina, were born. Pastel walls and the pillow's pink lace trim must be childhood memories too. They form an ironic contrast to the grisly scene.

Three heads—the Virgin's, the mother's, and the child's—are lined up on the painting's central vertical axis. All three figures are locked into place by horizontals and orthogonals whose rigid geometry underscores *My Birth*'s horrific stasis. Forced to bear witness from the obstetrician's vantage point, the viewer feels immobilized, for the bed's legs reach down to the top of a scroll unfurled across the sheet-metal panel's lower edge, leaving no place to step.

FRIDA KAHLO

9

Frida in 1937.

The goddess Tlazolteolt in the act of childbirth. Aztec, early sixteenth century.

Frida after the death of her mother, October 16, 1932. Photograph by her father, Guillermo Kahlo.

The Mater Dolorosa looks on, but she cannot save the situation. Frida never filled in the scroll that turns *My Birth* into a *retablo*—a votive painting, usually on a small sheet of tin, that depicts a person saved from disaster together with the holy agent of salvation. The scrolls of *retablos* are inscribed with thanks to the Virgin or a saint and with information about the miracle. In *My Birth* no words were necessary. There was no salvation; the drama of this double death is brutally clear.

Rivera compared the frankness of his wife's birth scene with a famous Aztec sculpture of parturition in which a full-grown man's head emerges from between the legs of a woman whose face is set in a grimace of pain. Frida was, Rivera said, "The only human force, since the extraordinary Aztec master who sculpted in black basalt, that has given plastic form to the real act of birth . . . the only woman who has expressed in her art the feelings, functions, and creative power of woman."[13]

Frida continued the "wonderful poem of her life" with *My Nurse and I,* 1937, a painting she rightly judged to be one of her best. Here she suckles in her dark Indian nurse's arms. Because it was the adult Frida who had the memory, the baby has an adult head, and because she could not remember her wet nurse's features, she covered her face with a pre-Columbian mask.[14]

Like *My Birth, My Nurse and I* could be a double self-portrait: the nurse has loose, stringy black hair like Frida's, and inscribed on her Teotihuacán mask are eyebrows that join. Thus, as in several later paintings, the weak, vulnerable half of Frida is nurtured by the strong, life-sustaining aspect of herself. Usually the strong side of Frida's duality is her Indian half; the pale-skinned Frida is more vulnerable. "I came out looking like such a little girl and she so strong and so saturated with providence, that it made me long to sleep."[15] In *My Birth* Frida is born from herself; in *My Nurse and I* she suckles herself. Two years later, in *The Two Fridas,* she would befriend herself; and later, in *Tree of Hope,* 1946, she would save herself. Frida's was a self-enclosed world. She was her beginning and her end, her creator, her nurturer and her destroyer. The small formats and the often hemmed-in spaces of her self-portraits underscore this closure.

Frida described her nurse as "saturated with providence." The nurse does embody a powerful feeling of fatalism. But it is a cruel fatalism, not a protective one, and to convey it, Frida borrowed from

My Nurse and I, *1937.*

two aspects of her heritage, the pre-Hispanic and the Christian. The black stone funerary mask, with its open mouth set in a stylized scream, is both savage and sorrowing. The wet nurse does not embrace or cuddle Frida: she displays her. Frida looks like a sacrificial offering.

That the sacrifice might also have Christian overtones is suggested by the similarity of the posture of Frida and her nurse to that of the Madonna and Child. Indeed, the painting makes a clear reference to the Madonna Caritas motif, in which, even as the Virgin suckles the Christ Child, she has foreknowledge of his crucifixion. Taking the Christian symbolism one step further, some viewers have seen *My Nurse and I* as a pagan Pietà. Frida herself acknowledged that the painting had some Christian symbolism when she said that from her nurse's nipples "milk falls as from the sky," and that the raindrops are "milk from the Virgin."[16] That was how her Indian nurse had explained the phenomenon of rain. Like *My Birth*, *My Nurse and I* has an unfurled blank scroll along its lower edge, indicating that Frida thought of it as a *retablo*. Here the holy image is the Indian nurse, who doubles as the Virgin. But, from the baby's bleak, piercing stare we know that Frida will not be saved.

There is another, more positive message in *My Nurse and I*. By painting herself as an infant with an adult head, Frida wanted, she said, to show the "continuity of life." The painting declares Frida's faith in her Indian ancestry, which she imbibes with her nurse's milk. The nurse is also an embodiment of the Mexican earth. The ducts and glands of her left breast are revealed as if in X-ray vision, just like the breast in Rivera's 1933 Rockefeller Center mural, and they recall also the plant patterns that decorate breasts in pre-Columbian sculptures from Jalisco. To show that nature and human beings are bound together in the same cycles, Frida enlarged one leaf in the wall of jungle foliage that forms the painting's background and gave it engorged, milk-white veins like those of the lactating nurse.[17] Just as Frida is nourished by her nurse's plantlike breast, so in the jungle a praying mantis and a caterpillar metamorphosing into a butterfly are nourished by leaves.

In *My Nurse and I*, Frida transformed the stereotypical mother and child image into an expression of loss and separation. "My mother could not suckle me because eleven months after I was born my sister Cristina was born. I was fed by a nana whose breasts they washed every time I was going to suck them.''[18] Frida lost first her mother and then her nurse, for the "nana" was fired when it was discovered that she was drinking alcohol.

All the fear and abandonment that Frida must have felt when her younger sister replaced her in her mother's arms comes out in *My Nurse and I*. Frida does not look like a satiated infant being lulled to sleep. On the contrary, the nurse's embrace is symbolic, not physical. Rather than looking tenderly down at the child, she stares straight ahead. For her part, Frida does not burrow into her nurse's bosom like a normal suckling child. She faces outward, and though milk drips into her mouth, she does not close her lips around the nipple. Her mouth is open, suggesting a spiritual ravenousness that would characterize Frida later in life. And, like the mouth on the nurse's mask, she shows her teeth—a disconcerting detail in a nursing scene.

ABOVE: *Frida's mother, Matilde Calderón, c. 1900.*

LEFT: *Frida, c. 1913* (front left) *with her sisters Matilde* (back left) *and Adriana* (front right) *and two cousins and an uncle.*

It is clear from this lack of bodily empathy that the wet nurse was no substitute for Frida's natural mother. In an article entitled "Frida Kahlo's Loneliness," the child psychiatrist Salomon Grimberg hypothesizes that because her mother fell ill soon after she was born, Frida never bonded with her. As a result, she could not fully separate from her mother, and she was plagued by an insatiable longing for connectedness. All through her adult life Frida would, by a thousand different means, including painting, flee from loneliness by attempting "to re-create the nurturing experience she had missed in childhood."[19]

Frida's longing to be embraced by a mother transformed itself into an intense need to bind herself to people, objects, plants, animals, even to painting and politics. Part of Rivera's attraction was his female aspect—Frida loved, she said, "the sensitivity of his wonderful breasts."[20] One of the most moving expressions of Frida's need is *Doña Rosita Morillo,* a 1944 portrait of the mother of her friend and chief patron, Eduardo Morillo Safa. Perhaps because when Frida painted portraits the projection of feeling and fantasy was inhibited by her concern with creating a likeness, her portraits are usually less intense and less original than her self-portraits. *Doña Rosita Morillo* is an exception. With the extremely refined realism that Frida mastered during the 1940s, she painted the kindly, wise grandmother with such minute detail that we feel we could reach out and touch her. Doña Rosita is what Frida's nurse is not—she is so strong and "saturated with providence" that she becomes an icon of comfort like van Gogh's *La Berceuse.* As in van Gogh's painting, a direct physical link connects viewer and subject. The bosomy maternal figure in *La Berceuse* holds a rope that leads out of the painting to an unseen cradle (in our space) that she is rocking. In Frida's portrait a length of red wool from Doña Rosita's knitting connects the woman to the viewer and, of course, to Frida.

In another autobiographical painting, *My Grandparents, My Parents, and I,* 1936, Frida portrayed herself as a sturdy, self-possessed two-year-old standing in the patio of her childhood home. With all the self-centeredness of a child's vision, she is the most important figure in her family tree. She made her house tiny compared to herself, and the neighboring houses are even smaller: from the standpoint of the enclosed world of Frida's patio, the rest of Mexico is a wilderness. The charming naïveté of the painting's style is in perfect

OPPOSITE: **Doña Rosita Morillo,** *1944.*

*BELOW: **The patio of the Blue House, 1933. Photograph by Guillermo Kahlo.***

ABOVE: *Wedding photograph of Guillermo Kahlo and Matilde Calderón, 1898.*

CENTER: *Sketch for* My Grandparents, My Parents, and I, *1936.*

RIGHT: *Frida at about two, c. 1909.*

accord with the child's-eye view. Every detail is in the right place, and so is Frida—in the center.

Frida holds the loop of a red ribbon that is her bloodline and that supports her family tree as easily as if it were the string of a balloon. One wonders, why did she loop the ribbon, and did she have a reason for placing the loop at the exact spot where her father's and mother's bodies overlap? One hint might be the fetus seen in X-ray vision on the skirt of her mother's wedding dress. This must be Frida before she was born. The red loop could be a reference to her mother's sex, for just below the fetus Frida painted her own conception. A school of sperm appears to have swum through the loop on the way to an egg that has already been fertilized by the fittest competitor. To Frida her conception was an event so important that nature had to respond: next to the embryo a red cactus flower opens to a stream of windblown pollen.

My Grandparents, My Parents, and I, *1936.*

Nestled in cloud puffs (a delightfully kitsch device borrowed from her parents' wedding photograph or from religious paintings), Frida's grandparents are identified as Mexican or German by their respective placement above the dry earth or over the sea. Frida's parents, also based on their wedding photograph, loom large above her. Frida said that she looked like both her parents: "I have my father's eyes and my mother's body."[21] She was lucky: her father's large eyes gleamed intelligence, and her wasp-waisted mother was beautifully formed. Frida placed herself directly in front of her father. It was with him that she most identified as a child.

The son of Hungarian Jews who lived in Baden-Baden, Germany, Guillermo Kahlo emigrated to Mexico in 1891 at the age of nineteen, and in the first decade of this century became one of Mexico's foremost photographers. For the government of the dictator Porfirio Díaz he recorded architectural monuments of the pre-Hispanic and colonial eras. His advertisement announced that he was a "specialist in landscapes, buildings, interiors, factories, etc.," and that he took "photographs on order, be it in the City, be it in any other point of the Republic."[22] He also took portraits, but preferred buildings because, he said, he didn't want to improve what God had made ugly.[23]

Soon after his first wife died giving birth to his second daughter, Kahlo married Matilde Calderón, a Mexican of mixed Indian and Spanish ancestry. "My mother was a great friend for me," Frida recalled, "but she could never make us participate in the religion thing. My mother was hysterical about religion. We had to pray before meals. While others concentrated on their inner selves, Cristi and I would look at each other, forcing ourselves not to laugh." Although she doted on her mother, Frida was critical. Matilde Calderón was, she said, "like a little bell from Oaxaca. . . . She did not know how to read or write; she only knew how to count money." The time her mother drowned a litter of rats stuck in Frida's mind: "Maybe she was cruel because she was not in love with my father."[24]

Frida described her taciturn, eccentric father as "very interesting, and he moved in an elegant way when he walked. Tranquil, hard working, brave, he had few friends."[25] He did have a special love for his fifth child. "Frida is the most intelligent of my daughters," he would say. "She is the most like me."[26] Having no son, and recognizing in Frida his own intellectual independence and curiosity, he loaned her books and took her for walks in nearby parks, where she

Frida's father, Guillermo Kahlo. Self-portrait, c. 1907.

collected insects and plants to examine under his microscope.

Kahlo also taught his daughter to use a camera, to develop film, and to use fine-pointed brushes to retouch and color photographs. Working as his studio assistant, she learned to be meticulous and methodical and to pay attention to the most minute details. These lessons served her well when she became a painter; with her fine sable brushes, she set down her image stroke by tiny stroke until it covered the whole panel. Watching the way Frida started in the upper left corner of her panel and worked her way across, her friend (and Rivera's assistant) Lucienne Bloch compared Frida's method to that of a mural painter.[27] Frida's method was also like the retouching and coloring of photographs in that she seemed to be filling in an image that preexisted in her mind.

Guillermo Kahlo was an amateur painter, and Frida must have been entranced to watch him paint his highly realistic candy-box style of watercolors of flowers, fruit, and farm scenes. But it was his portrait photographs and his interest in pre-Columbian art that affected her the most. Years later she told a friend that while her father made photographs for calendars, she painted the calendars of her inner vision.[28] Frida is thus yet another example of a woman painter whose artist father offered not only an example but also some early training.[29]

When Frida had polio, at the age of seven, Herr Kahlo, as she called him, nursed her back to health and encouraged her to take up various sports that were unusual for a Mexican girl of that time. His solicitousness may have provided Frida with a lesson in the power of a sick person to attract attention and to control other people's behavior. Later in life Frida exaggerated the suffering caused by her childhood disease. She said she had spent nine months confined to her room with polio. "It all began with a horrible pain in my right leg from the muscle downward. They washed my little leg in a small tub with walnut water and small hot towels."[30] In fact, the medical record she gave to a doctor in 1946 says that during her illness she led a normal life, had no pain, and could participate in sports. She told the doctor that after she hit her right foot against a tree, her leg turned out and became slightly thinner and shorter. Doctors diagnosed poliomyelitis. The treatment was sunbaths and calcium.[31]

Although Frida knew her father adored her, he was, she said, "a kind of fearful mystery, for whom she also had pity, for Guillermo

Portrait of Don Guillermo Kahlo, *1951.*

Kahlo suffered from epilepsy, and when his attacks came on, Frida would be hustled out of the way and nothing would be explained."[32] When she was old enough, she accompanied him on photography outings. "His temperament was such that it was difficult to believe that he had epilepsy. But many times when he went walking with his camera on his shoulder and me by the hand, he would suddenly fall. I learned to help him during his attacks in the middle of the street. On the one hand, I would make sure that he immediately breathed alcohol or ether, and on the other, I watched so that his camera would not be stolen."[33] That her father had health problems of his own must have made Frida's childhood illness more acceptable—or even admirable—to her. In her diary she wrote: "My childhood was marvelous, because, although my father was a sick man (he had vertigos every month and a half), he was an immense example to me of tenderness, of work (photographer and also painter) and above all of understanding for all my problems."

In 1951, ten years after her father's death, Frida painted his portrait based on a photograph that he took of himself and that he gave to each of his daughters, inscribing each copy with these words: "Every now and then remember the affection your father has always

ABOVE: *Guillermo Kahlo. Self-portrait, 1925.*

LEFT: *Frida painting her father's portrait, 1951.*

*Frida in her garden
with her pet* itzcuintli
dogs, c. 1945.

had for you. Guillermo Kahlo 1925." The photograph, like her father's portrait and like many of her paintings, was a kind of memento, a way of conveying and securing attachment. One year after she received her father's gift, Frida made a similar kind of gesture when she painted her first self-portrait and gave it to her boyfriend in the hopes that he would not forget her.

The sober brown tonality of Frida's portrait of her father suits his austere nature, while also recalling early sepia-toned portrait photographs. Guillermo Kahlo's brow is furrowed, and his gaze has an unsettling intensity that was to reappear in many of his daughter's self-portraits. His stiff, frontal pose is typical of his own formal portraits; indeed, Kahlo's studio portraits had a tremendous influence on the way Frida positioned her subjects in space. Her figures (usually herself) keep still as if they were posing for the camera, and they often seem to be set in front of space, not in it. Perhaps the peculiar schism between Frida and her setting in her self-portraits has its origin in the way her father placed sitters in front of fake backgrounds or next to luxurious pieces of furniture that he kept in his studio as props. Naturally the split between Frida and her surroundings also came from the fact that Frida's model was her mirror image. When she painted self-portraits, she concentrated on details of physiognomy and dress, ignoring the actual surroundings that she saw in the glass and substituting a symbolic space that she could never truly inhabit.

In her 1951 portrait, Guillermo Kahlo's shiny overly large eyes glance to his left just like the "eye" of his camera beside him. Their roundness is echoed also in his buttons (Frida put in more buttons than were shown in the photograph) and in a series of magnified cells or eggs that float in the background. Surrounding the cells/eggs are swarms of dark marks that suggest sperm and that give the portrait's background a van Gogh–like agitation. As similar marks create microscopic organisms in the sketch for *My Grandparents, My Parents, and I*, in that painting, Frida may have been referring to her genesis, or she may have been making an analogy between sexual and artistic fecundity.

As if in answer to the inscribed panel along the lower edge of the photograph her father gave her in 1925, Frida wrote in a scroll beneath her father's bust: "I painted my father, Wilhelm Kahlo of Hungarian-German origin, artist-photographer by profession, in character generous, intelligent and fine, valiant because he suffered for sixty years with epilepsy, but he never stopped working and he fought against Hitler. With adoration. His daughter Frida Kahlo."

In Frida's portrait of herself at two she held the ribbon of her family tree and was protected by the Blue House's patio walls. Two years later when she painted herself at about four in *Four Inhabitants of Mexico,* she addressed not ancestral ties but her ties to her Mexican heritage, embodied in a cast of characters based on artifacts that the Riveras owned. These include a Judas, a pre-Columbian idol from Nayarit, a clay skeleton of the type that children like to dangle on the Day of the Dead, and a straw man riding a donkey.[34] Again Frida is enclosed, but this time in a larger arena—a plaza near her home in Coyoacán. This square is vaster and emptier than most Mexican plazas. It has no balloons, no bandstand, no trees, no birds, no flowers. The few tiny specks indicating people only make the plaza's de Chiricoesque emptiness more lonely. In the far distance, the buildings that rim the square—including La Rosita, a pulque bar where

Frida and her students painted murals in the 1940s and 1950s—look desolate. The plaza is empty, Frida said, "because too much revolution has left Mexico empty."[35] Like *My Nurse and I, Four Inhabitants of Mexico* is a somewhat ambivalent celebration of her Mexican roots, for Frida, rather than ignoring the sorrows of her native land, identifies them with her own.

Sitting on the ground sucking her middle finger and clutching her skirt, Frida looks like a child feeling lost because her mother has left her alone. She stares in wonder at the pregnant clay idol; the skeleton, too, is in her line of vision. The idol, with her broken and repaired head, represents Mexico's past. Since the fronts of her feet are missing, we know she also stands for Frida, who had a number of foot operations in the 1930s, one of which (in 1934) involved the amputation of parts of the toes of her right foot. Despite the amplitude of the idol, this mother figure is no more comforting than the nurse in *My Nurse and I.* Indeed, none of the four inhabitants of Mexico takes any notice of Frida. She is connected to them only by the alignment of her shadow with theirs. The square's huge emptiness and the feeling of estrangement must reflect the child's vision. *Four Inhabitants of Mexico* is like a bad dream.

The menace of the Judas is made real by a network of fuses that covers him from head to foot. To Frida, however, he was a humorous figure: "It is burnt up," she said, ". . . it makes noise, it is beautiful and because it goes to pieces it has color and form."[36] The Judas is the stereotypical macho, the opposite of the passive pregnant female. His shadow moves between the pregnant idol's legs and lies on the earth next to hers, linking them as a couple. His girth and his blue overalls identify him with Diego, who at one point kept a nearly identical Judas next to his easel. These two "inhabitants" provide a kind of make-believe family for the child Frida, but they do not lessen her isolation.

The skeleton is a frequent player in the unfolding drama of Frida's art, for death was ever present within her. Frida said this one was "very gay, a joke," but it wouldn't have been funny to a child. Behind the skeleton, the straw man and his burro capture the fragility and pathos of Mexican life. Frida painted him, she said, "because he is weak, and at the same time has such elegance and is so easy to destroy."[37] Made of papier-mâché, straw, and clay, the four inhabitants of Frida's Mexico are ephemeral. In *The Wounded Table* from

Four Inhabitants of Mexico, *1938.*

the following year, the adult Frida, again accompanied by these artifacts, flaunts both her vulnerability and her *Mexicanidad* (Mexicanism), thus becoming the fifth inhabitant of Mexico.

From the same year as *Four Inhabitants of Mexico* come two small paintings (one is lost but recorded in a photograph) of a girl who must be Frida, again at about four. She is wearing a skull mask and standing alone in a vast plain. In the extant version the girl holds a yellow flower that looks like the flowers Mexicans place on graves. At her feet sits another mask, this one a monster carved in wood like the masks that hang in the dining room of the Frida Kahlo Museum. Neither mask seems appropriate for this tiny girl; they accentuate her innocence and hint at the cruelty of her fate.

Also from 1938 comes *They Ask for Planes and Are Given Straw Wings,* which, according to Rivera's biographer Bertram D. Wolfe, records "the time when her parents dressed her in a white robe and wings to represent an angel (wings that caused a great unhappiness because they would not fly)."[38] Frida holds a toy version of the planes that were asked for but not received. Her useless straw wings are suspended by ribbons descending from the sky, and she is also tethered by a ribbon that winds around her skirt and ends in bows nailed to the ground. As in other paintings from this period (see, for example, *Memory,* 1937), Frida combines festive ribbons with images of helplessness and pain.

It has been suggested that the self-portrait with straw wings refers to the disappointment of the Spanish Republican Army, when its request for airplanes was not fulfilled. Indeed, Frida was at this time deeply concerned about the civil war in Spain, and she was active in helping Spanish refugees.[39] It is possible that *The Airplane Crash*, a lost painting in which dead bodies litter the ground in front of a plane's burning wreck, is Frida's version of Picasso's protest in *Guernica.* A more likely interpretation of the painting is that it recalls the year when Frida's freedom of movement was (she said) curtailed by polio; her foot operations in the 1930s would have made the memory of that childhood suffering all the more vivid.

The girl tethered to the ground and to the sky is solemn and alone, as Frida must often have been when she had polio. As a child she tried to hide her atrophied right leg with three layers of socks, but as Frida's childhood friend the painter Aurora Reyes recalled, "We were quite cruel about her leg. When she was riding her bicycle we would

Frida, c. 1910.

**Girl with
Death Mask,**
1938.

**They Ask for Planes
and Are Given Straw
Wings,** *1938.*

yell at her, *'Frida, pata de palo!'* [Frida peg leg], and she would respond furiously with lots of curses."[40] Frida's differentness accentuated her loneliness. To counter it, she became purposefully different, first a tomboy and later an exotic personality. But, even though she became extroverted, she never lost the sick child's awareness of the distance between her inner and outer worlds, and she kept her inner world as a haven and a terrain for adventure.

Around the time that she had polio, Frida invented an imaginary friend who could dance instead of limp and who kept her company when she needed her. Another aspect of herself, this friend was the beginning of the alternate Frida who appears in her self-portraits. In her diary, while explaining the origin of *The Two Fridas,* a double self-portrait from 1939, Frida described her first meeting with this imaginary companion:

> I must have been 6 years old when I experienced intensely an imaginary friendship with a little girl more or less the same age as me. On the glass window of what at that time was my room, and which gave onto Allende Street, I breathed vapor onto one of the first panes. I let out a breath and with a finger I drew a "door." . . .
>
> Full of great joy and urgency, I went out in my imagination through this "door." I crossed the whole plain that I saw in front of me until I arrived at the dairy called "Pinzón." . . . I entered by the "O" of Pinzón and I went down in great haste into the *interior of the earth,* where "my imaginary friend" was always waiting for me. I do not remember her image or her color. But I do know that she was gay—she laughed a lot. Without sounds. She was agile and she danced as if she weighed nothing at all. I followed her in all her movements and while she danced I told her my secret problems. Which ones? I do not remember. But from my voice she knew everything about me. . . . Thirty-four years have passed since I experienced this magic friendship and every time that I remember it, it revives and becomes larger and larger inside of my world.

Frida told us she drew a door on glass and went through it. Later the "door" to her imaginary world would be the mirror through which she traveled into her self. Although she carefully modeled her face to look three-dimensional, her self-portraits have an uncanny flatness. She did not paint her face as a solid volume in space but as a reflection as hard and flat as the image in the mirror that was her model.

With Cristina and childhood friend Isabel Campos, 1919.

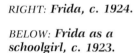

RIGHT: *Frida, c. 1924.*

BELOW: *Frida as a schoolgirl, c. 1923.*

In 1922 Frida entered the National Preparatory School, which not only offered the best education in Mexico but was also a center of ideological and political ferment in the postrevolutionary years. Its teachers were eminent, its students were the cream of Mexico's youth, and, most important for Frida, the school was caught in the crosscurrents of the nation's search for a Mexican identity. The philosophy professor Antonio Caso exhorted his students: "Turn your eyes to the soil of Mexico, to our customs and our traditions, our hopes and our wishes, to what in truth we are!"[41] The education minister José Vasconcelos declared that Mexican education should be founded on "our blood, our language and our people," and, as part of his crusade to educate Mexicans about their heritage, he hired such painters as Diego Rivera, José Clemente Orozco, and David Alfaro Siqueiros to decorate public walls—including those of the Preparatory School—with murals that glorified Mexican history and culture.

To a great extent, the values of Frida's generation were formed by this ferment. "That was a time of truth, of faith, of passion, of nobility, of progress, of celestial air and of very terrestrial steel," recalled Andrés Iduarte, a fellow Preparatory School student who became director of the National Institute of Fine Arts. "We were fortunate, together with Frida . . . our vitality coincided with that of Mexico; we grew spiritually while the country grew in the moral realm."[42]

When the fifteen-year-old Frida became one of thirty-five girls in a student body of some two thousand, she found a milieu suited to her enormous energies. From the beginning, she stood out. Her clothes were those of a German schoolgirl: white blouse, dark tie, navy blue pleated skirt, boots, a broad-brimmed black straw hat with long ribbons, and a knapsack full of private treasures. Frida was, if not exactly beautiful, arresting. Her glance was both direct and mysterious, loving and daemonic. If she fixed her eyes on you, it was hard to escape her power of enchantment.

Although she rarely studied, Frida was a brilliant student, and she chose a program to lead her to medical school. She was an avid reader, and, from the evidence of a poem entitled "Memory," published in the newspaper *Universal Ilustrado* on November 30, 1922, she was a gifted writer as well. In rough translation, her poem reads:

> *I had smiled. Nothing more. But clarity was in me and*
> *In the depth of my silence*
> *He followed me. Like my shadow, irreproachable and light.*
> *In the night he wept a song . . .*
> *the Indians withdrew, winding through the side streets*
> *of the town.*
> *After drinking mescal they went to the dance wrapped in*
> *ponchos.*
> *The music was a harp and a small guitar, and there was*
> *joy in*
> *the smiling dark-haired women*
> *In the distance, behind the city square, the river shone*
> *and it flowed like the*
> *moments of my life.*
> *He followed me.*
> *I ended up crying, forgotten in the entrance of the*
> *Parish church,*
> *protected by my silk shawl, which soaked up tears.*[43]

Preferring the company of boys, Frida joined a high-spirited and rebellious clique of seven boys and two girls known as the Cachuchas, after the caps they wore. One of the group remembered that "it was the joking attitude we had toward people and things that drew Frida to us."[44] Frida shared with her *cuates* (pals) a boyish, comradely loyalty that would characterize her friendships, and even her loves, for the rest of her life. Delighting in mischief, she became a ringleader

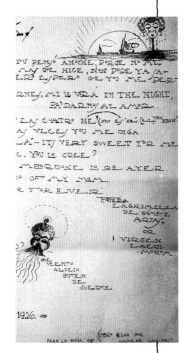

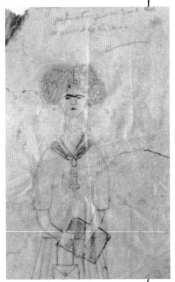

*ABOVE: **Letter to Alejandro Gómez Arias, 1926.***

*BELOW: **"Here I'm Sending You My Picture,"** c. 1922.*

in their endless pranks. One of the Cachuchas' targets was the mural painters. They set fire to wood shavings piled beneath newly built scaffolds, forcing the painters to descend and making them go to work armed with pistols.

Fat, loquacious Diego Rivera was Frida's favorite victim. After returning from fourteen years of living and working in Europe, Rivera had embarked on his first mural, an allegory entitled *Creation,* in the Preparatory School's theater. At thirty-six he was a fabulous monster. He looked like a cross between a Buddha and a frog, and he wore a Stetson hat, a gun belt, and baggy overalls. But that didn't deter women; they liked to play beauty to his beast. He attracted women also because he was a great listener (especially to women, whose way of thinking he preferred) and a charismatic storyteller, regaling his audience with tales of fighting beside Lenin and eating human flesh. The press followed him about, and the more he talked, the more fantastic his self-mythologizing became.

Naturally Frida was drawn to him, and when she took note of the succession of beautiful models that accompanied him on the scaffold, she teased him by yelling things like "Hey, Diego, here comes Nahui!" when his jealous wife, Lupe Marín, was there. Once Frida dared to inflame Lupe's jealousy herself. In his autobiography, Rivera told the story of Frida's turning up one evening and asking him, "Would it cause you any annoyance if I watched you at work?" She watched so long and so intently that Lupe Marín was enraged. Frida, Rivera recalled, "merely stiffened and returned Lupe's stare."[45]

Legend has it that Frida was infatuated with Rivera and that once when discussing her life plans with school friends she declared: "My ambition is to have a child by Diego Rivera. And I'm going to tell him someday."[46] The other girls were appalled, but Frida explained, "Diego is so gentle, so tender, so wise, so sweet. I'd bathe him and clean him. I'd really like to have a child by him."[47] Meanwhile, Frida had a boyfriend named Alejandro Gómez Arias, who was the school's most respected orator and the Cachuchas' undisputed leader. Erudite, ironic, and handsome, he attracted Frida, who grew up to love outstanding men. Her letters to him reveal her development from a spirited child into a passionate adolescent and finally into a wily and long-suffering woman. They also show her intense need to bind herself to another person by telling him every detail of her suffering—a compulsion that would later impel her long series of self-portraits.

Diego Rivera painting **Creation,** *his first mural, National Preparatory School, 1922.*

For three years Frida and Alejandro were almost inseparable. Then, on a rainy September afternoon in 1925, the bus they took home from school was smashed by a trolley. Frida recalled:

> It was a strange collision. It was not violent, but rather silent, slow and it harmed everybody, and me most of all. . . . I was an intelligent young girl but impractical, in spite of all the freedom I had won. Perhaps for this reason, I did not assess the situation nor did I guess the kind of wounds I had. The first thing that I thought of was a *balero* [Mexican toy] with pretty colors that I had bought that day and that I was carrying with me. I tried to look for it, thinking that what had happened would not have major consequences.
>
> It is a lie that one is aware of the crash, a lie that one cries. In me there were no tears. The crash bounced us forward and a handrail pierced me the way a sword pierces a bull. A man saw me having a tremendous hemorrhage. He carried me and put me on a billiard table until the Red Cross came for me.[48]

When bystanders saw Frida lying in the street after being thrown from the bus, they cried *"La bailarina! La bailarina!"* They thought she was a dancer; somehow her clothes had come off in the collision, and her blood-covered body sparkled from gold powder that a fellow passenger must have been carrying.

As soon as Alejandro was able to pull himself out from under the bus, he went to look for Frida. When he picked her up, he discovered to his horror the metal rod that had punctured her abdomen. A

Retablo *partially repainted by Frida Kahlo to show her accident. The inscription reads: "The couple Guillermo Kahlo and Matilde c. de Kahlo give thanks to the Virgin of Sorrows for having saved their daughter Frida from the accident that happened in 1925 on the corner of Cuahutemozin and Calzada de Tlalpan."*

17 de Septiembre de 1926 = FRIDA Kahlo (Accidente)

worker wearing overalls, whom Alejandro thought he recognized as an employee of the Preparatory School, said, "We have to take it out!" The man put his knee on Frida's body and pulled. Alejandro then carried the screaming and bleeding Frida to a billiard room, laid her on a table, and covered her with his coat. Her cries, he recalled, drowned out the ambulance sirens. "I thought she was going to die."

Doctors at the Red Cross Hospital thought so too. Seeing no hope for Frida, they left her alone while attending other survivors. Only after Alejandro pleaded with them did they take Frida to the operating table.

Frida's spinal column was broken in three places; her pelvis was fractured; her collarbone, two ribs, and her right leg and foot were all broken; her left shoulder was dislocated. In her medical record Frida said that the steel rod had entered a hip and come out through her vagina, which explains why she told a friend that she had lost her virginity in the accident.[49] Although she may have overdramatized the wound, just the way she exaggerated her sufferings from polio, it is likely that the association of sex with pain, seen in several of her paintings, is connected with her memory of being penetrated by the handrail.

When Frida had regained consciousness, she asked that her family be notified. Her parents were so upset that neither was able to come. "My mother was speechless for a month because of the impression it made on her," Frida remembered. "It made my father so sad that he became ill, and I could not see him for over twenty days."[50] Frida's older sister Matilde came to the rescue. "It was Matilde who lifted my spirits; she told me jokes. She was fat and ugly, but she had a great sense of humor. She made everyone in the room howl with laughter."[51]

For a month Frida lay on her back encased in a plaster cast and enclosed in a structure that looked like a sarcophagus. She wrote to Alejandro: "In this hospital death dances around my bed at night."[52] Death would continue to dance around Frida for the next twenty-nine years. Indeed, she invited it to dance, teasing and flirting with death, and keeping an eye on it so that she could hold it at bay. She dressed papier-mâché skeletons in her own clothes and hung them from her bed's canopy so that they jostled in the wind. One of her favorite possessions was a sugar skull of the type that children eat on the Day of the Dead. Frida ordered the skull to be made with her own name written in bold letters on its forehead.

Frida recovered from the accident, relapsed, and recovered again, but from 1925 on her life was a battle against slow disintegration. There were periods when she felt well and her limp was barely noticeable. And there were periods when she was either bedridden or hospitalized. She is said to have had some thirty-five operations, most of them on her spine and right foot. "She lived dying," said a friend, the writer Andrés Henestrosa.[53]

All of Frida's health problems may not have stemmed from the accident. In 1930 Frida's friend the San Francisco surgeon Dr. Leo Eloesser diagnosed a congenital deformation of her spine (scoliosis). More recently, Dr. Salomon Grimberg has argued that the deformation of Frida's spine was not congenital but rather a result of Kahlo's childhood bout with polio.[54] Years of walking on her shorter, thinner right leg, he says, could have deformed her vertebral column and pelvis. The damaged spinal column might, in turn, have injured nerves that control "motility, strength, and blood flow to the legs."

This, in turn, could have led to the trophic ulcers that Kahlo began to suffer in the 1930s or to the gangrene that eventually necessitated the amputation of her right leg.

In a recent letter to *The New York Times* ("Arts and Leisure," December 1990, p. 4) Dr. Philip Sandblom, professor emeritus of surgery at the University of Lund, in Sweden, has offered another theory. He believes that the main cause of Frida's misery was spina bifida, a congenital malformation that occurs when the lower spine does not close during fetal development and that sometimes leads to progressive trophic ulcers on the legs and feet.[55] In a letter to Dr. Eloesser written in May 1932, Frida said: "My foot continues to be sick and this is as a result of the toe that is naturally in worse condition than when you saw me since two years have already gone by. . . . In the Ford Hospital . . . I don't remember which doctor diagnosed that it was a 'trophic ulcer.' What is that? When I knew that I had such a thing in my foot, I was dumfounded." Dr. Leo Eloesser's unpublished reminiscences suggest that spina bifida was the cause of Frida's physical disability: "I doubt whether the accident was responsible. X-rays that I had taken later showed a spina bifida; her lower analgesia and anesthesia were characteristically compatible with this disorder. Her disability increased in time and various operations on her foot and leg made matters worse."[56]

Even if the accident was not the cause of what has been called Frida's "calvary," it was certainly traumatic. One friend noted that her accident turned Frida into a "mature, sad woman." Another friend said it was a rebirth.[57] In a letter to Alejandro Gómez Arias, Frida described the change:

> Why do you study so much? What secret are you looking for? Life will reveal it to you soon. I already know it all, without reading or writing. A little while ago, not much more than a few days ago, I was a child who went about in a world of colors, of hard and tangible forms. Everything was mysterious and something was hidden; guessing what it was was a game for me. If you knew how terrible it is to know suddenly, as if a bolt of lightning illuminated the earth. Now I live in a painful planet, transparent as ice; but it is as if I had learned everything at once in seconds. My friends, my companions became women slowly, I became old in instants and everything today is bland and lucid. I know that nothing lies behind; if there were something I would see it.[58]

That frozen world without "hard and tangible forms" appeared as the desolate dream landscape in the background of many paintings.

The accident and its painful aftermath made Frida into an artist. It forced her to try to find wholeness by painting self-portraits in which she turns her body inside out to chart her states of mind not in terms of action or facial expression, but in terms of things done to her body. In her paintings Frida is, like an accident victim, passive and immobilized; but when she set about painting that passive image, she was driven by an amazing force of will. Twenty-six days after the accident Frida wrote to Alejandro from her hospital bed:

> Alex *de mi vida:* you more than anybody know how sad I have been in this piggy filthy hospital, since you can imagine it and also the boys must have told you about it. Everyone says I should not be so desperate, but they don't know what three months in bed means for me, which is what I need, having been a *callejera* [person who loves strolling in the streets]. But what can one do, at least *la pelona* [the bald one, Frida's word for death] didn't take me away. Right?. . . . Speaking of something else I am wild with hunger . . . and I cannot eat anything but the few revolting things that I told you about before; when you come bring me chocolate cake, candy drops and a *balero* [Mexican toy] like the one we lost the other day. . . . Your *cuate* [pal] who has become as thin as a thread. Friducha[59]

Finally Frida was well enough to walk, and on November 12 she wrote to Alejandro from home: "On Sunday at seven for sure there will be the Mass to give thanks that I did not die, and it will be my first outing, but afterward I want to go out in the street, even if it is only to take the first steps and maybe you will come to take a stroll in the town, do you want to?"

Looking at the healthy if somber young woman in a photograph taken by her father on February 7, 1926, one can hardly believe that just a few months earlier she had nearly died. In another photograph from the same day, Frida wears a man's three-piece suit and sports a cane. Even in her youth, clothing not only distracted attention from her wounds, it played a key role in her self-invention. As the years went on, her exotic dress accentuated the contrast between chronic pain and her gallant facade of *alegría* (joy).

Around September 1926, Frida's health took a turn for the worse. For months she was forced to stay in bed imprisoned in a series of orthopedic corsets.[60] The following April she wrote to Alejandro:

On Friday they put the plaster apparatus on me and since then it has been a real *martyrdom,* which one can compare with nothing; I feel asphyxiation, a frightful pain in my lungs and in the whole back, I can't even touch my leg and I can hardly walk and even less sleep. Imagine, they had me hanging from nothing but the head, two and a half hours, and afterward supported by the tips of my feet, more than an hour, while it dried with hot air, but when I arrived home it was still completely wet. . . . They did not let Adriana [Frida's older sister] or anyone come and I was suffering horribly completely alone.

For three months I am going to have this martyrdom, and if I don't get better with this I sincerely want to die. Because I can't stand it anymore; it is not only the physical suffering, but also I do not have the slightest distraction, I do not leave this room, I can't do anything, I can't walk, I am completely desperate and above all, you are not here—and to all that add: having to listen constantly to sorrows, my mother continues to be sick, during this month she has had 7 attacks [in the early 1920s Frida's mother began to have seizures similar to those of her husband], and my father the same, and without money. . . .

How I need you, Alex! Come quickly! You can't imagine how I need you.

I adore you.

After the revolution, Frida's father's photographs were much less in demand. Beset by bills, her parents sold the French living-room

Frida (left) *in 1926 with members of her family, including* (back row) *her grandmother, her sister Adriana, and Adriana's husband, Alberto Veraza;* (middle row) *an uncle* (left), *her mother* (center), *a cousin* (right); *and* (seated) *Carlos Veraza and Frida's sister Cristina.*

LEFT: **La Adelita, Pancho Villa, and Frida,** *c. 1927.*

RIGHT: **The Cachuchas,** *1927.*

furniture, mortgaged the house, and took in paying guests. There was little Frida could do to help, and she also felt guilty, because worrying about her was detrimental to her parents' health. So she tried to control and hide her misery, developing the heroic Frida that would reappear in self-portraits.

She began painting because she was "bored as hell in bed," and it occurred to her that painting was a way she could earn a living at home.[61] She had, she said, "energies enough to do anything instead of studying to become a doctor. And without paying much attention, I began to paint." Frida's mother ordered a special easel so that Frida could paint lying down. Guillermo Kahlo allowed his daughter to use brushes and a box of paints that she had been coveting for years.

Except for the requisite high school art courses, Frida had no special art training. She had always enjoyed looking at art books, and she drew incessantly in schoolbooks and embellished her letters with sketches. At one point, when she was considering earning her living by making scientific illustrations for medical publications, she practiced drawing from slides under a microscope. (This might be the

source of the magnified cellular organisms in several of her paintings.) Just before the accident she had a brief paid apprenticeship in engraving with the printer Fernando Fernández, who thought she had "enormous talent" and taught her to draw by copying prints. Fernández and Frida are said to have had a brief affair.[62]

Her first subjects were those accessible to an invalid: portraits of friends, family, and herself. Although the early paintings show aptitude and ambition—even a degree of originality—they are awkward in the handling of space, gloomy in color, stiff in drawing, and iconographically somewhat stilted. Several canvases show a primitive version of Cubism. In a 1927 painting of the Cachuchas and in *La Adelita, Pancho Villa, and Frida,* c. 1927, for example, space is tipped up and divided into facetlike compartments. The objects in *Portrait of Miguel N. Lira* are placed in ladder perspective so as not to disturb the flatness of the picture plane. But Frida's primary inspiration came from Italian Renaissance painting, especially that of Botticelli, whom she mentions several times in letters. She also admired Bronzino's portrait *Eleonora di Toledo;* something of that woman's aristocratic

LEFT: **Portrait of Adriana,** *1927.*

RIGHT: **Portrait of Miguel N. Lira,** *1927.*

poise is seen in Frida's first *Self-Portrait,* 1926, and in her *Portrait of Alicia Galant,* 1927. In the 1926 *Self-Portrait* there are also traces of the linear refinement of the English Pre-Raphaelites and of Modigliani, whose elongated figures Frida knew and admired. Other sources for her highly stylized drawing—for example, of water and clouds—come from Art Nouveau illustrations and from Oriental art. In addition, she surely was influenced by the Mexican painter Adolfo Best Maugard, whose teaching method, based on pre-Columbian design, was widely adopted in Mexico during the 1920s.

Of the early portraits, only the *Self-Portrait* hints at the emotional tension that would charge Kahlo's later paintings. Perhaps this is because it was, like so many of her later self-portraits, a token of love by which she hoped to restore her lover's affection. She began it during her relapse in the late summer of 1926, when her relationship with Alejandro was foundering, apparently because he felt she had been promiscuous. Her letters promise that she will become a better person in order to deserve him, and the portrait presents him with that better person. Late in September, when it was finished, she wrote to Alejandro: "Within a few days the portrait will be in your house.

ABOVE: **Portrait of Alicia Galant,** *1927.*

RIGHT: Frida in 1926.

OPPOSITE: **Self-Portrait,** *1926.*

**Portrait of
Cristina Kahlo,**
1928.

Forgive me for sending it without a frame. I implore you to put it in a low place where you can see it as if you were looking at me."

Just as she gave school friends drawings of herself with captions asking them to remember her, she gave Alejandro the *Self-Portrait* so that he would keep her in his thoughts. In her wine-red velvet dress, Frida looks like a princess. Her elegant fingers are stretched in a gesture of discreet supplication. Her plea for love seems to have worked: not long after Alejandro received the portrait, he and Frida were rejoined. But then, in March 1927, he left for Europe, where his parents sent him in part to free him from Frida. When she wrote that she missed him, she identified herself with her *Self-Portrait,* calling it "your 'Boticeli' [sic]." "Alex," she said, "your 'Boticeli' has also become very sad, but I told her that until you come back, she should be the 'sound asleep one'; in spite of this she remembers you always." On July 15, anticipating his return, she wrote: "You cannot imagine how marvelous it is to wait for you, serenely as in the portrait." From the beginning, Frida intended her self-portraits to have magical powers that invoked her presence as a supplication for love.

The first *Self-Portrait* provided a substitute self that, like the make-believe friend in her childhood daydreams, understood Frida's problems. Below her signature on the back of the canvas, Frida wrote a German phrase that defies the painting's nocturnal gloom: "Heute ist Immer Noch" (Today still goes on). In 1928, when her health was restored, she painted her sister, Cristina, seated in a plain white dress before a cloudless dawn sky. The tenebrous atmosphere of the *Self-Portrait* has cleared; it is the difference between night and day.

Frida, c. 1927.

*Frida with Cristina
(second from right),
Carlos Veraza (left),
and other family
members, c. 1928.*

The year she painted Cristina, Frida met the Italian-born American photographer Tina Modotti, and through her was introduced to a lively new world of art and leftist politics. One of Modotti's friends (an ex-lover) was Diego Rivera. Frida recalled her first encounter with him since the days when, as a schoolgirl, she had teased Rivera while he painted murals: "The meeting took place in the period when people carried pistols and went around shooting the street lamps on Madero Avenue and getting into mischief. During the night, they broke them all and went about spraying bullets, just for fun. Once at a party given by Tina, Diego shot a phonograph and I began to be very interested in him in spite of the fear that I had of him."[63] Another time Frida told the story of her first meeting with Rivera this way:

> As soon as they gave me permission to walk and to go out in the street, I went carrying my paintings, to see Diego Rivera, who at that time was painting the frescoes in the corridors of the Ministry of Education. I did not know him except by sight, but I admired him enormously. I was bold enough to call him so that he would come down from the scaffolding to see my paintings and to tell me sincerely whether or not they were worth anything. . . . Without more ado I said: "Diego, come down." And just the way he is, so humble, so amiable, he came down. "Look, I have not come to flirt or anything even if you are a woman-chaser. I have come to show you my painting. If you are interested in it, tell me so, if not, likewise, so that I will go to work at something else to help my parents." Then he said to me: "Look, in the first place, I am very interested in your painting, above all in this portrait of you, which is the most original. The other three seem to me to be influenced by what you have seen. Go home, paint a painting and next Sunday I will come and see it and tell you what I think." This he did and he said: "You have talent."[64]

In his autobiography Rivera said that Frida's canvases "revealed an unusual energy of expression, precise delineation of character, and true severity. They showed none of the tricks in the name of originality that usually mark the work of ambitious beginners. They had a fundamental plastic honesty, and an artistic personality of their own. They communicated a vital sensuality, complemented by a merciless yet sensitive power of observation. It was obvious to me that this girl was an authentic artist."[65]

Rivera admired the painter as well as the paintings, and he began to spend Sunday afternoons at her home in Coyoacán. Before long

Frida and Diego at a
demonstration of the
Syndicate of Technical
Workers, Painters, and
Sculptors, 1929.

Frida distributes arms
to revolutionaries in
Insurrection, part
of Rivera's mural
sequence at the
Ministry of Education
in Mexico City, 1928.

Frida appeared in Rivera's *Ballad of the Proletarian Revolution* mural series on the third floor of the Ministry of Education. Wearing a red work shirt emblazoned with an even redder star, Frida, along with Tina Modotti and other militant Communists, hands out rifles and bayonets. Frida had recently joined the Young Communist League; clearly she was a fit companion for the Communist leader that Rivera was until his expulsion from the party in 1929. In this fresco, as in other Rivera murals, Frida is portrayed not simply as herself but as an ideological symbol within the panorama of history. When Frida painted Rivera, on the other hand, she always depicted him as an individual, her husband, the man she adored. In his vast murals illustrating his Marxist vision, Rivera took a broad, abstract view; on her small sheets of Masonite or tin, Frida zeroed in on herself.

In his autobiography Rivera recalled that on one of his visits to Coyoacán, Frida's father took him aside and said, "I see that you are interested in my daughter, eh?" When Rivera replied that he was, Guillermo Kahlo said, "She is a devil."

"I know it," said Rivera.

"Well, I've warned you," said Kahlo, and he turned on his heel and left.[66] Another time Kahlo warned: "Notice that my daughter is

ABOVE: *Frida and Diego on their wedding day, August 21, 1929.*

OPPOSITE: **Self-Portrait,** *1929.*

a sick person and all her life she will be sick; she is intelligent, but not pretty. Think it over if you want, and if you wish to get married I give you my permission."[67] Kahlo must have realized that he himself could not give Frida, his only unmarried daughter, the financial support her variable health required. Mrs. Kahlo took less kindly to her daughter's liaison. From her point of view, the forty-two-year-old Rivera was too old and too fat. Worse still, he was a Communist and an atheist. Frida's friends, according to Gómez Arias, were at first shocked at her choice, but some of them realized that marriage to Rivera would be an advantage to the aspiring artist.

In any case, nothing could dissuade Frida from her attachment. Indeed, from the evidence of a letter dated September 30, 1929, from the Communist journalist Joseph Freeman to Kenneth Durant, director of the New York office of TASS, she had few options: "She is already at this early stage in the happy union, pregnant," wrote Freeman forty days after Frida and Diego were married in a civil ceremony in the town hall of Coyoacán.[68] Frida recalled: "I arranged everything in the court of Coyoacán so that we could be married the 21st of August, 1929. I asked the maid for skirts, the blouse and *rebozo* [shawl] were also borrowed from the maid. I arranged my foot with the apparatus so that it couldn't be noticed and we got married." Frida's parents said "it was like the marriage between an elephant and a dove."[69]

When Frida married Diego, she espoused the nativist faith that he shared with other postrevolutionary artists and intellectuals reacting against the worship of European culture during the dictatorship of Porfirio Díaz. Frida was one of the first women in the Mexican art world to wear regional costumes, and she and Rivera loved native theater, dance, and music, just as they extolled and collected indigenous forms of visual art. When Frida became involved with Rivera, her painting changed along the same lines. "I began to paint things that he liked. From that time on he admired me and loved me."[70]

The Frida that Rivera loved appears in the *Self-Portrait* she painted the year she married. Here she has replaced the luxurious Renaissance-style gown she wore in her first self-portrait with a cheap peasant blouse, and she wears Mayan jade beads and colonial earrings. No longer the winsome, melancholy aristocrat, she is now a contemporary Mexican girl possessed of all the candor and spunk she needed to lure Rivera down from his scaffold.

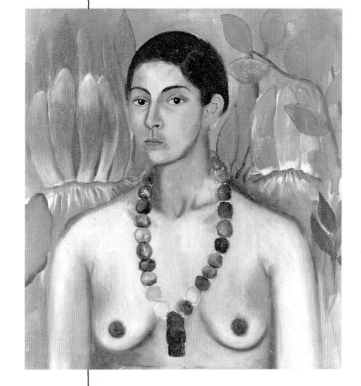

LEFT: **Indian Woman Nude,** *c. 1929.*

RIGHT: **Portrait of a Girl with a Ribbon Around Her Waist,** *c. 1929.*

In other paintings, Frida now followed Rivera's lead in depicting Mexican Indian women with strong, dignified, impassive faces that recall Gauguin's Tahitians. In *Two Women,* 1929, and *Indian Woman Nude,* c. 1929, she placed her figures before a wall of foliage that reveals her admiration (shared with Rivera) of Henri Rousseau. Also inspired by Rivera, she painted a series of Mexican Indian children in the bright and often jarring color combinations so often seen in Mexican popular art. "Diego showed me the revolutionary sense of life and the true sense of color," she later recalled.[71] With its broad expanses of high-keyed color and its Mexicanist content, *Portrait of Virginia* (also called *Niña*), 1929, could be a detail taken from a Rivera mural. At this early stage Frida used primitivism to camouflage her real artistic naïveté, but the childlike qualities of style, subject, and artist combine to give the painting a definite charm. Frida's paintings of Indian children lack the stereotypical cuteness of Rivera's. With the closely observed details of dress and facial expression, Frida's Virginia is, one feels, the result of a tender interchange between artist and model.

Frida on the patio of the Blue House, 1930.

Portrait of Virginia (Niña), *1929.*

Two Women,
1929.

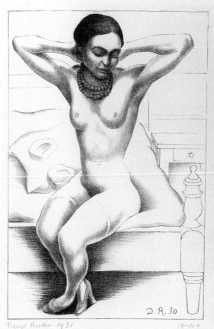

ABOVE: **The Bus,
1929.**

RIGHT: **Frida, 1930.**
*Lithograph by Diego
Rivera, one of the few
images in which
Rivera depicted his
wife not as a symbol
or political figure but
as herself.*

Rivera's political attitudes turn up again in *The Bus,* 1929, a Mexicanized, tongue-in-cheek version of Daumier's *Third-Class Carriage.* Sitting in a row on a bench in a rickety bus are representatives from different levels of Mexican society. Frida, like Rivera, demonstrated her sympathy for the dispossessed. Her heroine is clearly the Madonna-like, barefoot Indian mother suckling her baby. Nor is there any question as to the villain: he is the blue-eyed gringo who, like Rivera's fat capitalist in his *Night of the Rich* panel at the Ministry of Education, holds a moneybag loaded with coins.

"I suffered two grave accidents in my life," Frida Kahlo once said. "One in which a streetcar knocked me down. . . . The other accident is Diego."[72] Her collision with Rivera transformed Frida into a sacred monster: thanks to Diego's mania for publicity, the Riveras' loves, battles, politics—even their health—became manna for the press.

Their union was both carnal and comradely, bound by mutual dependence and yet surprisingly open and free. One of their most powerful bonds was their admiration for each other's art. To her he was the world's greatest artist, the "architect of life."[73] To him Frida was "a diamond in the midst of many inferior jewels" and "the best

LEFT: **Portrait of Lupe Marín,** *c. 1930.*

RIGHT: **Portrait of a Woman in White,** *c. 1930.*

painter of her epoch."[74] Frida became Rivera's most trusted critic. His encouragement of her art was essential to her, and part of her impetus to paint came from her desire to please him. She was, he said, a better artist than he, and he loved to tell of Picasso's reaction to Frida's work. "Look at those eyes," Picasso is said to have written to Rivera, "neither you nor I are capable of anything like it."[75]

She called him *"mi niño, Dieguito,"* and he called her his *"niña chiquita."* These diminutives masked their troubles. Rivera was an unabashed philanderer. Once he excused himself, saying that his doctor had pronounced him unfit for fidelity.[76] Like his mural painting, his love affairs were spectacular and public. The movie stars Paulette Goddard and María Félix were just two of his infatuations, and his hospitality to American tourists who felt that a visit to Rivera was as much of a "must" as a trip to the pyramids was more than cordial. Frida gave him back in kind. Rivera did not mind her attachments to women—often to women who were intimate with him as well. But he did mind her affairs with men. When a friend asked why, he replied, "I don't want to share my toothbrush with anyone."[77] Frida was more tolerant. Although she was often hurt by Rivera's more serious affairs, she pretended to scoff, saying "I do not believe that the banks of a river suffer for letting the water run."[78]

Most of her affairs—especially those with men—she kept secret. Rivera would be "capable of killing you," she warned the sculptor

LEFT: Frida and Diego with Sergei Eisenstein (right) *at the Blue House in Coyoacán in 1931, before Eisenstein embarked on his film* Viva Mexico.

RIGHT: At the Cortéz Palace, Cuernavaca, August 6, 1931. Left to right: *Frida's great friend Dr. Leo Eloesser; Frances Flynn Paine, art adviser to the Rockefellers; Frida; Jean Charlot, mural painter; Elie Faure, French critic; and Diego Rivera.*

OPPOSITE: Self-Portrait, 1930.

Frida going out to welcome the exiled Russian revolutionary leader Leon Trotsky and his wife, Natalia, as they arrived in Tampico, Mexico, January 12, 1937. With Frida are members of the American Communist Party and Tampico port authorities.

ABOVE: **With Trotsky, with whom Frida had a brief love affair in the early summer of 1937.**

Isamu Noguchi, who in 1935 escaped from the pistol-wielding Rivera by climbing an orange tree to the roof. When her affair with Leon Trotsky was in danger of becoming known, both she and Trotsky drew back into the safety of friendship. (Rivera had secured asylum for Trotsky and his wife in 1937, and Frida loaned them her house in Coyoacán.) Even after the liaison was over, Frida flirted openly with Trotsky, as if she wanted to pique her husband's jealousy by flaunting her intimacy with a man whom she knew he admired. Perhaps to tantalize Trotsky she also acted kittenish with Rivera in Trotsky's presence.[79] Another form of gentle torture might have been the self-portrait she gave Trotsky on November 7, 1937, his birthday and the anniversary of the Russian Revolution. It is one of her most seductive self-portraits. She presents herself to the great revolutionary not as a Tehuana, nor as a political activist, but as a colonial aristocrat dressed "fit to kill," holding a sheet of paper on which she dedicates the portrait to him "with all love." No doubt she wanted to keep herself in the forefront of her former lover's mind and heart. Frida was pure mischief—what Breton described when he said that "there is no art more exclusively feminine, in the sense that, in order

LEFT: **Leon and Natalia Trotsky on the Tampico pier after disembarking from the Norwegian tanker Ruth. Behind Frida on the left is the American Trotskyite Max Schachtman. Rivera, who secured asylum for Trotsky from President Cárdenas, was ill and unable to travel to Tampico to meet the boat.**

Self-Portrait (Dedicated to Leon Trotsky), *1937.*

Frida and Diego Rivera, *1931.*

to be as seductive as possible, it is only too willing to play alternately at being absolutely pure and absolutely pernicious."[80]

Frida chronicled the ups and downs of her marriage in paint, starting with *Frida and Diego Rivera,* 1931, a wedding portrait completed after nearly two years of conjugal life. Here Frida adopted the stiff, frontal pose favored by naive nineteenth-century limners such as José María Estrada, whose work influenced Rivera as well. An informative inscription on a ribbon in the beak of a dove (a device both Frida and Diego borrowed from such artists as Estrada and from popular art) is as ingenuous in tone as the painting is folkloric in style: "Here you see us, me Frieda Kahlo, with my beloved husband Diego Rivera. I painted these portraits in the beautiful city of San

LEFT: **Frida and Diego in San Francisco, 1930–31.**

BELOW: **Girl in a Red Dress,** *by José María Estrada, active 1830–1860.*

LEFT: *Diego Rivera and Frida Kahlo in San Francisco, 1930. Photograph by Edward Weston.*

RIGHT: *Rivera (December 11, 1931) painting* The Liberation of the Peon *(a movable mural panel) for his exhibition at the Museum of Modern Art, New York.*

Francisco California for our friend Mr. Albert Bender, and it was in the month of April of the year 1931." (Bender, a Rivera patron, had secured permission for Rivera to enter the United States after he was refused a visa because of his well-known Communism.)

The painting hints at what the Riveras' marriage would become. As firmly planted as an oak, Rivera looks immense next to his bride. Turning away from her, he brandishes his palette and brushes—he is the great maestro. Frida, whose tiny feet barely brush the ground, cocks her head and reaches toward her monumental mate. She plays the role she liked best: the genius's adoring wife.

Her hand lies on his in the lightest possible clasp. Frida knew that Diego was unpossessable. Even as she worked on this painting, Rivera was entranced with the tennis champion Helen Wills, whom he painted nude on the ceiling of the Luncheon Club of the Pacific Stock Exchange in San Francisco, and whom, to the outrage of some good citizens, he also depicted as "California's representative woman."

Frida, 1930.
Photograph by
Edward Weston.

**Portrait of
Mrs. Jean Wight,**
1931.

LEFT: **Portrait of Lady Cristina Hastings,** *1931.*

RIGHT: **Portrait of Dr. Leo Eloesser,** *1931.*

*Frida in
San Francisco,
1931.
Photograph by
Imogen
Cunningham.*

ABOVE: ***Frances Flynn Paine, Diego, Frida, and Mrs. William C. Hammer,*** *director of the Philadelphia Grand Opera Company, February 26, 1932, in preparation for the presentation of Carlos Chávez's ballet* **Horsepower** *on March 31, 1932, for which Rivera designed the sets and costumes. Frida called the ballet a "porqueria" (a disgusting mess) and said the dancers were "a crowd of insipid blonds pretending they were Indians from Tehuantepec and when they had to dance the Zandunga, they looked as if they had lead instead of blood."*

ABOVE: ***Frida and Diego in 1930 or 1931.***

CENTER: **Frida Kahlo and Diego Rivera, 1930.**

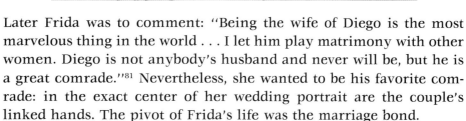

Later Frida was to comment: "Being the wife of Diego is the most marvelous thing in the world . . . I let him play matrimony with other women. Diego is not anybody's husband and never will be, but he is a great comrade."[81] Nevertheless, she wanted to be his favorite comrade: in the exact center of her wedding portrait are the couple's linked hands. The pivot of Frida's life was the marriage bond.

In the early months of her marriage, Frida learned that one way to make that bond firm would not be available to her. She miscarried the child she was carrying at the time of her wedding. In a drawing

ABOVE: **Nude of Eva Frederick,** *1931.*

RIGHT: **Portrait of Eva Frederick,** *1931.*

Retrato de Eva Frederick, nacida en Nueva York, pintado por Frieda Kahlo.

of herself holding hands with Diego, dated December 1930, she conveyed her loss by drawing a baby on her stomach and then erasing it. "We could not have a child, and I cried inconsolably but I distracted myself by cooking, dusting the house, sometimes by painting, and every day going to accompany Diego on the scaffold. It gave him great pleasure when I arrived with the midday meal in a basket covered with flowers."[82] Her thwarted wish to bear a child became an underlying theme in many of her paintings.

Frida's injured (and possibly malformed) pelvis did not prevent conception, but she could not bring a child to term. The most traumatic of her several miscarriages (she also had therapeutic abortions) happened during the year that the Riveras lived in Detroit while he completed his Detroit Institute of Arts murals. On July 4, 1932, after three and one half months of pregnancy, Frida hemorrhaged and was rushed to the Henry Ford Hospital. "I miscarried in the wink of the eye," she wrote to Dr. Leo Eloesser. "I had such hopes to have a little Dieguito who would cry a lot, but now that it has happened there is nothing to do but put up with it."[83]

To combat depression, Frida began to paint, and now, as if pain and loss propelled her to a new level of intensity, she found her own

ABOVE: *Frida and Diego, early 1930s.*

LEFT: *Frida and Diego in the interior court of the Detroit Institute of Arts, where Rivera painted murals, 1932.*

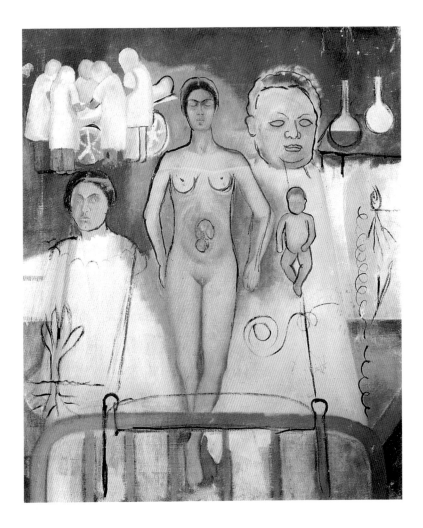

Frida and the Caesarean Operation, c. 1932.

vision. In *Henry Ford Hospital* Frida lies naked, weeping and hemorrhaging onto the single sheet of her hospital bed. As in *Four Inhabitants of Mexico,* space is a nightmarish void in which Frida has no grounding. She said that she painted the ground earth color in order to express her loneliness. On the horizon, distant and unavailable, lies the Ford Motor Company's Rouge plant, where Rivera, full of enthusiasm for modern industry, was busy making preparatory sketches for his murals. Frida looks diminutive in relation to her bed and to the plane in which it floats. Disjunctive scale and the way the bed is tipped up in intentionally incorrect perspective add to the feeling of disconnection and helplessness. Her discomfort is made

ABOVE: **Henry Ford Hospital,** *1932.*

LEFT: *Frida and Diego at the Ford Motor Company's Rouge Plant, Detroit, 1932. When Frida was in the Henry Ford Hospital after her miscarriage, Rivera was making studies at the Rouge for his Detroit Industry murals at the Detroit Institute of Arts.*

**Self-Portrait,
9 July 1932,**
1932.

vivid by the odd twist in her body: from the waist up she turns toward the viewer; from the waist down she turns away.

Six objects symbolic of her feelings at the time of her miscarriage are suspended from the ends of veinlike red ribbons that she holds against her stomach as if they were umbilical cords. Indeed, one of these ribbons is tied to the stump of the umbilical cord of a male fetus, the little "Dieguito" she had longed to have. Frida based the fetus on medical illustrations procured for her by Rivera while she was still in the hospital, and wanted to draw what she had lost. Other symbols of maternal failure include the orchid, which looks like an extracted uterus. It was, she said, a gift from Diego when she was in the hospital. "When I painted it I had the idea of a sexual thing mixed with the sentimental." The snail, she said with poetic inconsistency,

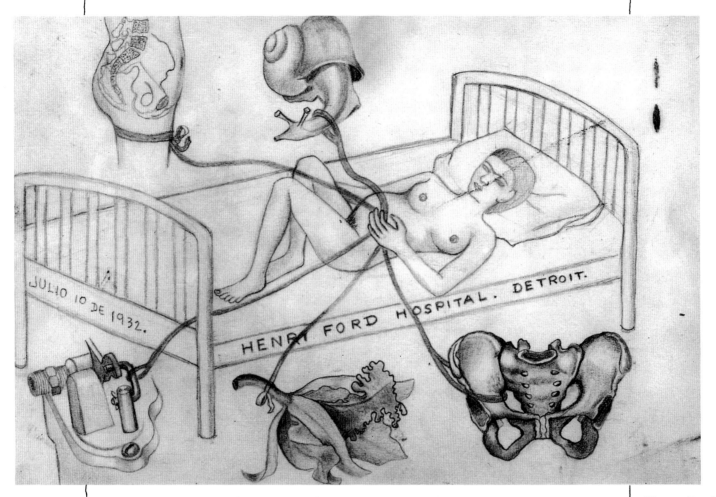

referred to the slowness of the miscarriage, which was "soft, covered and at the same time, open." The salmon-pink female torso is a plaster model of the type used to illustrate anatomy in medical schools. Frida said it was her "idea of explaining the insides of a woman." The cruel-looking machine is an autoclave, a device for sterilizing surgical instruments.[84] She told one friend that she had invented it "to explain the mechanical part of the whole business." Frida did not share Rivera's passion for modern industry; to her, machines represented "bad luck and pain."[85]

Henry Ford Hospital is the first painting in which Frida used sheet metal as its support. It was Rivera who, hoping to improve Frida's mood, suggested that she try, like a *retablo* painter, to paint on tin panels. And, if she couldn't think of anything she wanted to paint,

Henry Ford Hospital,
1932.

ABOVE: **Retablo,** *1937.*

BELOW: **Self-Portrait Dreaming,** *1932.*

she could, he said, start by painting all the years of her life. Like a *retablo, Henry Ford Hospital* makes no distinction between fact and fantasy, and the drama is recorded in a straightforward, primitivistic style. Whereas in Frida's earlier portraits naive style masked the awkwardness of inexperience, now primitivism was a sophisticated choice: it distanced the viewer—and herself—from horrific subject matter. It would be unbearable to look at subjects such as birth or miscarriage if they were not mitigated by the gentle abstraction of primitivism. Even with the heightened realism of her 1940s paintings, Frida continued to use primitivism as a distancer. For both Riveras, *retablos* were an important source, but, because Frida's work was so essential to her well-being, it was she who understood the magic function of the retablo on the deepest level.

Also from the period that followed her miscarriage comes a lithograph entitled *Frida and the Miscarriage*. In it the naked, weeping Frida bleeds the life she had begun into the earth, which shoots forth plants shaped like the eyes, hands, and genitals of her miscarried child. A male fetus near Frida's feet is attached to a less developed fetus inside her womb by a long umbilical cord that spirals around her leg. On one side of Frida embryonic cells divide. On the other, a moon, like Frida, weeps two tears. Frida is divided into light and dark halves, and from her dark half springs an extra arm—the arm of the stal wart, life-sustaining Frida that holds a palette as if it were an escutcheon. Frida seems to be saying that painting must replace maternity. "Many things prevented me from fulfilling the desires which everyone considers normal," she said, "and to me nothing seemed more normal than to paint what had not been fulfilled."[86] Another time she put it this way: "My painting carries with it the message of pain. . . . Painting completed my life. I lost three children. . . . Painting substituted for all of this. I believe that work is the best thing."[87]

Frida's sorrow at her childlessness expressed itself both directly and indirectly. In *Me and My Doll,* painted in 1937 when Frida probably had another miscarriage, she took the conventional mother and child theme and drained it of its usual rhetoric. Instead of holding a baby in her arms, she sits next to an ugly ceramic doll. Her stiff posture is clearly a pose, but she refused to ham for the camera. She looks straight out at us, not at her "baby." Her hands are folded in her lap, and, in complete defiance of sentiment, she smokes.

Me and My Doll,
1937.

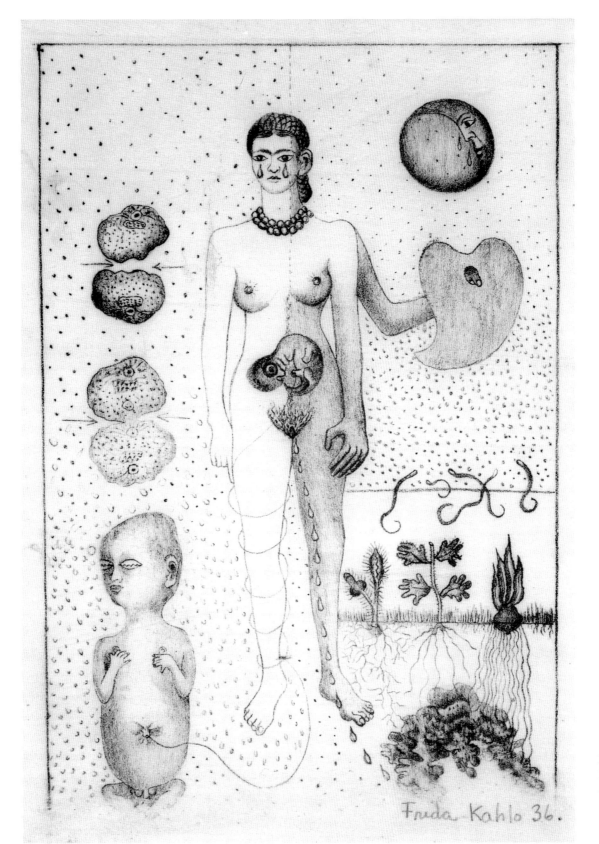

Frida Kahlo 36.

**Frida and the
Miscarriage,
*1932.***

ABOVE: *Painting by an anonymous folk artist of a dead child hanging over Frida's bed in the Frida Kahlo Museum.*

BELOW: *Frida with unidentified child, mid-1940s.*

It was perhaps the loss of a child that prompted one of her most striking paintings, *The Deceased Dimas,* 1937. Like Frida in *My Nurse and I,* the dead boy "dressed up for paradise" (as Frida once titled this painting) looks like a sacrificial offering in some pagan ritual. The child decked out as a holy figure in fact represents a traditional Mexican child's lying in state. Moreover, Frida followed a Mexican tradition of postmortem portraiture that goes back to colonial times. That she was drawn to this tradition we know: above her bed in the Frida Kahlo Museum hangs a portrait of a dead child decked with flowers. The contrast between Dimas's royal robes and his bare brown feet is poignant, as is the simple faith signaled by the cheap reproduction of Christ's flagellation that lies on his pillow. Frida painted the corpse in an unconventional foot-first perspective that puts the viewer in the position of a mourner kneeling on the straw mat upon which Dimas lies. Thrust close to him, we cannot avoid Dimas's deathly gaze or the blood dripping from the corner of his mouth. Frida's view of death was sardonic and unsparing. She did not allow transcendence: Dimas will be rolled up in his straw *petate,* the common man's bed and shroud, and buried.

Besides her dolls, Frida found other substitutes for offspring. She had her sister Cristina's two children, who treated her like a second mother. From the evidence of her portrait *Mariana,* 1944, she doted on friends' children as well. Not content with that, she assembled a

El difuntito Dimas Rosas —
a los tres años de edad. 1937.

The Deceased Dimas,
1937.

**Itzcuintli Dog
with Me,**
1938.

menagerie in her Coyoacán home—among her animals was a pack of *itzcuintlis* (Mexican dogs), one of which appears in a 1938 self-portrait in which Frida did to the conventional master/pet theme what she did to the mother and child image in *Me and My Doll*. She sits alone smoking (what may, given the shape of her cigarette holder, be marijuana). Just as in the earlier painting she has no contact with her substitute baby, here she has no contact with her dog.

Frida may have meant the spider monkeys that populate her self-portraits to have a sexual reference, as they do in Mayan myths and in Western tradition. Certainly she believed in being natural and uninhibited about sex, and she would have liked monkeys all the better for knowing that they symbolize lust. Often her portraits make it clear that simians are her next of kin through parallels between their appearance and her own. She also binds her pets to herself with silk ribbons, which in Frida's symbology are life-lines. Although they are meant to provide companionship, and they sometimes put their arms around her as if to console her, they actually heighten her isolation, for they are neither children nor her longed-for Diego. They are wild animals captured in domesticity. As such, they are full of the possibility of movement while Frida is immobilized. Their rest-

Frida with her pet monkey in her garden in Coyoacán, 1943.

Self-Portrait with Monkeys, *1943.*

Self-Portrait with Monkey, *1945.*

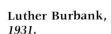

Luther Burbank,
1931.

lessness hints at an energy trapped inside Frida that is so explosive
it borders on rage.

Frida's childlessness lent urgency to her connections with all
forms of life. She nurtured the plants in her garden as if they were
offspring; she painted flowers and fruit with such passion that they
look alive. Not being able to root her body in the world by bearing
children, she dug her roots into the universe, embracing a philosophy
that saw all aspects of life as intertwined.

Luther Burbank, painted in San Francisco in 1931, is an early example of Frida's vision of human and vegetable life working in uni-
son. The portrait turns the Californian horticulturist known for his
work in creating hybrid fruits into a hybrid himself. Burbank (who
appears in a more literal portrait in Rivera's Pacific Stock Exchange
Luncheon Club mural from the same year) holds an uprooted plant,
no doubt one of his hybrids, but instead of planting it, he himself is
planted. His lower legs are transformed into a tree trunk whose roots
are fed by what Frida said was his own corpse. Thus *Luther Burbank*

Luther Burbank,
1931.

is the first statement of a favorite Kahlo theme: the fertilization of life by death.[88]

The portrait is also the first indication that Frida was to become a painter of fantasy. Contact in San Francisco with Surrealism could partly account for the change, but Frida's inventiveness also came straight from Mexican popular culture, where the metamorphosis of humans into plants or animals is common. In addition, she had Rivera's fascination with hybrid creatures as a model. In his murals at the National Agricultural School at Chapingo (1926–27), for example, Tina Modotti's legs, like Burbank's, are transformed into a tree trunk.

Frida's still lifes—for example, *Fruits of the Earth, Pitahayas,* and *Tunas (Still Life with Prickly Pear Fruit),* all 1938—are full of sexual references as well as allusions to the life/death cycle. She often opens or wounds fruit the way she opens or wounds her own body in self-portraits. The halved papaya in the center of a still-life tondo from 1942 is so disconcertingly female that its commissioner, the wife of Mexico's president Camacho, refused to accept the painting when it was finished.

Still Life *(tondo),*
1942.

Fruits of the Earth, *1938.*

FRIDA
KAHLO
8 8

ABOVE: **Tunas (Still Life with Prickly Pear Fruit),** *1938.*

BELOW: **Pitahayas,** *1938.*

In *Xochitl, Flower of Life,* 1938; *Flower of Life,* 1944; and *Sun and Life,* 1947, Frida projected her obsession with fertility onto flowers by transforming them into even more obvious male and female genitals. Cosmic and sexual forces join as the sun generates life, sperm bursts from phallic stamen, vaginalike lilies open, and fetuses grow in petaled wombs. Though Frida rejoiced in the notion of fecundity, it also made her weep: in *Sun and Life* a plant's ejaculation is echoed by a tear in the sun's third eye and in a weeping fetus. *Moses,* 1945, gives the fertility theme epic scope. Drawing on Freud's *Moses and Monotheism,* Frida painted Moses' birth beneath a life-engendering sun flanked by gods, heroes, common humanity, and the all-embracing

Xochitl,
Flower of Life,
1938.

Flower of Life,
1944.

hands of death. In the foreground a conch spurting fluid into a concave round shell is, Frida said, a symbol of love. Fresh, leafy branches sprouting from dead tree trunks refer to the cycle of life.

Frida's most lucid statement of her faith that all life participates in a single flow is *Roots*, 1943, a childless woman's dream of fertility in which her torso opens up like a window that gives birth to a vine. Frida's blood courses through the vine and into red vesicles that extend beyond the vine leaves' veins to feed the parched earth. With her elbow propped on a pillow, she dreams that she is a tree of life. Possibly, too, given her Catholic upbringing, she was making an analogy between her blood flowing into the world and the wine that came from Noah's grapevine and that predicted Christ's sacrifice. Thus, as in several other paintings, Frida may have alluded to herself as a sacrificial victim. *Roots* can also be seen as a reversal of *My Nurse and I.* In the latter Frida is a baby nourished by the plantlike breasts of a Mexican earth mother; in *Roots* the adult Frida nourishes the Mexican earth. But there is something ominous in this dream of fulfillment: a crevasse opens in the ground next to Frida. If she is to continue to float over this pitted terrain, she must not waken from her dream.

Sun and Life, *1947.*

Moses, *1945.*

Roots, *1943.*

After her miscarriage in Detroit, Frida was miserable, and she longed to go home to Mexico. Detroit seemed charmless and boring to her. She missed the sparkle and the strong light-dark contrasts of Mexico. The summer was torrid. Rivera was working around the clock, but most of the time she didn't feel like working at all. On August 31, when the temperature rose to ninety-nine degrees, Frida watched a solar eclipse through smoked glass. She was, Lucienne Bloch (who was living with the Riveras) recalled, "disgusted . . . she said it was not beautiful at all, [no better than] 'a cloudy day when the full business was showing itself.' "[89]

Despite Frida's deprecation of the eclipse, that day she felt inspired to start a new painting, *Self-Portrait on the Border Line Between Mexico and the United States,* in which she juxtaposed the sun and the moon for the first time. Their joint presence was to recur often in her art. It referred to her (and Rivera's) belief that a number of dualities—light-dark, night-day, male-female, life-death—underlay the workings of the world. For Frida the sun and moon paralleled her own duality, such as the light and dark aspects of herself evident, for example, in the lithograph she made in Detroit. These dualities had

Showcase in Detroit, *1932.*

their root in the pre-Columbian notion of an eternal war between light and dark, the sun being the masculine principle and the moon the feminine principle. The sun and moon also light up the skies of many Mexican crucifixion scenes, where they refer either to the solar eclipse at the time of Christ's sacrifice, to the idea that all nature was in mourning, or to the Old and New Testaments.

In *Self-Portrait on the Border Line Between Mexico and the United States* the sun and moon hold sway only over Mexico, which was, this

ABOVE: **On the roof of the Detroit Institute of Arts during an eclipse of the sun on August 31, 1932. Right to left:** *Diego, Frida, Mrs. Jean Wight (the wife of one of Diego's assistants and a portrait subject for Frida), and Rivera's assistant Lord Hastings and Lucienne Bloch.*

LEFT: **Frida at the Mexican border on her way from Detroit to Mexico to see her dying mother, September 7, 1932.**

Frida in Detroit painting **Self-Portrait on the Border Line Between Mexico and the United States, 1932.**

painting tells us, where Frida wanted to be. While Rivera was busy eulogizing modern industry on the walls of the Detroit Institute of Arts, Frida was yearning for the ancient agrarian culture of Mexico. In her painting she is dressed up in an uncharacteristically sweet pink frock and lace gloves. But she herself is far from demure. As in her first self-portrait, her nipples show beneath her bodice. Her face is poised for mischief, and, again in defiance of propriety, she holds a cigarette. She also holds a small Mexican flag, which tells us where her loyalties lie.

Frida stands on a boundary stone that marks the border between Mexico and the United States. The stone is inscribed "Carmen Rivera painted her portrait in 1932." Perhaps she used her Christian name and her husband's last name as part of her pretense of being proper—she loved to shock Grosse Pointe dowagers by seeming to be shy and

Self-Portrait on the Border Line Between Mexico and the United States, *1932.*

then coming out with off-color expressions delivered in slightly incorrect English to make it seem as if she didn't know what they meant. (In Spanish, too, Frida swore like a mariachi.) Or she could have used the name Carmen Rivera instead of her habitual Frida Kahlo because that is what the press called her in articles describing her as Rivera's petite wife who sometimes dabbled in paint. Rivera knew better—once in his awkward English, he introduced her to Detroit journalists by saying "His name is Carmen," and another time he called her *"la pintora mas pintor,"* using both the feminine and masculine terms for painter in recognition of her strength and perhaps also of her androgynous nature. It is probable that he called her Carmen because he did not want to use the German name Frida during the rise of Nazism.[90] For the same reason, about 1935 Frida herself would drop the *e* with which she had always spelled her name (Frieda).

In *Self-Portrait on the Border Line* a fire-spitting sun and a quarter moon are enclosed in cumulus clouds that, when they touch, create a bolt of lightning. By contrast, the single cloud over the United States is nothing but industrial smoke spewed from four chimney stacks labeled FORD. And instead of encompassing the sun and moon, the American cloud besmirches the American flag, whose artificial stars have none of the dazzle of Mexico's real sun and real moon. Whereas the Mexican side of the border has a partially ruined pre-Columbian temple, the United States has bleak skyscrapers. Whereas Mexico has a pile of rubble, a skull, and pre-Columbian fertility idols, the United States has a new factory with four chimneys that look like automatons. And whereas Mexico has exotic plants with white roots, the United States has three round machines with black electric cords. The machine nearest Frida has two cords. One connects with a Mexican lily's white roots, the other is plugged into the United States side of the border marker, which serves as Frida's pedestal. She, of course, is as motionless as a statue, which is what she pretends to be. With the high-voltage irony of her withering glance, Frida looks, once again, like a "ribbon around a bomb."

In 1933, while Rivera was at work on his Rockefeller Center mural (left unfinished and later destroyed because Nelson Rockefeller objected to the inclusion of Lenin's portrait), Frida produced her own manifesto, entitled *My Dress Hangs There,* 1933. Whereas Rivera, taking a broad view, contrasted the evils of capitalism with a Marxist

*OPPOSITE: **Frida in 1932. Photograph by Lucienne Bloch.***

*BELOW: **Frida at the New Workers' School, in front of Rivera's mural panel** Communist Unity, New York, 1933.*

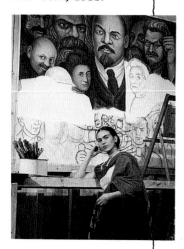

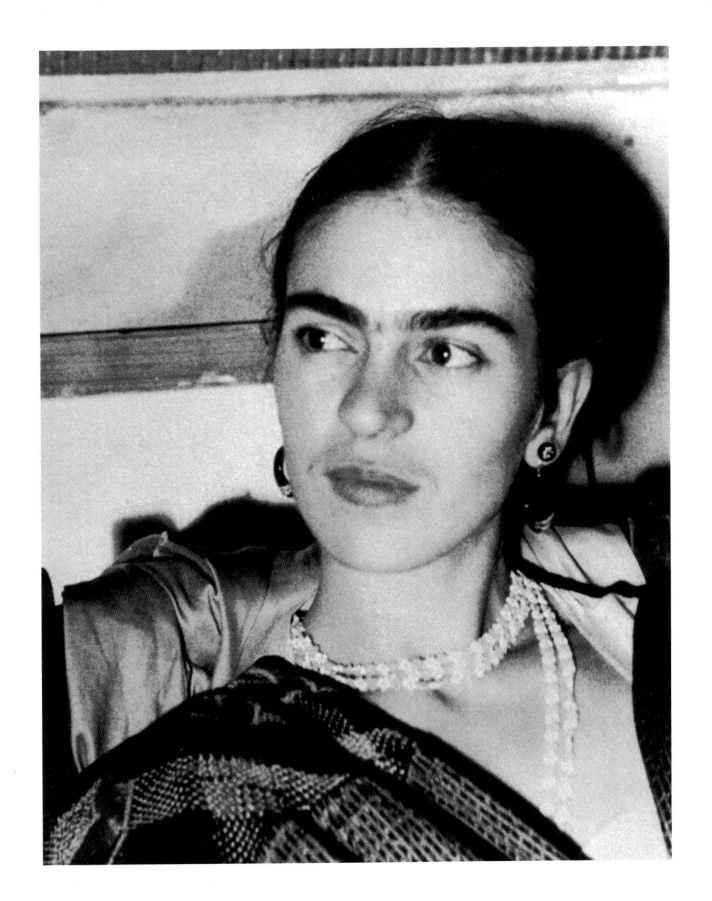

My Dress Hangs There, *1933.*

utopia and placed an idealized worker in the center of his mural, Frida painted a personal and sardonic view of New York in the Depression years and placed her own Tehuana costume in the middle. Like Rivera's mural, *My Dress Hangs There* is crammed with details that are given coherence by a rather primitive brand of Synthetic Cubism.

Frida's Cubism went so far as to include bits of collage: fragments of newspaper photographs of breadlines, a military parade, the audience at a baseball game, and political demonstrators. The steps of Federal Hall, presided over by a statue of George Washington, are made out of a collaged graph showing "weekly sales in millions." She poked fun at American values—sports and plumbing—by setting a golf trophy and a toilet on top of classical columns. A skyscraper forms the pedestal for the almighty telephone, whose cord snakes in and out of city buildings so depersonalized they resemble tombstones. Trinity Church with a dollar sign in its window is linked by a red ribbon to Federal Hall, which in Frida's view stood for capitalism. Other false values that Frida gently remonstrates against are the commercialization of sex seen in the sex goddess Mae West (whom Diego worshiped) vamping Manhattan from a peeling billboard above

BELOW: **Frida typing a letter dictated by Diego on May 11, 1933, two days after he was expelled from Rockefeller Center.**

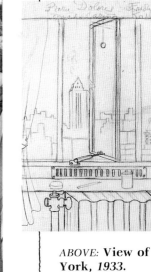

ABOVE: **View of New York, 1933.**

RIGHT: **Rivera's Rockefeller Center mural (destroyed) repainted at the Palace of Fine Arts, Mexico City, 1934.**

ABOVE: *Frida (eating an ice-cream cone) and Diego (smoking a cigar) at Jones Beach, Long Island, New York, 1933.*

BELOW: *Frida and Diego with Lucienne Bloch at the New Workers' School, New York, where Rivera painted a series of mural panels after being fired by Nelson Rockefeller, 1933.*

OPPOSITE: **Self-Portrait "Very Ugly,"** *1933.*

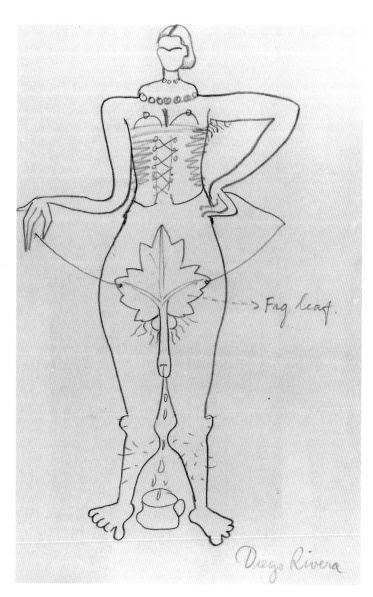

> Fig leaf.

Diego Rivera

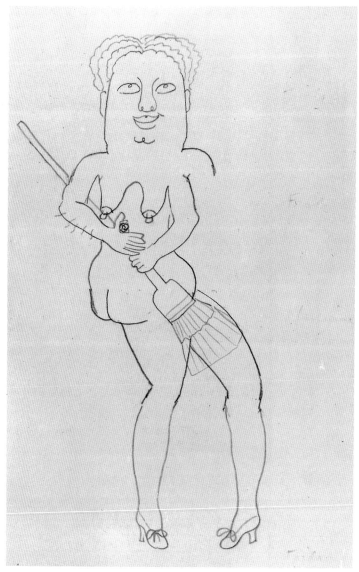

Two "exquisite
corpses" (drawn by
Frida in collaboration
with Lucienne Bloch
and Rivera), c. 1933.

LEFT: **Self-Portrait, 1933.**

BELOW: Frida and Lupe Marín (Rivera's second wife) in New York, 1933.

buildings going up in flames, and conspicuous waste suggested in a garbage pail stuffed with detritus, including a human hand. Suspended from a blue ribbon tied with bows to the toilet and the trophy, Frida's Tehuana dress hangs empty. Disgusted with watching millionaires sip cocktails while the poor starved, she wanted to flee to Mexico, a longing hinted at by the collaged steamship chugging out of New York Harbor while the Statue of Liberty appears to wave.

ABOVE: *Diego and Frida in front of the organ-grinder cactus fence that enclosed their San Angel home, c. 1934.*

CENTER: *The Riveras' linked houses in San Angel. The large pink one on the left was Diego's, the smaller blue one on the right was Frida's. Frida lived here with Diego from 1933 to 1939.*

When Frida and Diego returned to Mexico late in 1933, Rivera was disconsolate. He wanted to continue painting murals for an industrial society, where, in his view, the Marxist revolution would eventually occur. Unfairly, he blamed Frida for persuading him to leave the United States, and it may have been in retaliation that he had an affair with her younger sister, Cristina, the person besides Diego whom Frida loved the most. When Frida learned of this betrayal, she wrote to a friend: "I have suffered so much in these months that it is going to be difficult for me to feel completely well soon, but I have done everything I can to forget what happened between Diego and me and to live again as before." A month later, she wrote: ". . . I am in such a state of sadness, boredom, etc. etc. that I can't even do a drawing. The situation with Diego is worse each day. . . . Now, after many months of real torment for me, I forgave my sister and I thought that with this, things would change a little, but it was just the opposite."[91]

Early in 1935, the Riveras separated, and Frida moved into an apartment in the center of Mexico City. In July she flew to New York, where, after confiding her troubles to Lucienne Bloch and Bertram

TOP, RIGHT: *Frida with her sister Cristina's children, Isolda (b. 1929) and Antonio (b. 1930), at the Blue House, c. 1934.*

BOTTOM, RIGHT: *Frida and Cristina Kahlo, c. 1934.*

*Frida and Cristina
Kahlo hold out
Communist literature
in a detail from
Rivera's* **Mexico
Today and Tomorrow**
*mural at the National
Palace, Mexico City,
c. 1934.*

and Ella Wolfe (Bertram Wolfe was Rivera's friend and biographer),
she decided that she wanted to go back to Diego. On July 23 she wrote
to him: "[I know that] all these letters, liaisons with petticoats, lady
teachers of 'English,' gypsy models, assistants with 'good intentions,'
'plenipotentiary emissaries' from distant places, only represent *flir-*

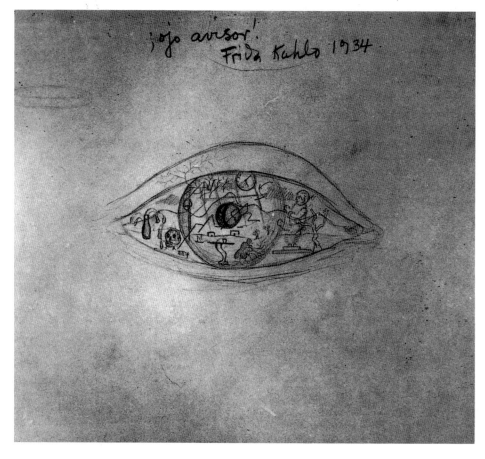

All-Seeing Eye,
1934.

tations, and that at bottom *you and I* love each other dearly, and thus we go through adventures without number, beatings on doors, imprecations [*mentadas de madres*], insults, international claims—yet we will always love each other." All this, Frida said, made her "understand in the end that I love you more than my own skin, and that, though you may not love me in the same way, still you love me somewhat. Isn't that so? . . . I shall always hope that that continues, and with that I am content."[92]

But Frida was not content, as her letters from 1935 and her inability to work reveal. After their reunion, she and Rivera may have had some kind of understanding that, though they adored each other, they would be free to have love affairs with others. Perhaps to balance Rivera's philandering and as a reaction to his liaison with her sister, in 1935 Frida had an affair not only with Noguchi but also with the graphic artist and mural painter Ignacio Aguirre.

Self-Portrait with
Curly Hair, *1935.*

In 1934 Frida produced no paintings. In 1935 she painted only a
bust-length self-portrait in which her hair is short and curly (to spite
Diego, who loved her hair worn long) and *A Few Small Nips,* in which,
her own pain being too great to depict, she projected it onto another
woman's calamity. In the latter a naked, bloodied woman lies on a
bed beneath her dagger-wielding murderer. Like Frida's in *Henry Ford
Hospital* her wretchedness is intensified by the way her upper and
lower body twist in opposite directions.

The scene is based on a newspaper report that told of a drunk
who killed his girlfriend by stabbing her over and over again. Brought
before the judge, he explained, "But I only gave her a few small nips!"
Inspired by the great turn-of-the-century Mexican printmaker José
Guadalupe Posada, whose leaflets illustrating newsworthy events
frequently depict men stabbing women, Frida produced a painted
broadside. With her Mexican black humor, she found the story both

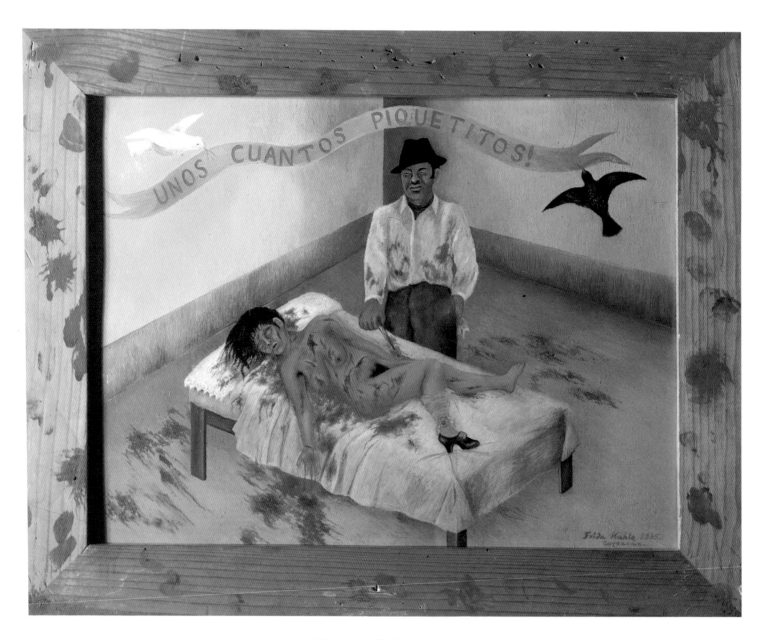

A Few Small Nips, *1935.*

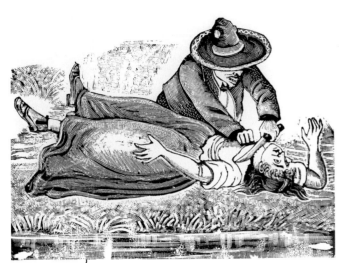

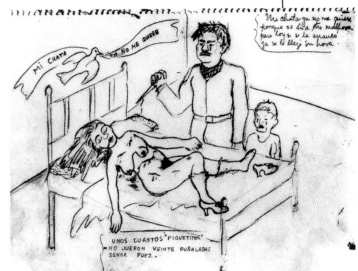

horrible and funny. A banner held by love doves—of all things!—
bears the painting's title. One dove is black, the other white, alluding
perhaps to the light and dark sides of love. As in *My Birth,* there is
irony in Frida's choice of sweet pastel colors and a wry humor in
such details as the lace-trimmed pillow, the single high-heeled shoe,
the fancy lace garter, and the fallen stocking worn by what must have
been a "fallen" woman. Frida inscribed a cartoonlike preparatory
drawing for *A Few Small Nips* with the words of what must be a popular song: "My sweetie doesn't love me anymore because she gave
herself to another bastard, but today I snatched her away, her hour
has come." In the drawing a small boy stands weeping by what must
be his mother's deathbed.

The man is the stereotypical macho. The woman is the victim, *la
chingada.* To a friend Frida confided that she had painted the murderer "because in Mexico, killing is quite satisfactory and natural."
She added that she had needed to paint *A Few Small Nips* because she
herself had come close to being "murdered by life."[93] At a later date,
when she must again have felt murdered by life, Frida continued the
splotches of blood that make this her goriest painting out onto the
picture frame, thus implicating the viewer in the murder. Indeed, as
in *My Birth,* Frida set up this painting so that the viewer feels cor-
nered by its violence: walls press the bloody bed toward us, and, because one bed leg is cut off by the lower edge of the painting, there
is no way for us to skirt the disaster.

LEFT: *José Guadalupe
Posada,* **A Victim of
Francisco Guerrero,
"El Chalequero,"
1890.**

RIGHT: *Sketch for*
A Few Small Nips,
1935.

RIGHT: *Frida in New York during the period when she was separated from Diego in 1935. She wears the jacket in which she appears in her 1937 painting* Memory.

ABOVE: *Frida and Diego raising their fist in Communist salute during an antifascist demonstration in Mexico City, November 23, 1936*

Two years later Frida was able to express her misery over the Rivera/Cristina affair in a self-portrait entitled *Memory,* 1937. As always, she used bodily wounds to suggest psychic injury. Her face, though tearful, is expressionless. Her hair is cropped, and she wears the European-style clothes she favored when she was separated from Rivera. Flanked by alternative identities—her schoolgirl outfit and her Tehuana costume, each set of clothing equipped with one arm— Frida herself stands armless and helpless. Her dividedness is underscored by the way she stands with one foot on dry land and the other on a sea. The foot placed over water wears an apparatus that looks like a sailboat and that surely refers to recent foot operations.[94]

Memory is as simple and direct as a valentine: torn from her body, Frida's huge heart lies at her feet pumping rivers of blood into the landscape. To create an extraordinarily accurate visualization of the sensation of pain in the chest caused by extreme sorrow, Frida pierced the hole left by her extracted heart with a steel rod and put seesawing cupids on either end. The puttis' blithe indifference to her everexpanding wound recalls Diego's propensity to thoughtless frolic. The poetry of blood in *Memory* joins the cruelty of Aztec sacrifice with

Memory, *1937.*

**Remembrance of
an Open Wound,
*1938.***

the violence of Spanish Catholic martyrdoms.[95] The greater the pain she wished to convey—especially pain caused by rejection from Diego—the bloodier Frida's self-portraits became.

If the rod penetrating the hole in Frida's chest has an obvious sexual connotation, the reference to sex is even more blatant in the equally bloody *Remembrance of an Open Wound,* 1938 (destroyed in a fire), in which Frida again expressed her unhappiness at Rivera's affair with her sister. Here Frida sits with her legs apart as she pulls up the ruffle on her Tehuana skirt in order to display her wounds. Her foot wound is real. The other wound, an open gash on her inner thigh, is invented, and it alludes to the injury to her sense of herself as a sexual being. Next to the gash Frida placed a sprig of leaves as if it were a commemorative wreath. The leaves may also be another example of Frida's enlisting plants as players in her personal drama.

Frida was festive and candid about her pain. She told friends that her right hand is hidden under her skirt because she is masturbating. Once again, sex and pain are linked, and once again Frida is, underneath the flamboyant behavior and exotic clothes, alone. The veinlike roots that dangle from her flowered headdress and that cover her like a wedding veil remain as unconnected and unrooted as was Frida without Diego.

LEFT: Study for **Remembrance of an Open Wound,** *1938.*

CENTER: **Self-Portrait with Bandaged Foot,** *c. 1938.*

RIGHT: **Self-Portrait Drawing,** *c. 1937.*

RIGHT: **Frida with (left) Trotsky, seated; Diego, in back; Natalia Trotsky; Reba Hansen; André Breton, the Surrealist poet and essayist; and Jean Van Heijenoort, Trotsky's secretary with whom Frida had an affair, 1938.**

ABOVE: **Self-Portrait (miniature), c. 1938.**

When André Breton went to Mexico in 1938, he was charmed by Frida and by her work. "My surprise and joy," he wrote, "was unbounded when I discovered, on my arrival in Mexico, that her work has blossomed forth, in her latest paintings, into pure surreality, despite the fact that it had been conceived without any prior knowledge whatsoever of the ideas motivating the activities of my friends and myself."[96] Breton's welcoming her into the ranks of Surrealism advanced Frida's career. Soon she was invited to have a show by New York's Surrealist-oriented Julien Levy Gallery. Of her exhibition, *Time* magazine noted that the "flutter of the week in Manhattan was caused by the first exhibition of paintings by famed muralist Diego Rivera's German-Mexican wife, Frida Kahlo." In the work *Time* discerned "the playfully bloody fancy of an unsentimental child."[97] *Art News* praised Frida's "remarkable craftsmanship" and her "openness." The show was, it said, "definitively a beautiful achievement."[98]

Following her New York debut, Frida traveled to Paris, where André Breton had promised her a show. When she arrived, she discovered that nothing had been organized. "The question of the exhibition

TOP: *Frida at the opening of her first exhibition, Julien Levy Gallery, New York, November 1, 1938. Behind Frida is her painting* What the Water Gave Me, *1938.*

BOTTOM: *Frida in New York, 1938. Photograph by Julien Levy.*

LEFT: *Frida in New York, 1938. Photograph by Nickolas Muray.*

FRIDA
KAHLO
—■—
1 1 8

TOP: *A gathering in Lupe Marín's apartment, Mexico City, 1938.* **From left: Luis Cardoza y Aragón, Frida, Jacqueline and André Breton, Lupe, Diego, and Lya Cardoza.**

BOTTOM: *Gathering at the Riveras' San Angel home, 1938.* **Right to left: Frida; Miguel Covarrubias, the Mexican painter and caricaturist; Diego; Nickolas Muray; Rosa Covarrubias, the former American dancer Rosa Rolando; and two Tehuanas who served Rivera as models.**

LEFT: **Left to right:** *Diego; Frida; Natalia Trotsky; an unidentified woman; André Breton; Trotsky; three unidentified Mexicans, probably policemen; and* (right) *Jean Van Heijenoort on an outing near Mexico City, June 1938.*

is all a damn mess," she wrote (in English) to her friend and lover Nickolas Muray, a photographer living in New York.

With Nickolas Muray (the Hungarian-born photographer with whom Frida had an affair) in Coyoacán, 1938.

> Until I came the paintings were still in the custom house, because the s. of a b. Breton didn't take the trouble to get them out. . . . So I had to wait days and days just like an idiot till I met Marcel Duchamp (marvelous painter), who is the only one who has his feet on the earth, among all this bunch of coocoo lunatic sons of bitches of the surrealists. . . . Well, after things were more or less settled as I told you, a few days ago Breton told me that the associated of Pierre Colle, an old bastard and son of a bitch, saw my paintings and found that only *two* were possible to be shown, because the rest are too *"shocking"* for the public!! I could of kill that guy and eat it afterwards, but I am so sick and tired of the whole affair that I have decided to send everything to hell, and scram from this rotten Paris before I get nuts myself.[99]

Duchamp rescued Frida's paintings from customs and arranged for the Pierre Colle Gallery to present the show, "Mexique," whose curator was Breton. It included eighteen paintings by Frida, as well as photographs by Manuel Alvarez Bravo, some pre-Columbian pieces,

ABOVE: **I Belong to My Owner**, *1937*.

RIGHT: **Portrait of Alberto Misrachi**, *1937*.

Portrait of Diego Rivera, *1937.*

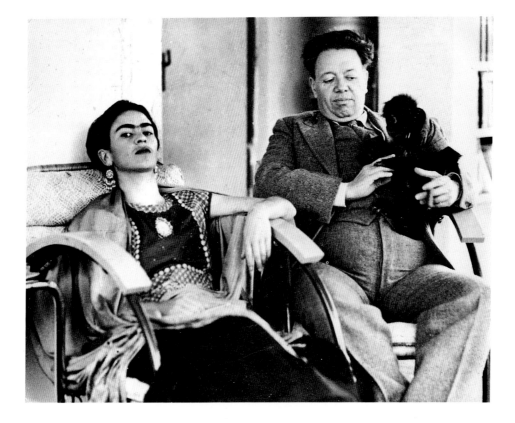

*Frida and Diego
with their pet monkey
Fulang-Chang,
c. 1938.*

and a selection of such popular art objects as *retablos,* toys, sugar skulls, masks, ceramics, baskets, and even some dressed fleas. Frida was not entirely pleased to have her show diluted by what she called "all this junk" that Breton had picked up in Mexican markets, but she was delighted with the vernissage on March 10, 1939. "There were," she wrote to friends, "a lot of people on the day of the opening, great congratulations to the 'chicua,' amongst them a big hug from *Joan Miró* and great praises for my painting from *Kandinsky,* congratulations from *Picasso* and *Tanguy,* from Paalen and from other 'big cacas' of Surrealism."[100] Preoccupied with the menace of war, the French public didn't pay much attention to Frida's paintings, but the Louvre bought a self-portrait entitled *The Frame,* c. 1938 (in which Frida framed her face with decorative birds and flowers painted on the back side of glass), and the critic L. P. Foucaud gave her a favorable review in *La Flèche,* saying that each painting was a "door opened on the infinite and on the continuity of art." In a period when "guile and swindle are in style," he wrote, "the striking

Dora Maar's portrait of Frida, taken in 1939, in Paris, where André Breton and Marcel Duchamp helped to organize an exhibition entitled Mexique, *which included a large group of Frida's paintings.*

probity and exactitude of Frida Kahlo de Rivera spare us many strokes of genius.''[101]

Although Breton claimed that Frida was a self-invented Surrealist, she was neither ignorant of this European movement nor was she truly part of it.[102] Her work differs from Surrealism in that her fantasy was always rooted in concrete fact and immediate experience. Frida did not want to mystify. She wanted to communicate her feelings with the greatest possible clarity and directness. "I never knew I was a Surrealist," she said, "till André Breton came to Mexico and told me I was."[103] Increasingly as the years went on, she rejected the Surrealist label: "I never painted dreams," she pointed out. "I painted my own reality."

Yet Surrealism encouraged Frida to follow her own fantasy, a fantasy deeply imbedded in her native culture. Moreover, there is a change in her work after her direct contact with Surrealism during

The Airplane Crash,
c. 1938.

Breton's visit in 1938. A comparison between the naive style and straightforward drama of such early works as *Henry Ford Hospital* and the more complex and allusive *What the Water Gave Me,* 1938, reveals Frida's fascination with Surrealism's unsettling enigmas.

What the water gave Frida was a bathtub revery. As she soaked her aching body, her mind began to drift. Toes doubled in reflection looked like fleshy crabs. Beside her wounded toes she envisioned a vein emerging from the drain and dripping blood into the bathwater. On her right thigh she saw her imaginary wound with sexual-looking pods, red petals and roots floating above it. The water's lulling light also precipitated images of past and present, life and death, comfort and loss. In the midst of this vision is Frida, drowned in her imaginings and bleeding from the corner of her mouth. She is kept afloat by a lasso that serves as a tightrope for insects and a minute dancer. Beside the drowned Frida floats her Tehuana costume, once again empty, and once again an emblem of her spiritual disconnection.

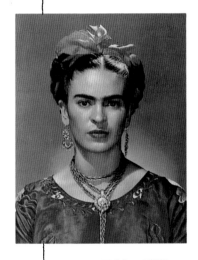

ABOVE: **Frida, 1938. Photograph by Nickolas Muray.**

LEFT: **The Frame, c. 1938.**

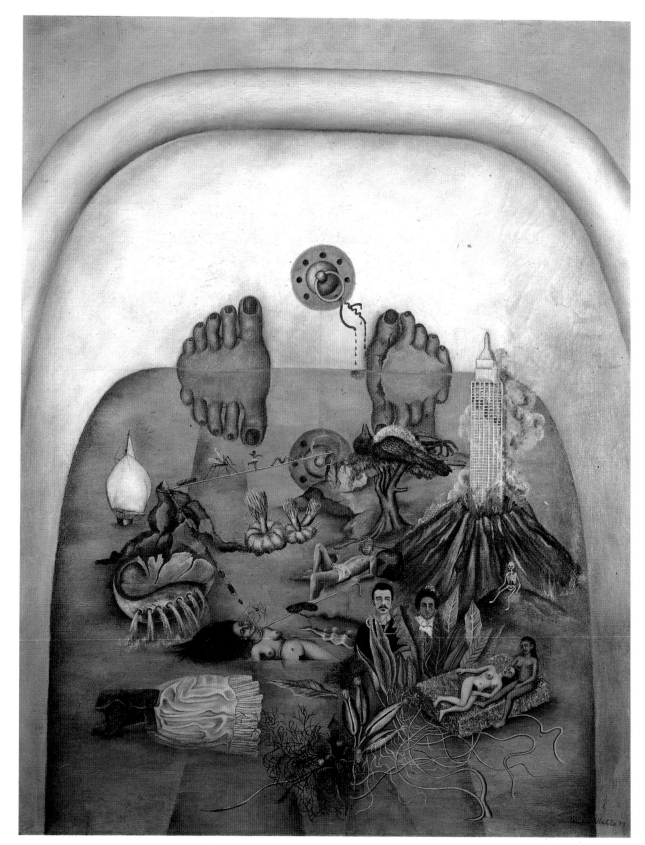

**What the Water
Gave Me,** *1938.*

To the right of Frida are her parents, based on their wedding photograph. Their light and dark complexions reappear in two female nudes, who use a sponge as a raft. These women are aspects of Frida's duality, the Indian and the European, the comforter and the comforted. They may also refer to her bisexuality, and they turn up again the following year, in a painting called *Two Nudes in a Forest,* which Frida made for an intimate woman friend.

The broken conch shell in *What the Water Gave Me* might refer to Frida's inability to bear a child. The ship heading for a rock means death. To the right is an island with a skeleton and a dead bird whose one red foot seems analogous to Frida's bleeding foot. It is unclear whether Frida intended the Empire State Building, caught in the molten red crater of an erupting volcano, to signal the death of capitalism or the rape of Mexico. The Bosch-like masked man lying on the island's shore holds one end of the tightrope that winds around Frida's neck and waist. The other end is attached to a phallic rock. If either end were released, Frida would sink farther into the watery depths of her dream.

Unlike most of Frida's self-portraits, *What the Water Gave Me* has no dominant central image. Details come in and out of focus as the

Two Nudes in a Forest, *1939.*

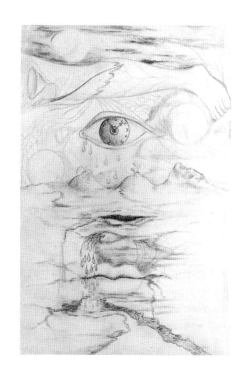

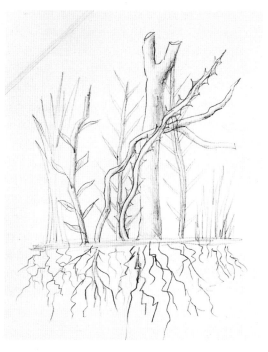

TOP, LEFT: **Fantasy, 1944.**

TOP, RIGHT: **Roots, c. 1946.**

BOTTOM: **Karma II, c. 1946.**

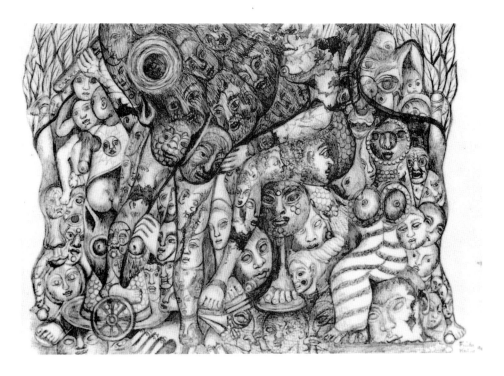

Karma I, *c. 1946.*

viewer scans the water's surface and partakes in the flux of the artist's imaginings. The canvas's subdued tones and thin, relatively transparent paint surface enhance the mood of revery. Although *What the Water Gave Me* is Frida's most Surrealistic painting, each detail is so intimately connected to the painter's life that the work remains a realistic depiction of the dreamer and her daydream.

Frida came closest to Surrealism in the diary that she kept during the last decade of her life. Often the entries are like stream of consciousness poems. Color and line burst free of the images they depict. Figures are fragmented, distorted, reassembled. Using a Surrealist method for incorporating accident into art, Frida occasionally made a drop of ink her starting point. Or a splotch of color formed by closing the diary when the ink was still wet could be transformed into exotic flora and fauna. Of such imagery, she wrote in her journal, "Who would say that spots live and help one to live?! Ink, blood smell. I do not know what ink I would use that would want to leave its tracks in such forms. I respect its wishes and I will do what I can to flee from myself, worlds, inked worlds—land free and mine. Faraway suns that call me because I form part of their nucleus. Foolishness . . . What would I do without the absurd and the fleeting?"

FRIDA
KAHLO
130

Diary pages: "El horrendo 'ojosauro.' "

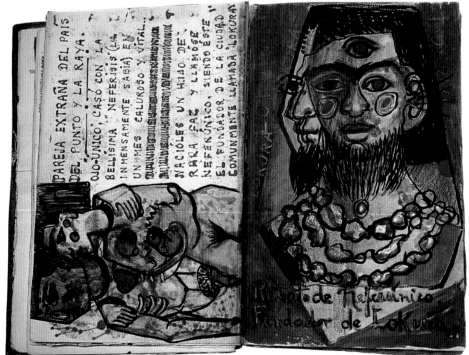

Diary pages: "Portrait of Neferúnico, Founder of Madness."

Diary pages: "Bird."

Diary pages: "Masked Dancers."

When Frida rejoined Diego in Mexico in the spring of 1939 after her New York and Paris exhibitions, her marriage collapsed, and she moved into the Blue House in Coyoacán. Whether the trouble came from her own or his infidelities is not certain. By mid-October they had petitioned for a divorce by mutual consent before the court of Coyoacán, and by the end of the year the divorce had come through. An inveterate fabulist, Rivera said the divorce was "purely a matter of legal convenience in the spirit of modern times."[104] To other reporters he said, "There are no sentimental, economic or artistic questions involved. . . . I believe that with my decision I am helping Frida's life to develop in the best possible way. She is young and beautiful. She has had much success in the most demanding art centers. She has every possibility that life can offer her, while I am already old and no longer have much to offer her. I count her among the five or six most prominent modernist painters." When the same reporters went to interview Frida, she cited "intimate reasons, personal causes, difficult to expain" as the motive for divorce.[105] To Nick-

RIGHT: **El verdadero vacilón**
(The True Tease),
c. 1946.

OPPOSITE: Diego and Frida on the roof of the San Angel house in April 1939, just after her return from Paris. Marital difficulties led to their separation by the summer of 1939. On November 6, 1939, they were divorced.

olas Muray she wrote on October 13: "Two weeks ago we began the divorce. I have no words to tell you how much I been suffering and knowing how much I love Diego you must understand that this troubles will never end in my life, but after the last fight I had with him (by phone) because it is almost a month that I don't see him, I understood that for him it is much better to leave me. . . . Now I feel so rotten and lonely that it seems to me that nobody in the world has suffer the way I do, but of course it will be different I hope in a few months."

Frida's health declined. Her doctor ordered a twenty-kilogram weight to stretch her spine. A photograph shows her trapped in a contraption that appears to pull her head away from her body. By the end of 1939 she was drinking a bottle of brandy each day.

She told Muray she had "no words" to express her pain, but she did have paint. During the period of her divorce she worked harder than ever before, and she produced some of her most powerful self-

*ABOVE: **Rivera painting Paulette Goddard, who may have been a contributing cause to the divorce, and an Indian woman in his San Angel studio, 1940.***

*RIGHT: **Rivera and Paulette Goddard arriving at the Los Angeles airport June 5, 1940. Rivera, divorced from Frida for seven months, said that the actress had helped him to "escape from Mexico with my life," after he became a suspect in the May 24, 1940, attempt on Trotsky's life by a group of Stalinists.***

portraits, "sublimating," as Rivera put it, "her anguish in her painting."[106] There was an economic motive as well: to Muray she said, "Since I came back from New York I don't accept a damn cent from Diego. . . . I never will accept money from any man till I die."[107]

The self-portraits from the divorce period are no longer pretty, folkloric, or charming. They are full of repressed rage, and Frida's tearless face has been hardened into an accusing mask. In the fall of 1939, while the divorce was in process, Frida worked on *The Two Fridas,* which her diary says had its origin in her memory of an imaginary childhood friend. But the double self-portrait's split identity seems more charged than that reading would allow, and Frida admitted to a friend that it recorded her unhappiness at being separated from Diego. The Frida in the Tehuana costume represents, she said, the woman that Rivera had loved. The other Frida, clad in a white costume, the blouse of which looks like a Victorian wedding dress, is, she said, the Frida whom Rivera no longer loved.[108] Like the women in *Two Nudes in a Forest,* the two Fridas also stand for Kahlo's dual heritage; once again the Indian side is stronger. The painting may, in addition, refer to Frida's love for women. At the center of the canvas, the two women's hands are joined in a stiff ceremonial clasp. Both Fridas' hearts are extracted—the same straightforward device to show pain in love that she used in *Memory.* The unloved Frida's heart is broken; the other Frida's heart is whole. Each woman has one hand in her lap near her genitals; the Tehuana Frida holds a miniature portrait of Diego as a boy. From its red oval frame springs a vein that travels through both women's hearts and is finally cut off by surgical pincers held in the lap of the rejected Frida. A poem by Elias Nandino, part of which Frida copied in her journal as a love note to Diego, says, "My blood is the miracle that travels in the veins of the air from my heart to yours." In her despair, Frida tries to stop the flow of blood from Diego, but it keeps dripping, and some of the red flowers embroidered on her white skirt are transformed into blood stains.

Defiant in their perfect composure, the two Fridas are set against a stormy sky that recalls El Greco's view of Toledo. Agitated clouds, like the rents in the land in other self-portraits, hint at the women's inner turmoil. As usual, the figures are completely disconnected from the vast empty space in which they are set. Frida's world is self-enclosed. Rejected by Diego, she holds her own hand, binds herself

Frida in traction during the year she was divorced from Rivera, 1939–40.

to herself with a strong red vein. She is her only companion.

Many people who knew Frida well felt her dividedness. Her paintings, Rivera remarked, "always portray her own life: the two Fridas, at once the same person and two different people."[109] Alejandro Gómez Arias said, "The personality of this woman was so contradictory and multiple that you could say there were many Fridas. Maybe none the one she wanted to be."[110] Frida herself spoke of the "duality" of her personality, perhaps referring to the Frida she felt herself to be from within and the Frida she saw from without—the observer and the observed. There was the flamboyant creature whom she presented to the world, the woman full of laughter, compassion, and heroic strength who served as the priestess in Rivera's temple. This persona

FRIDA
KAHLO
1 3 6

RIGHT: *Frida at her easel, c. 1945.* **The Two Fridas** *hangs on the wall and the shelves are full of pre-Columbian sculptures.*

OPPOSITE: **The Two Fridas,** *1939.*

ABOVE: Frida painting **The Wounded Table,** *1940. During the period of her divorce, Frida painted some of her most powerful works. This lost painting was one of her two large canvases; the other is* **The Two Fridas.**

hid the dark side of Frida, the needy, manipulating woman who in part embraced the role of victim in order to be admired for her martyrdom.

Frida's self-portraits are schismatic: she painted her body as subject for the artist's scrutiny, the female in the passive role of pretty object, victim of pain, or participant in nature's cycles. Her face, by contrast, is regal, self-willed, almost androgynous. To judge from her more obviously feminine prettiness in photographs, it is clear that she exaggerated her mustache and gave her features a somewhat steely cast. Perhaps as she examined her face in the mirror, Frida decided to depict the depicter, not the passive model. Her face she painted as the dispassionate investigator of what it feels like to be a woman; her body was the repository of feminine emotions.

The blood that drips on Frida's Tehuana skirt in *The Two Fridas* keeps on dripping in *The Wounded Table,* 1940, her only other large painting and one that a January letter to Muray says she was "working like hell" to finish before the January 17 opening of the "International Exhibition of Surrealism" (to which she also sent *The Two Fridas). The Wounded Table* has human legs that are flayed like those

BELOW: **The Wounded Table,** *1940.*

of an *écorché,* and several knots on its surface bleed. As a place where people gather, the table stands for domesticity; Frida's sense of home was battered by divorce.

Like *The Two Fridas,* the painting is a dramatization of loneliness. In the double self-portrait Frida accompanies herself; in *The Wounded Table* she is accompanied by her sister Cristina's children, by her pet fawn Granizo, and by three of the *Four Inhabitants of Mexico.* Theater curtains are pulled aside to reveal a stage where the seven characters are arranged on three sides of a table in a scene that recalls the Last Supper. In the center, Frida plays Christ, and a papier-mâché Judas wearing overalls that identify him as Diego plays the role of Judas.[111] Looking back on the divorce, Rivera admitted his betrayal: "I simply wanted to be free to carry on with any woman who caught my fancy . . . was I simply the depraved victim of my own appetites?"[112] We know that even as the Judas embraces Frida, he deceives her, for he leans on the table, as did Judas at the Last Supper when Christ said "But, behold, the hand of him that betrayeth me is with me on the table" (Luke 22:21).[113]

Inspired by a Nayarit sculpture of an embracing couple (now in the Frida Kahlo Museum), Frida elongated the arm of the idol that sits on her left. And, perhaps to emphasize her link with pre-Columbian culture, she made the idol's arm continuous with her own. The clay skeleton, with its pelvic bone tied to a chair to keep it upright, lifts a lock of her long hair in the coiled spring that forms his forearm. He seems intimately linked with Frida, as well.[114] Indeed, all three Mexican artifacts are probably aspects of Frida, for the idol has peg legs, and the skeleton and the Judas have broken and bloodied right feet.

Frida's suicidal feelings during her separation from Rivera ricochet through space in *Suicide of Dorothy Hale,* 1939, commissioned by Clare Boothe Luce as a gift for the dead woman's mother. When the painting arrived from Mexico, Mrs. Luce was shocked. There was, she recalled, an angel waving an unfurled banner that said "The suicide of Dorothy Hale, painted at the request of Clare Boothe Luce, for the mother of Dorothy." Horrified at the painting's violence, Clare Boothe Luce had the angel and the banner removed.[115] Frida clearly thought of the painting as a *retablo,* for she included an informatory panel inscribed in red script that turns into dripping blood just above her own signature.

En la ciudad de Nueva York el día 21 del mes de Octubre de 1938, a las seis de la mañana, se suicidó
la señora DOROTHY HALE tirándose desde una ventana muy alta del edificio Hampshire House.
En su recuerdo,   [...] retallo, habiéndolo ejecutado FRIDA KAHLO.

As in *A Few Small Nips*, Frida projected her feeling of being killed by Diego onto another woman's tragic demise, depicting her friend Dorothy Hale's eerily graceful leap to death from a high window of Manhattan's Hampshire House in three successive stages. Blood-spattered, but not battered, the fallen actress looks lovely in her Mme X gown decked with a corsage that was a gift from Noguchi. Frida painted Dorothy Hale's death as though it were just a rehearsal—perhaps a tryout for her own suicidal fantasies. Yet, as in *A Few Small Nips*, the emotional pressure is so high that the painting's contents explode onto the frame: extending the frothy sky onto the frame makes the whole painting seem a Magrittean fiction. Blood dripping down the frame's bottom section shocks the viewer into feeling like a witness to the catastrophe.

Frida's attraction to death is revealed again in *The Dream*, 1940, where the bed in which she is sleeping ascends into a lavender-and-white sky. As in Frida's dream of floating over the earth in *Roots*, she is in danger of falling, should her dream be interrupted. In her sleep, she pairs herself with a skeleton in the form of a papier-mâché Judas,

ABOVE: **Frida in 1940, with a baby goat in her arms, sitting beside her bed, on whose canopy lies a papier-mâché "Judas" skeleton laced with fireworks—Rivera called the skeleton Frida's "lover".**

LEFT: **The Dream, 1940.**

OPPOSITE: **The Suicide of Dorothy Hale, 1939.**

which actually did rest upon her bed's canopy. To Frida the skeleton was an amusing reminder of mortality. Rivera teased her by calling it her lover. A thorny vine embroidered on her bedspread grows free from its needlework. At her feet its roots appear to have been yanked from the earth when the bed took flight. Over her head it bursts into foliage.

Like Frida the skeleton lies on its side with its head resting on two pillows. In the place of Frida's vine, the skeleton has a network of explosives and a bouquet of lavender flowers. He is awake while Frida sleeps: at any moment, one feels, he could explode, making Frida's dream of death come true.

Both the thorny vine and the threat of death turn up again in a 1940 *Self-Portrait* that Frida sold to Nickolas Muray. Now the vine is woven into a necklace of thorns that draws blood from Frida's neck.[116] By wearing Christ's crown of thorns, Frida again presents herself as a Christian martyr. Several of the necklace's twigs are broken: Frida had an empathy for broken things—broken tables, broken veins, broken hearts. Hanging from the thorn necklace is a dead hummingbird, whose outstretched wings echo Frida's joined eyebrows. The bird must point to Frida's feeling of being cut down in flight or to her rejection by Diego: in Mexican folk tradition dead hummingbirds were used as charms to bring luck in love. In Aztec mythology the hummingbird symbolized reincarnation—the spirits of dead warriors returned in the form of hummingbirds.[117] In Christian symbolism birds in general stand for the winged soul. Given the religious atmosphere of this painting, in which Frida looks as solemn as a Pantocrator, the bird might also refer to the Holy Ghost.

Behind her shoulders, Frida's cat and monkey are black and menacing.[118] The cat is ready to pounce on the bird, and the monkey Caimito de Guayabal (meaning Guavapatch Fruit), a gift from Diego, fingers the necklace of thorns in a way that could deepen Frida's wounds. As in many of her bust-length self-portraits, a wall of large leaves closes off space. Every leaf presents its full veiny front or back to the spectator, just as Frida addresses us with her full frontal view. Among the leaves two flowers transformed into dragonflies may be symbols of transcendence, as are the filigree butterfly brooches attached to Frida's headdress. (Years later, Frida gave these butterfly pins to a lover as a token of her love.)

In letters Frida called her physical trials a "martyrdom." In paint-

Self-Portrait,
1940.

ings she dignified her grief by comparing it to Christ's suffering. Although she left Catholicism when she was about twenty-one, she remained steeped in it, and her paintings have a religious function. By painting herself as a martyr transcending pain, Frida made herself into an icon for herself and others to worship. Like the holy image in a votive painting, she is at once an abstract symbol and a powerful physical presence. Her self-portraits were, like ex-votos or magic talismans, crucial to her survival. This feeling of magical efficacy gives Frida Kahlo's paintings the peculiar magnetism that pulls the viewer into her cult.

Christian imagery, especially the theatrically bloody martyrdoms that hang in Mexican churches, pervades Frida's iconography. Her house in Coyoacán displays a particularly gruesome Road to Calvary, in which the overemphasis on Christ's wounds seizes the spectator on the most primitive physical level. This bloodiness and self-mortification hark back to preconquest times, when the Aztecs tore out human hearts and punctured their own skins to ensure life's continuance. But it was Spanish Catholicism that brought to Mexico the depiction of pain in veristic and human terms, creating images so real and so frightening that the Indians could not help but be awe-struck and, of course, converted. Borrowing the rhetoric of Catholicism, Frida used the same combination of pain and realism to attract devotees to her cause.

In another 1940 *Self-Portrait* (inscribed to Dr. Eloesser, "my doctor and my best friend. With all love") Frida's necklace of thorns is just a single strand, but it draws even more blood. In the background, leafless broken-off twigs profiled against an opalescent sky look like the dead twigs woven into Frida's necklace in the self-portrait with the hummingbird. No doubt the dry white buds that mingle with the twigs (and that droop from Frida's headdress as well) likewise refer to her desolation. Although Frida has flowers in her hair and wears the earrings in the shape of hands that Picasso gave her when she was in Paris, she looks like someone dressed for a ball for which she has no escort.

Frida's work from the year in which she and Rivera were separated demonstrates a heightened awareness of color's capacity to drive home emotional truths. As a self-taught artist, she began with a highly personal and unorthodox feeling for color. Her palette came out of her love for the startling combinations of bougainvillea pinks,

Pinté mi retrato en el año de 1940
para el Doctor Leo Eloesser, mi médico y
mi mejor amigo. Con todo mi cariño.   Frida Kahlo

Self-Portrait, *1940.*

Self-Portrait, *1940.*

purples, and yellows seen in the decorative arts of Mexico. She chose colors the way she chose her clothes—with exquisite aesthetic calculation. In such early works as *Henry Ford Hospital,* pastels create an ironic disjunction with the painful subject matter. In later paintings the choice of colors is just as odd and often even more dissonant and complex. The soft, pearly sky and the bright flowers in the Eloesser *Self-Portrait,* for example, only accentuate the chill of Frida's predicament. Their richness recalls the way statues of the scourged Christ in Mexican churches are often surrounded by flowers, lace, velvet, and gold.

Frida's idiosyncratic approach to color is revealed in a kind of prose poem in her diary, where she wrote a list of colors next to patches of colored lines, and where, in a characteristically unsystematic way, she told each color's meaning:

GREEN: warm and good light

REDDISH PURPLE: Aztec. Tlapali [Aztec word for "color" used for painting and drawing]. Old blood of prickly pear. The most alive and oldest.

BROWN: color of *mole,* of the leaf that goes. Earth.

YELLOW: madness, sickness, fear. Part of the sun and of joy.

COBALT BLUE: electricity and purity. Love.

BLACK: nothing is black, really *nothing.*

LEAF GREEN: leaves, sadness, science. The whole of Germany is this color.

GREENISH YELLOW: more madness and mystery. All the phantoms wear suits of this color. . . . . .or at least underclothes.

DARK GREEN: color of bad news and good business.

NAVY BLUE: *distance.* Also tenderness can be this blue.

MAGENTA: Blood? Well, who knows!

Yellow is "madness, sickness, fear." Several of Frida's 1940 paintings are dominated by a yellow that only exacerbates the dour mood. This yellow is not sunny, it is glaring. The yellow background in the *Self-Portrait* commissioned by the American engineer Sigmund Firestone, for example, makes Frida's black veil even more funereal. The yellow bedspread in *The Dream* is hallucinatory, and the yellow kitchen chair in the bleak *Self-Portrait with Cropped Hair* has the inappropriate gaiety of the yellow bed and chair that van Gogh painted at Arles.

**Fulang-Chang
and I,** *1937.*

**Self- Portrait
with Monkey**
1940.

**Self-Portrait
with Cropped Hair,
1940.**

The darkness in the interstices of a wall of leaves in a nocturne entitled *Self-Portrait with Monkey,* 1940, seems a more straightforward expression of Frida's gloom. Here a blood-red ribbon braided through her hair winds around her neck four times and around her pet monkey's once. The mood is claustrophobic; beginning in the year of her divorce, Frida began to encircle her neck in self-portraits with ribbons, necklaces, veins, vines, or a monkey's long arms that threaten to choke her. To identify the monkey as her close relative, Frida made his left arm continuous with her braid. Although she may have wanted to show her feeling of connectedness, the effect is sinister.

Compared to *Fulang-Chang and I,* 1937, in which a lavender ribbon links a softer, younger, and happier Frida with her spider monkey, the Frida in *Self-Portrait with Monkey* is grim. The circumstances under which these two portraits were made could not have been more different. When Frida painted *Fulang-Chang and I* in March 1937, she was at the height of her beauty, and her seductive powers were confirmed by her love affair with Trotsky. When Frida gave *Fulang-Chang and I* to her close friend Mary Sklar, she also gave her a mirror in a similar folkloric frame. Frida's idea was that the mirror and the painting should hang side by side so that Mary Sklar could always see herself next to Frida. The Frida in the 1940 *Self-Portrait with Monkey* is much more solitary: Frida's only companion was the mirror she looked into as she painted her features. As we submit to Frida's stare, we realize that she is not looking at us, but at herself in the mirror. Her eyes seem to bore holes through us and look beyond us, for in looking at her mirror reflection Frida was in fact looking at someone twice as far from her (and much smaller) than the viewer.

Shortly after her divorce came through, Frida wrote to Nickolas Muray: "I have to give you bad news: I cut my hair, and look just like a ferry [fairy]. Well, it will grow again, I hope!" One story has it that Frida warned Diego that if he continued his affair (probably with Paulette Goddard), she would again crop off the long hair he so admired. Perhaps the skeleton holding up a strand of her hair in *The Wounded Table* was another warning.

In *Self-Portrait with Cropped Hair* Frida looks like one of those mutilated saints dear to Mexican Catholicism. In her left hand she holds a lock of her shorn hair like an emblem of her sacrifice. In her right, she holds the scissors with which she martyred her femininity. A mood of suppressed fury resonates through colors so acid they set our teeth on edge. That same rage is expressed in Frida's aggressively ugly clothes. She has stripped off the Tehuana costume that gave such pleasure to Rivera and put on a dark suit that is too big for her and that must be his. Because of the importance Frida gave to clothes, wearing a baggy man's suit was like wearing a hair shirt or a nun's habit. The only vestige of her femaleness is pendant earrings.

Surrounded by the evidence of her violence, she sits alone in a vast expanse of uninhabited earth that suggests the reach of her despair. (By contrast, in bust-length self-portraits walls of foliage shut Frida and her miseries into a space that is uncomfortably narrow.) Strands of hair that look frighteningly alive are spread all over the ground. Since they do not diminish in size as they recede in space, they appear to hover like something in a horror film, and they recall the unrooted vines and veins that in other paintings symbolize Frida's yearning for connectedness. As in *The Two Fridas,* Frida has severed her connections, especially her link to Diego. She holds the scissors that did the severing near her genitals, precisely where she placed the surgical pincers that cut the vein in *The Two Fridas.* Both paintings dramatize Frida's will to take revenge by excising the part of herself that possessed the capacity to love and to be loved. Revenge is a boomerang: the cutting away of femininity does not reduce her vulnerability nor excise mourning. The shorn hair is alive and stays close to her, just as the blood in *The Two Fridas* keeps on flowing.

Typical of Frida's sardonic humor is her decision to add a caption that turns her self-portrait into a song illustration, like those printed by José Guadalupe Posada. Against the lowering sky she wrote the words and the notes of a popular song: "Look if I loved you, it was for your hair. Now that you are bald, I don't love you anymore."

On May 24, 1940, Trotsky's home was machine-gunned by a group of Stalinists, and Rivera, who had had a well-publicized falling out with Trotsky the previous year, came under suspicion. He went into hiding and then left for San Francisco, where he was invited to paint a mural on the theme of pan-American solidarity for the Golden Gate International Exposition. Following the attempt on Trotsky's life, Frida became gravely ill, and three months later, when he was assassinated by an agent of the GPU (the Soviet secret police at the time), she was interrogated by the police and jailed for two days. Concerned about her health, Rivera suggested that she come to San Francisco to

Frida and Diego applying for a marriage license in San Francisco on December 5, 1940.

see Dr. Eloesser. Acting as a go-between, the doctor wrote to Frida: "Diego loves you very much, and you love him. It is also the case, and you know it better than me, that besides you, he has two great loves—1) painting 2) women in general. He has never been, nor ever will be, monogamous, something that is imbecilic and anti-biological. Reflect, Frida, on this basis. What do you want to do?"[119]

Frida flew to San Francisco, where her illness was diagnosed as a combination of a "crisis of nerves" and osteomyelitis. From New York, where she had gone for a brief visit, she wrote to Sigmund Firestone: "I was very ill in Mexico. Three months I was lying in an awful apparatus on my chin which made me suffer like hell. All the doctors in Mexico thought I had to be operated on my spine. . . . I got so scared that I was sure I was going to die."[120] To Frida's relief, the doctors at Saint Luke's Hospital in San Francisco did not recommend surgery. "You can imagine," Frida went on, "how happy I was . . . Besides, I saw Diego, and that helped more than anything else . . . I will go back to San Francisco and marry Diego again. (He wants me to do so because he says he loves me more than any other girl.) I am very happy."

Meanwhile, in San Francisco, Rivera told an assistant: "I'm going to marry Frida because she really needs me."[121] He needed her, too, for Frida saw to his every desire, making sure, for example, that his shirts were washed, his letters written, and his finances more or less straight, and that his favorite meals appeared on time—whatever time he chose to come home. Just as she loved his vulnerability and his womanly breasts, he loved her grit and her "Zapata" mustache. Her mordant wit and her lively, critical mind never bored him, and Rivera, above all, hated to be bored. And, of course, he was proud of having such a striking woman at his side.

The separation, he said, "was having a bad effect on both of us."[122] There were, however, several conditions upon which Frida agreed to remarry him. She insisted, Rivera recalled, that "she would provide for herself financially from the proceeds of her own work; that I would pay half of our household expenses—nothing more; and that we would have no sexual intercourse. In explaining this last stipulation, she said that, with the images of all my other women flashing through her mind, she couldn't possibly make love with me, for a psychological barrier would spring up as soon as I made advances.

"I was so happy to have Frida back that I assented to everything."

Perhaps to consecrate their reunion, Rivera painted Frida—now back in her Tehuana costume—into his Golden Gate mural. As usual, she is a symbolic figure. She represents, Rivera said, the "Mexican

Detail of Rivera's Treasure Island mural painted at the Golden Gate International Exposition in 1940 (now at the City College of San Francisco). When Frida joined him in San Francisco in Fall 1940, Rivera put her into his mural as a symbolic figure who, he said, "personifies the cultural union of the Americas for the South." Paulette Goddard, shown to the right holding hands with Rivera around the tree of love and life, stood for "American girlhood . . . shown in friendly contact with a Mexican man." Rivera and Goddard's joined hands, he said, meant "closer Pan-Americanism."

artist with [a] sophisticated European background who has turned to native plastic tradition for inspiration; she personifies the cultural union of the Americas for the South."[123] Behind Frida, Paulette Goddard looks amorously into Rivera's eyes as she and he hold hands around the tree of love and life. The film star, in the muralist's mind, stood for "American girlhood . . . shown in friendly contact with a Mexican man."[124] This, he baldly explained to a newspaper photographer, "means closer Pan-Americanism."[125]

On December 8, 1940, Rivera's birthday, Frida and he remarried. Conjugal life soon fell into its old patterns. In March 1941, she wrote to Dr. Eloesser: "you must have an idea of how he needs to be taken care of and how he absorbs time, since as always when he arrives in Mexico he is in a devilish bad humor until he acclimatizes himself once again to the rhythms of this country of craziness. This time the bad mood lasted more than two weeks, until they brought him some marvelous idols from Nayarit and seeing them he began to like Mexico again. Also, the other day, he ate a very delicious duck *mole,* and this also helped to give him back his pleasure in life." In July she reported again to the doctor: "The remarriage functions well. A small quantity of quarrels—better mutual understanding and on my part, fewer investigations of the tedious kind, with respect to other women,

LEFT: **Frida and Diego after their wedding ceremony, performed in a San Francisco courtroom by a municipal judge on December 8, 1940, Rivera's fifty-fourth birthday.**

RIGHT: **Frida and Diego after their remarriage, in the dining room in Coyoacán, 1941.**

Self-Portrait, *1941*

LEFT: *Frida's kitchen in Coyoacán. "Frida" and "Diego" are spelled out in mosaic on the wall.*

BELOW: *In a luncheon alcove in Frida's garden.*

who frequently occupy a preponderant place in his heart. Thus you can understand that at last—I have learned that *life is this way* and the rest is painted bread [just an illusion]. If I felt better healthwise one could say that I am happy—but this thing of feeling such a wreck from head to toe sometimes upsets my brain and makes me have bitter moments."

With the death of her father in April 1941, Frida's health worsened. The war in Europe depressed both Riveras, and Frida's somber mood informs her 1941 self-portraits—*Self-Portrait with Bonito*, for example, in which she is dressed in mourning, and *Self-Portrait with Braid*, in which serrated leaves twisting from arterylike stems seem ready to attack Frida's flesh. The painting suggests that the second marriage had all the problems of the first one, but it has an auspicious note: Frida has gathered up the hair she cut off in *Self-Portrait with Cropped Hair*, braided it into a pretzel, and reaffirmed her femininity by placing it on top of her head. In a 1941 nocturne entitled

**Self-Portrait
with Bonito,**
1941.

Self-Portrait with Braid, *1941.*

RIGHT: **Portrait of
Marucha Lavin
(tondo), 1942.**

BELOW: Frida painting
**Portrait of Marucha
Lavin,** *1942.*

TOP: **Portrait of Lucha María, a Girl from Tehuacán,** *1942.*

BOTTOM, LEFT: **Portrait of Lupita Morillo Safa,** *1944.*

BOTTOM, RIGHT: **Portrait of Natasha Gelman,** *1943.*

The Flower Basket (oddly enough, she painted this still-life tondo for Paulette Goddard) the hummingbird that hung dead at Frida's neck in the self-portrait from the divorce period now flies over luxuriant blossoms, perhaps rejoicing in its success in bringing luck in love.

Rivera continued to be an incorrigible womanizer, and Frida's thwarted desire to possess him expressed itself in *Self-Portrait as a Tehuana,* 1943.[126] Framed by her starched Tehuana headdress, Frida's face looks as devouring as a carnivorous flower. White and black tendrils that spring from her headdress are like conducting wires carrying her positive and negative energy out into the world. But, once again, these connectors are disconnected: the black threads that are continuations of the veins of leaves adorning her hair are unrooted and dangle in the air.

Like a female spider, Frida watches from the center of her web. She has consumed her mate and trapped the thought of him inside

ABOVE: **The Flower Basket** *(tondo), 1941.*

LEFT: With Nickolas Muray, c. 1939. Frida's **Me and My Parrots** *was finished in 1941.*

OPPOSITE: **Me and My Parrots,** *1941.*

La novia que se espanta de ver la vida abierta.

ABOVE: **The Bride Frightened at Seeing Life Opened,** *1943.*

OPPOSITE: **Self-Portrait with Monkey and Parrot,** *1942.*

Thinking
About Death,
1943.

LEFT: *Frida wearing a Tehuana headdress, standing in the Blue House's dining room, c. 1940. This ceremonial headdress derived from a petticoat found in a woman's trunk lost in a shipwreck. The Tehuantepec natives thought the petticoat should be worn on the head.*

her forehead in the form of a miniature portrait. Still, Rivera does not look possessable. His gaze lifts upward and far away, even as Frida, in this portrait, dresses up to capture his regard.

In *Thinking About Death* from the same year, Frida's desire has turned in the opposite direction. Instead of thinking about Diego, she focuses on a skull and crossbones, which appear in a circular window opened in her forehead. In *Self-Portrait as a Tehuana* she is tethered to the picture's frame by a radiating network of threads. In *Thinking About Death* stems with blood-red thorns and veins of leaves that form a wall behind her create a similar web: again there is no exit from obsessional thoughts. Yet Frida's confrontation with death is almost Egyptian in its imperturbability; indeed, her portrait recalls the famous bust of Nefertiti, of whom she said, "I imagine that besides having been extraordinarily beautiful, she must have been 'a wild one' and a most intelligent collaborator to her husband."[127]

RIGHT: *Painting* Self-Portrait as a Tehuana, *c. 1940, with Rivera looking on. Frida's* The Wounded Table, *1940, hangs in the background.*

Self-Portrait,
1948.

From the following year comes *Diego and Frida 1929–1944*, an anniversary gift for Rivera at a time when the couple had once again separated. (Frida painted another version of this double portrait to keep for herself.) This time Frida's urgent need to be tied to her husband made her merge her identity with his, creating a single head out of half of each of their faces. Male and female—the duality alluded to also by the sun and the moon and by a conch and a scallop shell—are joined, but the union is not stable: the spouses' faces do not line up, and their head must be held together by a necklace made of leafless branches. For Frida, the marriage bond was a martyrdom.

In 1948 Frida painted a second *Self-Portrait* in which she wears a Tehuana headdress; here its lace ruff closes off space and makes her look trapped. There is a peculiar disjunction between Frida and her costume. She looks like a face poking through one of those stage flats used by photographers at Mexican fairs. The split between face and clothes underscores psychological dividedness. It is poignant in an-

LEFT: **Diego and Frida 1929–1944,** *1944.*

RIGHT: **Frida's** *birthday note to Diego, December 8, 1945. She wrote, "Diego, my child, my love. You know what gifts I would give you, not only today, but always, but this year I had the bad luck of not being able to give you anything made by my hands nor anything that you would really like. I offer you everything that has always been mine and yours, my love, that is born and lives every hour because you exist and you receive it. Your little girl, Fisita [Frida's nickname] (your old occultress)."*

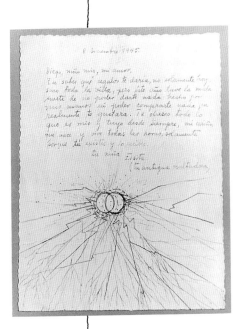

*In bed with a mirror
attached to the
canopy. Two of the
many dolls she
collected are in the
doll bed on the right.*

other way as well. She dressed herself in the Tehuana headdress as a plea for Rivera's love, but her clothes are off-putting. She is over-dressed. Her finery is a mask. The greater Frida's pain, emotional or physical, the more desperately festive her packaging became.

Though she decks herself in lace, she does not cosmeticize the depredations of age. The contours of her face are fuller and coarser now; although she had for years painted the slight mustache that surmounted her voluptuous red lips, the hardening of her features makes it look more obviously masculine. Years of pain have taken

their toll. That this toll continues to mount is shown by three tears glistening on Frida's cheeks like the tears of the Madonna of Sorrows. Turning to the mirror to find solace in the companionship of an alternate self, Frida became the voyeur of her own grief. Painting both the griever and the observer, she drowned in the narcissism of sorrow. In the end, the mirror offered no companionship. It didn't even give Frida her real face, but rather a reverse image flattened across hard, shiny glass—an image that was ultimately unavailable and so became the perfect object for Frida's chronic longing.

ABOVE: Frida, c. 1945.

LEFT: Looking in the mirror, c. 1943. Photograph by Lola Alvarez Bravo.

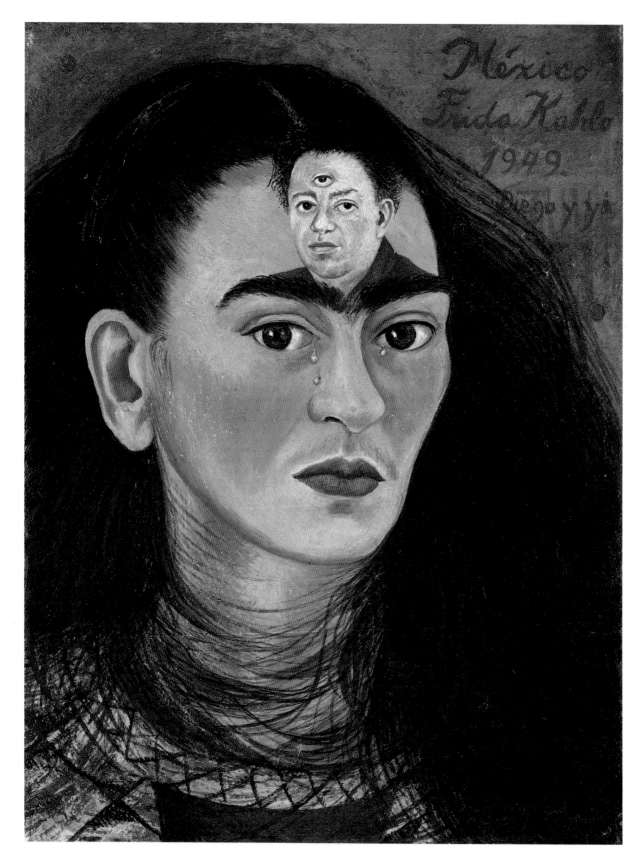

Diego and I,
1949.

Frida's anguish intensifies in *Diego and I,* painted the following year, when Rivera almost divorced her to marry María Félix. The beautiful film star was an intimate friend of Frida's as well, and though Frida pretended to joke about this affair, as she had about Rivera's other escapades, *Diego and I* shows that she was hurt. For once she almost loses her mask of reserve. Instead of a web of lace or leaves closing her in, she is now surrounded by a mass of her own loose hair, which swirls around her neck suggesting strangulation.[128] The cause of her distress is indicated by a small bust of Diego, for which her eyebrows serve as pedestal. A third eye, which refers to Rivera's superior mental and visual acuity, opens in her husband's forehead. Of the pyramid of five eyes that look out of this painting, only Frida's meet ours. Diego, whose artistic venue was panoramic and epic, looks out over our heads (and over the head of Frida in the mirror) into the beyond.

That Rivera was the constant intruder in Frida's thoughts is revealed also in her journal, much of which is a love poem to him: "DIEGO. I am alone." Then a few pages later: "My Diego. I am no longer alone. You accompany me. You put me to sleep and you revive me." Another time she drew two faces that look like vases. "Don't cry at me," one of them says. The other answers: "Yes. I'll cry at you." In a more romantic moment, she wrote: "Diego: Nothing is comparable to your hands and nothing is equal to the gold-green of your eyes. My body fills itself with you for days and days. You are

*TOP: **Diego with Fulang-Chang.***

*BOTTOM: **Frida with her pet monkey, c. 1945.***

*LEFT: **Rivera with the film star María Félix beside his portrait of Félix, 1949. At this time Rivera wanted to divorce Frida in order to marry María Félix (who was also an intimate friend of Frida's).***

Frida Kahlo. 4

the mirror of the night. The violent light of lightning. The dampness of the earth. Your armpit is my refuge. My fingertips touch your blood. All my joy is to feel your life shoot forth from your fountain-flower which mine keeps in order to fill all the paths of my nerves which belong to you."

As the years went on, Frida took a more and more motherly role in relation to her husband. He loved to be pampered, and she discovered that playing mother made it easier to indulge his mischief. Just as she could scold when he dropped his underwear on the floor or gobbled three scoops of pistachio ice cream, she could laugh at his sexual misadventures. She confided her maternal feelings to her journal: "At every moment he is my child, my child born every moment, diary, from myself." In her "Portrait of Diego," written for the catalogue of Rivera's 1949 retrospective at Mexico City's Palace of Fine Arts, Frida said, "Women—among them I—always would want to hold him in their arms like a new-born baby."[129] That is exactly what she does in *The Love Embrace of the Universe, the Earth (Mexico), Diego, Me, and Señor Xolotl,* 1949, a self-portrait that celebrates the final resolution of the Riveras' marriage. Here Frida is the earth mother/ Madonna nurturing the baby she could never have—her "Dieguito." Now she does not need to clasp him tightly, for the couple's union is sustained by a series of love embraces that roots them in the Mexican

LEFT: **Portrait of Diego Rivera, c. 1940.**

RIGHT: **Portrait of Frida Kahlo, c. 1940.**

OPPOSITE: **The Love Embrace of the Universe, the Earth (Mexico), Diego, Me, and Señor Xolotl, 1949.**

TOP: *Frida's studio upstairs in the Blue House, with* The Love Embrace *on the easel, 1949.*

BOTTOM: *In the patio with* The Love Embrace*, 1949. Photograph by Florence Arquin.*

OPPOSITE: *Frida and Diego, in the mid-1940s, in front of the stairway to Frida's bedroom. Frida's studio is on the left.*

earth and in the ancient dark/light duality of a pre-Columbian universe. Even Frida's *itzcuintli* dog, Xolotl, is encompassed by this vast interlocking pyramid of love.

Yet for all Frida's contentment in possessing her spouse, she knew, as she wrote in 1949, that "Diego has never been and never will be anyone's husband." Although she looks calm, tears still dot her cheeks, and a bright red crevasse cracks open her neck and chest. From it a magical fountain of milk sprays forth. In sympathy, the Mexican earth has a cracked breast from which one drop of milk appears. The baby Diego holds an orange maguey plant, which looks like fire and might stand for what Frida called his "fountain-flower" (his penis), or it might stand for the fire of his genius, rooted in the Mexican soil. In "Portrait of Diego" Frida described the Diego she painted in her portrait. His bulging, wide-set eyes were, she said, "constructed especially for a painter of spaces and multitudes." The third eye opened in his forehead is the invisible eye of "Oriental wisdom," and his "Buddha-ish mouth" is set in "an ironic and tender smile. . . . Diego is an immense baby with an amiable face and a slightly sad glance . . . seeing him nude, you immediately think of a boy frog standing on his hind legs. His skin is greenish white like that of an aquatic animal.[130]

To Frida, Rivera was everything. She wrote in her diary:

Diego. *beginning*
Diego. *constructor*
Diego. *my baby*
Diego. *my boyfriend*
Diego. *painter*
Diego. *my lover*
Diego. *"my husband"*
Diego. *my friend*
Diego. my mother
Diego. me
Diego, universe
Diversity in *unity*

Why do I call him *My* Diego? He never was nor ever will be mine.
He belongs to himself.

TOP, LEFT: **Pulqueria bar La Rosita, with murals painted by Frida's students, 1943.**

TOP, RIGHT: *With three of the students to whom Frida taught painting in the 1940s, c. 1944. From left: Fanny Rabel, Arturo Estrada, and Arturo García Bustos.*

BOTTOM: *Nelson A. Rockefeller (center) with Frida (on his left) and Rosa Covarrubias (on his right), at Miguel and Rosa Covarrubias's house in Mexico City, in the mid-1940s.*

In the mid-1940s Frida's health declined. She lost weight and had fainting spells. To support her back she had to wear a series of orthopedic corsets, which she described as a "punishment." Now more than ever, painting was a weapon for survival. Determined to confront and communicate her predicament, she painted herself as the heroic sufferer. Yet even her most grueling depictions of pain are not obviously self-pitying. From having had polio as a child and from her accident, Frida knew that it was best to play the "brave girl" if she wanted to keep her family and friends' admiration and love. Her attitude, frequently expressed in letters, was that "one must put up with it—there is no recourse." This fortitude is evident in her queenly bearing and unflinching gaze in her self-portraits.

Frida declared both her strength and her vulnerability in *The Broken Column,* 1944, painted during the five-month period when she was "punished" by a steel corset. An entry in her diary underscores the painting's almost paralytic tension: "To hope with anguish retained, the broken column, and the immense look, without walking, in the vast path . . . moving my life created of steel." Of all her paintings, this is the one that makes Frida's inability to move around in

Wearing a plaster cast, which she decorated with the hammer and sickle, c. 1950.

The Broken
Column, *1944.*

or to truly inhabit the landscape that stretches behind her almost unbearable. She wrote to Dr. Eloesser, "I got a little better with the corset but now I feel just as sick again, and I am now very desperate because I do not see anything that improves the condition of my spine."

In *The Broken Column* Frida's anguish is communicated in the most physical and harrowing way, by nails stuck into her face and flesh and by a split in her torso that resembles an earthquake fissure. The opening is echoed in the dark ravines cut into the earth behind her, and it suggests the horror of surgical intervention. Inside the gap a cracked Ionic column replaces her own deteriorating vertebrae. Penetrating from loins to chin, the column looks phallic, and the sexual connotation is all the more obvious because of the beauty of Frida's breasts and torso. (At first she had painted herself completely nude, but after deciding that her genitals were distracting, she covered them with what looks like a hospital sheet.)

The Chick,
1945.

A Mexican Saint Sebastian, Frida displays her wounds and demands that we marvel at her miraculous survival. Like many Saint Sebastian paintings, *The Broken Column* combines the sexual attraction of a well-formed nude with physical mortification to convey the message of spiritual triumph. But Frida is no saint. Instead of lifting her eyes heavenward to pray for salvation, she stares straight ahead, challenging both herself (in the mirror) and her audience to face her situation. Tears dot her cheeks, but her features are as masked as those of a pre-Columbian idol.

The painting's style is as steely as its content. Everything is pared down to essentials. There are no virtuoso flourishes of the brush, and every stroke has been laid down firmly to build a simple, clear image. Colors are as neatly contained within contours as those in a conscientious child's coloring book. All through her career Frida kept a slight primitivism that mitigated the violence of her imagery. In paintings from the 1940s that do not depict bodily wounds—that is, portraits, still lifes, and bust-length self-portraits—she did not need a naive style to mask pain, and these paintings are often highly realistic. Another reason for the greater realism in such works is that they were based not on *retablos,* but on nineteenth-century Mexican portraits and still lifes that aimed for a minutely detailed realism.

Besides its ability to distance pain, there are other aspects of primitivism that coincide perfectly with *The Broken Column*'s meaning. The awkward drawing and handling of space and the rudimentary modeling (Frida used little black in her shadows) make Frida look like a paper cutout—or an icon—set in front of, rather than integrated into, the landscape. Like an icon, too, the figure is strictly frontal, and its meaning comes from the emotional charge it directs out at the viewer, not from any active connections to objects inside the painting. Frida's doll-like stiffness underscores her helplessness and makes the bondage imposed by her corset's white straps all the more emphatic. This helplessness locks in with the painting's suggestion of sexual aggression. In spite of her fierce will, Frida does not act; she is always acted upon. Her arms, for example, look as incapable of movement as those of a china doll. Primitivism turns her into both a votive and a sex object.

Three self-portraits from 1945 and another entitled *The Circle* from about that time show that Frida's physical condition continued to deteriorate. In *The Circle* Frida's headless nude body disintegrates

**Self-Portrait with
Small Monkey,** *1945.*

into the surrounding landscape. In *Self-Portrait with Small Monkey* she is tied to her dog, to her monkey, to a pre-Columbian idol, and to her signature by a yellow ribbon that also loops around a nail driven into the beige clouds that form the painting's background. The trompe l'oeil nail (borrowed from Rivera, who in his Cubist phase borrowed the device of the illusionistic nail from Braque) teases the viewer with the reminder that no matter how real the image looks, it is just paint on a flat surface. But the nail is also premonitory. In Catholic Mexico it would be seen as an emblem of Christ's passion.

In *The Mask* Frida hides behind a weeping purple-haired mask that expresses her feeling of craziness. The disjunction between the masked and the real Frida is more disconcerting than in other self-portraits, because here the real Frida watches us through holes in the mask's eyes. In substituting a weeping mask for her own face masked by denial, Frida revealed that playing roles can literally disintegrate the self.

The faults and fissures of Mexico's volcanic terrain once again symbolize the violence done to Frida's passive body in *Without Hope,*

The Mask, *1945.*

Without Hope, *1945.*

Magnolias, *1945.*

where Frida lies in bed crying and vomiting or screaming a cornu-copia of gore out onto an easel that straddles her bed. The presence of the easel could refer to the connection between her illness (or possibly a recent miscarriage) and her need to make art. The funnel of butchery is topped with a sugar skull that has her name on its forehead. On the back of the canvas she wrote: "Not the least hope remains to me. . . . Everything moves in tune with what the belly encloses." Perhaps Frida is being force-fed, and the painting is meant to convey her disgust when doctors made her eat pureed foods every two hours or when, after an operation, they said, "Now you can eat anything!"

Again Frida is naked, but partially covered by a sheet. Nakedness for her usually implies helplessness, possibly because she was familiar with the experience of being stripped in preparation for surgery or because she remembered landing in the street with her clothes torn off during the bus crash. Frida's sheet is dotted with microscopic or-ganisms, which, by echoing the blood-red sun and the pale moon, ex-tend the drama of Frida's suffering from microcosm to macrocosm.

In February 1946, after almost four months of being bedridden, Frida decided to go to New York to put herself in the hands of Dr. Philip Wilson, a prominent surgeon at the Hospital for Special Surgery who had been recommended by her friend Arcady Boytler, who also suffered from back problems. On May 3, one month before flying to New York, Frida gave Arcady Boytler and his wife, Lina, one of her most poignant self-portraits. *The Little Deer* arrived at their house together with a ballad of thanks.[131]

The deer walked alone
very sad, and very wounded
until in Arcady and Lina
he found warmth and a nest.

When the deer returns
strong, happy and cured
the wounds he has now
will all be erased.

Thank you, children of my heart,
Thank you for so much advice,
in the forest of the deer
the sky is brightening.

I leave you my portrait
so that you will have my presence
all the days and nights
that I am away from you.

Sadness portrays herself
in all my paintings
but that's how my condition is
I no longer have structure.

Nevertheless, I carry
joy in my heart
knowing that Arcady and Lina
love me as I am.

Accept this little painting
painted with my tenderness
in exchange for your affection
and your immense sweetness.

Frida

Frida with her
pet fawn, Granizo,
c. 1938.

In *The Little Deer* Frida presents herself with the body of a young stag and her own head crowned with antlers. Like Frida, the deer is

The Little Deer, *1946.*

prey to suffering. Pierced by nine arrows, he stares out at the viewer from a forest enclosure. Although the stormy, lightning-lit sky in the distance is, as Frida's poem points out, "brightening," we know that the deer will never reach the sea. One meaning of the word "CARMA," which appears in the painting's lower-left corner, is destiny or fate, and, as in most of her self-portraits, Frida presents herself as incapable of changing destiny.

The deer's youthful vigor contrasts with the decay of old tree trunks, whose broken branches and knots correspond to his wounds. Beneath him a slender branch broken from a young tree alludes to Frida's and the deer's broken youth and imminent death. It may also refer to the pre-Hispanic custom of placing a dry branch on a grave to help the dead person enter paradise. With resurrection, the dry branch is transformed into a green branch.[132]

In Aztec belief the deer was the sign for the right foot; even with Frida's various operations, the condition of her right foot continued to worsen, and the deer could have been a kind of talisman.[133] The arrows in the deer may, like the arrows in valentine hearts, point to pain in love. In Mexico a frequently used colloquialism describes a cuckolded man as having antlers or horns. Perhaps because this expression usually refers to a man, Frida painted herself with the tes-

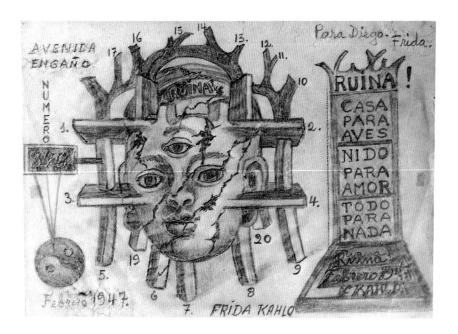

Ruin, *1947.*

ticles of a male deer.[134] Supporting the idea that *The Little Deer* expresses the misery of betrayal is the fact that the deer has nine arrows and nine points to his horns. Thus each arrow could refer to a Rivera escapade, just as the numbered projections from a structure that holds together a fractured male/female head in a 1947 drawing entitled *Ruin* refer to Rivera's myriad affairs. (The drawing, inscribed "deceit avenue," was a sour anniversary gift to Rivera.) Then again, Frida may simply have made her deer a male because Granizo, the fawn she once kept as a pet, was male. Or the deer has testicles because she recognized her bisexuality. Like the stag, Frida had the "balls" (this slang expression is used in Spanish, too) to put up with her sufferings.

On May 21 Frida flew to New York, and in June Dr. Wilson performed a spinal fusion in which four vertebrae were fused with a piece of bone extracted from her pelvis and with a metal rod fifteen centimeters long. During the two months she spent in the hospital, her recovery was good, and her spirits were high, in part because she was given frequent injections of morphine to kill her pain. On June 30 she wrote to Alejandro Gómez Arias:

> They do not allow one to write very much, but this is only to tell you that *the big* operation already took place. Three weeks ago they proceeded with the cutting and cutting of bones. And he is so marvelous this doctor, and my body is so full of vitality. . . . The first two weeks were full of great suffering and tears so that I do not wish my pains on anybody. They are very strident and evil, but now, this week, my yelling diminished and with the help of pills I have survived more or less well. I have two huge scars on my back. . . . Five vertebrae were damaged and now they are going to be like a rifle [in popular usage, "in terrific shape"]. The bother is that the bone takes a long time to grow and to readjust itself and I still have to spend six weeks in bed before they release me and I will be able to flee from this terrifying *city* to my beloved Coyoacán.

When Frida returned to Mexico, she was first bedridden and then enclosed in a steel corset for eight months. Instead of improving, her health grew worse. She had shooting pains in her spine, she lost weight, and she became anemic. Nevertheless, she painted, and in a letter to a friend she called her next self-portrait, *Tree of Hope,* 1946, "nothing but the result of the damned operation!"[135]

Beneath a cloudy sky in which the sun and moon divide the paint-

Tree of Hope,
1946.

ing into light and dark halves sits a weeping Frida clothed in a red Tehuana costume. She keeps vigil over the body of a second Frida, who lies anesthetized on a hospital trolley, her surgical incisions still open and dripping with blood. The seated Frida holds a pink orthopedic corset as if it were a trophy. But her real support comes from a flag emblazoned in red with words taken from a song—her motto, "Tree of Hope, keep firm."[136] The flagpole's pointed red tip looks like a paintbrush dipped in red paint or, in this context, like a surgical instrument stained with blood. The two Fridas are flanked by a grave-like trench and a precipice; as always, the fissured earth is a metaphor for Frida's wounds. The precipice and the trench point to danger averted: in describing *Tree of Hope* to Eduardo Morillo Safa, the patron to whom it was destined, Frida said, "There is a skeleton (or death) that flees in the face of *my will to live.*"[137] Perhaps to please him, she removed the skeleton, but she could not erase death's menace. Joining Frida the tragic victim and Frida the heroic survivor in one image, *Tree of Hope* is an act of faith, like a *retablo.* But in Frida's *retablo* there is no miracle worker; Frida takes charge of her salvation and becomes her own holy intercessor.

The spinal fusion of 1946 has been called the beginning of "the calvary" that led to Frida's death. Although she consulted numerous, perhaps too numerous, doctors, her condition grew steadily worse.

Rivera's Hotel del Prado mural of 1947–48, detail, showing Rivera as a boy, with Frida standing behind him in the motherly role that she assumed more and more in the 1940s. Holding hands with Rivera is the "Calavera Catrina," an invention of the printmaker José Guadalupe Posada, who stands to the skeleton's left.

TOP: *In the patio,
c. 1947.*

BOTTOM: *Frida and
Diego, c. 1941.*

Very likely she sabotaged her well-being by choosing to have unnecessary operations as a peculiar form of narcissism.[138] Having operations was a cry for attention. Being a surgical patient could alleviate her feelings of disconnection. Each new surgical procedure, each new doctor offered renewed hope. Each operation brought her admiration and sympathy and, most important, the attention of Diego. One of her doctors said that her health depended on her feelings about Rivera. When he was away or she felt abandoned by him, she would precipitate a crisis. When he was at her side, she recovered.[139] This pattern must have had its origin in her childhood, when she had polio and her father took it upon himself to restore his favorite daughter to health.

In 1950 Frida entered the British Hospital in Mexico City. When she left a year later, she had had at least seven operations on her spine. Her healing process was complicated by an infection, probably osteomyelitis. Frida maintained her humor and her stoicism, delighting visitors with her gaiety and, instead of complaining, listening to their problems. "We healthy people who went to visit her came away comforted, morally fortified," a woman friend recalled.[140] Frida dec-

Aqui me pinté yo, Frida Kahlo, con
la imágen del espejo. Tengo 37 años,
y es el mes de Julio de mil novecientos
cuarenta y siete. En Coyoacán, México,
lugar donde nací.

**Self-Portrait with
Loose Hair,** *1947.*

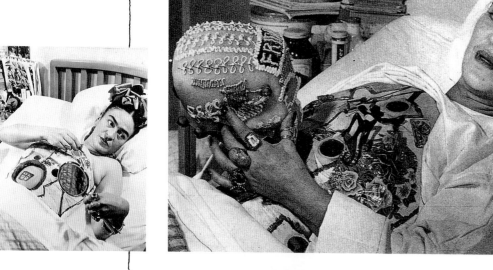

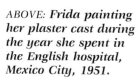

ABOVE: *Frida painting her plaster cast during the year she spent in the English hospital, Mexico City, 1951.*

TOP, RIGHT: *Holding a sugar skull in the English hospital, 1951.*

BOTTOM: *Frida using a semicircular apparatus (designed to keep her right foot warm) as a puppet stage, 1951.*

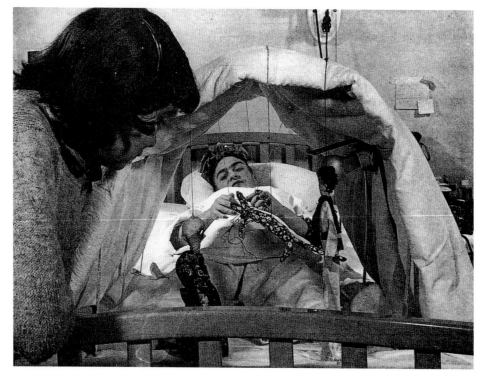

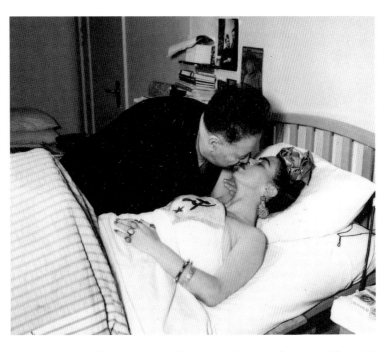

*With Diego in the
English hospital, 1951.*

orated her room with sugar skulls, wax doves, clay candlesticks from
Matamoros, and the Soviet flag. She hung sheets of paper on the wall
and asked visitors to sign their names for the Stockholm Peace Petition. With the help of friends she decorated her various plaster casts
with signatures, feathers, mirrors, decals, and the red star and hammer and sickle painted in iodine.

When she had been injected with painkillers, Frida was exuberant
to the point of being manic. She put on puppet shows, using as a
stage the semicircular metal apparatus designed to keep her right leg
warm. If she saw her doctor with a pretty girl, she'd cry, "Lend her
to me! I'll smoke that one myself!"[141] She had all kinds of plans and
all kinds of enthusiasms. Of the nine-year-old Indian boy from Oaxaca who became her disciple, for example, she said, "He has great
talent, and I am going to pay for all his education and send him to
the San Carlos Academy."[142] After having a bone from a donor named
Villa grafted onto her spine, she cried, "With my new bone I feel like
shooting my way out of this hospital and starting my own revolution."[143]

Lying flat on her back, she used a special easel to paint *My Family,*
a second version of her family tree (started years before and never
finished). It has a special poignancy: at the time when her engage-

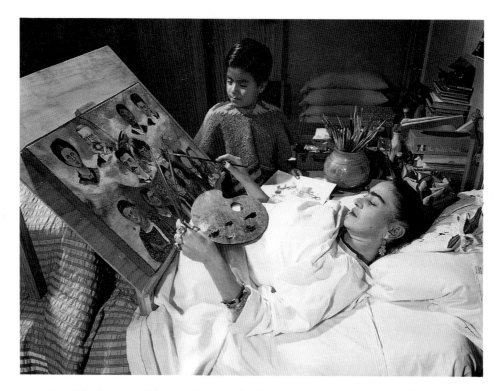

*Frida painting her
family tree in the
English hospital.
Looking on is a boy
who may be her
apprentice Vidal
Nicolás.*

ment with the world was increasingly curtailed, she looked for inter-connection by surrounding herself with relatives. Recalling her hospitalization, Frida said, "I never lost my spirit. I always spent my time painting, because they kept me going with Demerol, and this animated me and it made me feel happy. . . . I joked around, I wrote, they brought me movies. I passed three years [actually one] in the hospital as if it were a fiesta. I cannot complain."[144]

She should have complained. Instead, she was proud: "I hold the record for operations," she announced.[145] And she was grateful. While convalescing at home in 1951 she painted a secular *retablo* entitled *Self-Portrait with the Portrait of Dr. Farill.* Sitting in her wheelchair before her doctor's portrait on her easel, Frida is the saved victim of narrowly escaped danger. Her surgeon is the savior. In painting her-self with her doctor as an act of gratitude, Frida may have been think-ing of Goya, who, when he was old and sick in 1820, painted *Goya Attended by Doctor Arrieta* and added a dedicatory inscription telling of his gratitude to his doctor for saving his life.

Painting herself with her doctor was, one feels, as crucial to Fri-da's survival as an ex-voto. "I have been sick a year," she wrote in

My Family, *c. 1950–51.*

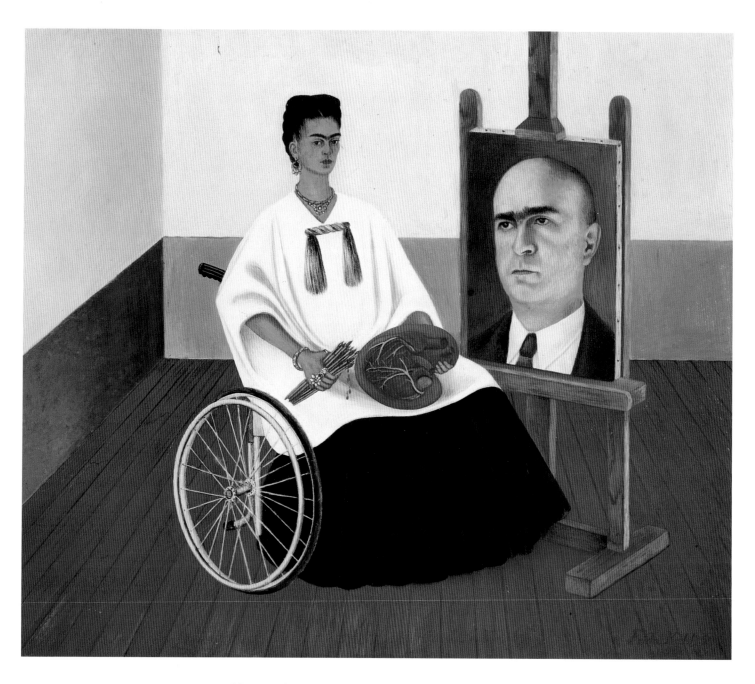

Self-Portrait with the Portrait of Doctor Farill, *1951.*

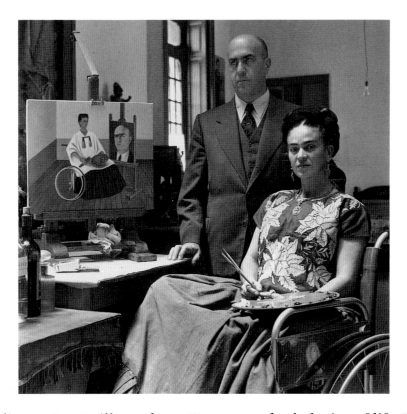

her diary. "Dr. Farill saved me. He gave me back the joy of life. I am still in a wheelchair and I do not know if soon I will be able to walk again. I have a plaster cast, which, in spite of being a frightful bore, helps my spine feel better. I do not have pains. Only a weariness . . . and as is natural, often desperation. A desperation that no words can describe. Nevertheless, I want to live. I already have begun to paint the little painting that I am going to give to Doctor Farill and that I am doing with all my affection for him."

With its drained, somewhat acid colors and its simple composition, *Self-Portrait with the Portrait of Dr. Farill* is charged with an intensity held in check. Confined by invalidism, Frida painted her world as a kind of prison. The corner of the room she occupies is defined by two windowless, pale yellow walls with gray-blue wainscoting, and her location in space is fixed by interlocking compositional lines that recall the tight, closed structure of *My Birth*.

Frida's extracted heart lies on her palette—an offering to her beloved doctor and a way of saying that she painted from the heart. Red paint drips from her brushes, which are, like the flagpole in *Tree*

Frida and Dr. Farill beside her Self-Portrait with the Portrait of Doctor Farill, *1951.*

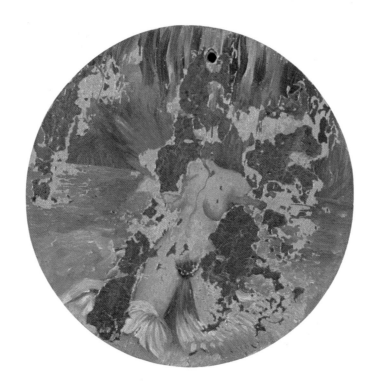

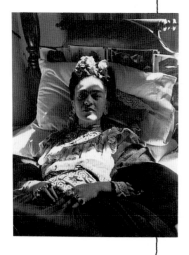

RIGHT: **The Circle (tondo), c. 1951.**

BELOW: In bed at home after spending a year in the hospital, 1952.

of Hope, as pointed as surgical instruments. The palette/heart and brushes are emblems both of her martyrdom and her salvation.

Home from the hospital, Frida continued to deteriorate. When she was well enough, she worked, but starting in 1952, her paintings lost their miniaturist precision and became rather crude both in conception and execution. This was in part because it was difficult for her to sit for long periods and in part because since 1946, when she was given morphine after her spinal fusion, she increasingly took refuge in drugs, especially Demerol. As one of her doctors put it, "The style of her last paintings shows anxiety with states of excitation of the type that comes from drug addiction."[146] Brush strokes seem to have been laid down with frenetic haste. Color is no longer clear and vibrant, but strident and grating. She used fewer colors, and those she chose—lots of red, yellow, and orange—do not convey subtle nuances of feeling and meaning. The paintings seem overexuberant. They recall the hollowness that saddened friends when Frida, in her last years, put on her mask of joy.

Fruits that formerly would have been arranged with precision and sly wit on a table are now spread on the earth beneath an open sky.

Still Life with Parrot, *1951.*

Fruit of Life, *1954.*

TOP: **Still Life with Legend,** *c. 1953.*

BOTTOM: **Still Life,** *1951.*

TOP: **Coconuts,** *1951.*

BOTTOM: **Still Life with Parrot and Flag,** *1951.*

ABOVE: **Naturaleza viva,** *1952.*

RIGHT: *Painting* **Naturaleza viva,** *1952.*

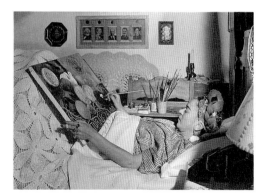

Frida acknowledged the preternatural animation in her still lifes when she titled one of them *Naturaleza viva,* meaning "alive nature," as opposed to the usual Spanish term for still life, which is *naturaleza muerta,* or "dead nature." In this still life a peace dove is nestled among Mexican fruits, some scarred, some cut open. The fruits' roundness is echoed in the sun and moon, and the sun is surrounded by a pointillism of orange dots that look as life-giving as the fruits' seeds. Golden roots embrace the fruit and grow into the earth, where they form the letters of the painting's title.

As the months passed, Frida's paintings became increasingly apocalyptic in mood. One 1953 still life entitled *Fruit of Life* is divided into four quarters (earth and sky, day and night); the sun's face, with its Frida eyebrows and its Rivera lips, looks berserk. Sun rays are transformed into a web of crimson roots that could be veins. Against the earth they spell out the word "LUZ" (light), plus Frida's name. Despite its roughness, this painting testifies to the courage with which Frida continued to devour life.

As her world became more and more restricted, her attachments to objects, friends, politics, and Diego intensified. Her engagement with painting became more charged as well. Whereas before she had maintained a coquettish, debunking attitude toward her work, often pretending not to take it seriously, now she would say that all she wanted to do was paint.[147]

In the spring of 1953 Frida's painting connected her to the world in a very concrete way: she was honored with her first one-person

ABOVE: Rivera, c. 1954.

RIGHT: Frida with her friend Teresa Proenza, 1952.

OPPOSITE: Frida with her household servants, c. 1952.

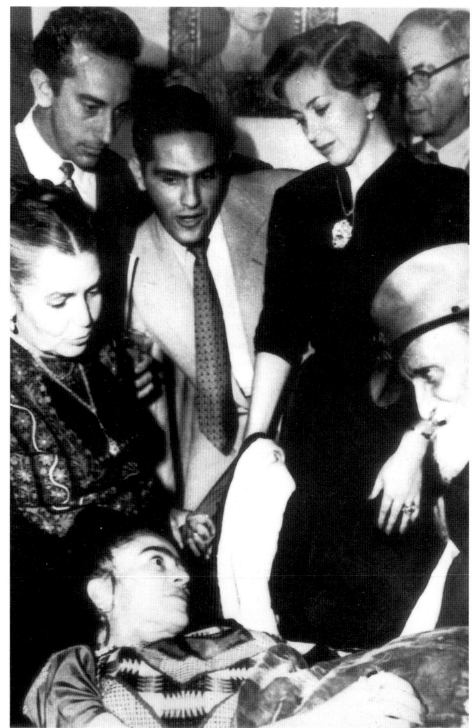

*RIGHT: **Frida being carried into the Galería de Arte Contemporaneo for the opening of her first exhibition in Mexico, April 13, 1953. Looking on are** (left to right) **Concha Michel** (ballad singer), **Antonio Peláez** (painter), **Dr. Roberto Garza, Carmen Farell,** and (lower right) *the painter Doctor Atl.*

*BELOW: **In a wheelchair, c. 1952.***

exhibition in her native land. Although her doctors had forbidden her to attend the opening, she arrived at the Galería Arte Contemporaneo in an ambulance. Enthroned on her own four-poster bed, installed in the gallery, she greeted guests, sang Mexican ballads and drank tequila until past midnight. For the invitation to her show she wrote a charmingly folkloric ballad, two of whose six verses say:

> *With friendship and love*
> *born from the heart*
> *I have the pleasure of inviting you*
> *to my humble exhibition. . . .*
>
> *These paintings*
> *I painted with my own hands*
> *and they wait on the walls*
> *to give pleasure to my brothers.*

The paintings gave such pleasure that the show was extended for a month by popular demand. The press was full of praise for Frida's heroic accomplishment. In an article entitled "Mexican Autobiography" *Time* magazine noted that Frida was a celebrity in her own right. Frida told *Time*'s stringer, "I am not sick. I am broken. But I am happy to be alive as long as I can paint."[148]

Another thing that broadened and gave value to her life was politics. After Frida had rejoined the orthodox Stalinist flock in the late 1940s, Communism became a religion. "Now I am a communist being," she wrote in her journal. "I understand clearly the materialist

Frida talking with Josephine Baker during the unveiling of Rivera's mural The Nightmare of War and the Dream of Peace *at the Palace of Fine Arts, Mexico City, 1952.*

Rivera painting Frida handing out Stockholm peace petitions in his **The Nightmare of War and the Dream of Peace,** *1952.*

dialectic of Marx, Engels, Lenin, Stalin and Mao Tse. I love them as the pillars of the new communist world." Portraits of these pillars hung like icons at the end of her bed.

The personal nature of the subject matter in her paintings began to trouble her. "I am," she wrote in her diary, "very worried about my painting. Above all to transform it, so that it will be something useful, since until now I have not painted anything but the honest expression of my own self, but absolutely distant from what my painting could do to serve the Party. I should struggle with all my strength for the little that is positive that my health allows me to do in the direction of helping the Revolution. The only real reason to live." She tried to politicize her still lifes by inserting flags, political inscriptions, and peace doves. But Frida's paintings remained a hymn to herself and to life.

In her political self-portraits she once again turned to *retablos* to express her faith and gratitude. In *Marxism Will Give Health to the Sick,* 1954, Frida, dressed in an orthopedic corset and clutching a red book that must be Marx's *Capital,* is the victim saved by the miracle-making saint, Karl Marx. Two enormous hands, one with an extra eye signifying wisdom, descend from the vicinity of Marx to support

Frida with José Clemente Orozco, Manuel Sandoval Vallarta, and Jaime Torres Bodet, 1946. Orozco received the National Art Prize; Frida received the Ministry of Education prize for her painting Moses, 1945; Vallarta received the National Science Prize; Torres Bodet was Minister of Education.

Frida's studio upstairs, designed by Rivera in the 1940s.

Marxism Will Give Health to the Sick, *1954.*

Frida so that she can cast aside her crutches. Another hand projects from Marx's head and strangles an American eagle, which is a caricature of Uncle Sam. Beneath the eagle rivers run red and an atomic bomb explodes. The other side of Marx's head is touched by a peace dove that hovers protectively over both Frida and a globe dominated by the Soviet Union, where the rivers are blue. Until 1954 Frida had painted only one quasi-political painting. By comparison with the lighthearted spoof on the false values of capitalist society seen in *My Dress Hangs There*, *Marxism Will Give Health to the Sick* is declamatory. Whereas the earlier painting gently mocks, the 1954 painting sees Communism versus capitalism as day versus night, holy peace dove versus evil eagle.

Early in 1953 Frida's doctors began to talk about the possible amputation of her right leg at the knee because of gangrene. Frida said she wanted to die. In her diary she drew herself as a doll breaking into bits as she falls from a pedestal, and she captioned the drawing "I am DISINTEGRATION." A sketch of herself nude and winged came with the words "Are you going? No." The reason: "BROKEN WINGS." Another day she felt bolder, and she drew her legs with a wash of crimson ink. The right leg is severed at the ankle. Thorny branches grow from its top. "Feet," she wrote, "what do I want them for if I have wings to fly?"

Perhaps the most heartrending of the diary's drawings shows Frida lying as she does in *Roots*, with her head propped on one elbow. But instead of a vine issuing from her torso to fertilize the soil, her whole body dissolves into the earth and becomes a network of roots. Above her are the words "color of poison," perhaps referring to gangrene. The sun and moon are in the sky and earth; in the sky next to a disembodied foot she wrote "Everything backwards, sun and moon, feet and Frida." On the opposite page a tree loses its leaves to the wind. Bent, not broken, it is strong. Yet it is not a tree of hope, but of despair. During these last years Frida replaced her motto "Tree of Hope, keep firm" with another: "Night is falling in my life," *"Esta anocheciendo en mi vida."*[149]

In August the doctors made their decision, and Frida wrote in her diary, "It is certain that they are going to amputate my right leg. I know few details, but the opinions are very serious. . . . I am very worried, but at the same time, I feel that it will be a liberation. I hope that I will be able, when I am walking, to give all the strength that I have left to Diego, everything for Diego." The night before the operation Frida chided her friends for looking morose: "It's as if there were a tragedy! What tragedy? They are going to cut off my *pata*. So what?"[150] She dressed in a Tehuana costume and delivered herself to the surgeon's knife.

Although the operation was a success, and Frida was able to walk short distances with her artificial leg, spiritually she never recovered. Even in moments when she summoned her habitual *alegría* and twirled in front of friends to show off her wooden leg shod in a red boot decorated with bells, her gaiety was a false mask. Rivera recalled, "Following the loss of her leg, Frida became deeply depressed. She no longer even wanted to hear me tell her of my love affairs,

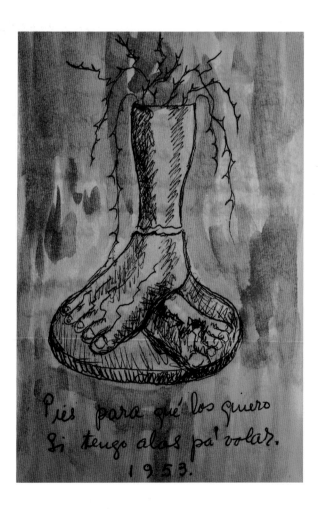

Diary page: "Feet, What Do I Need Them For If I Have Wings to Fly," 1953.

Diary pages: "I Am Disintegration," 1953.

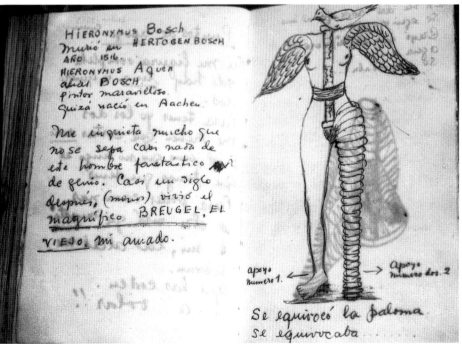

Diary pages: "The Dove Made a Mistake," 1953.

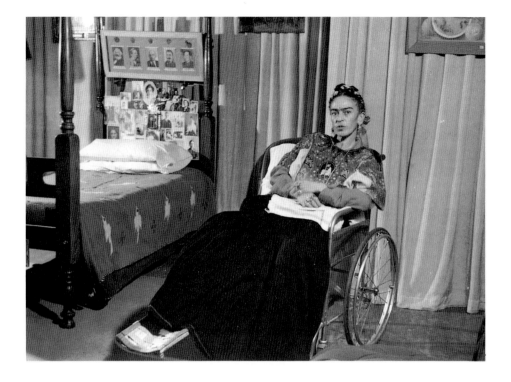

Frida after the amputation of her leg, 1953. Five photographs of her Communist heroes are framed above her bed.

which she had enjoyed hearing about after our remarriage. She had lost her will to live.''[151] Her drug addiction became more severe. She made several attempts at suicide, and she was frequently violent toward others as well. Much of the time she slept in a drug-induced stupor. On February 11, 1954, she wrote in her diary: ''They amputated my leg six months ago, they have given me centuries of torture and at moments I almost lost my 'reason.' I keep on wanting to kill myself. Diego is the one who holds me back because of my vanity in thinking that he would miss me. He has told me so and I believe him. But never in my life have I suffered more. I will wait a little while.''

On July 2, while recuperating from bronchopneumonia and against doctor's orders, she left her bed to participate in a demonstration against the fall of the leftist government of Jacopo Arbenz in Guatemala which was brought about by CIA intervention. Prominent figures from the world of Mexican culture followed in her wake as Frida, looking ravaged and with her head covered only by a wrinkled scarf instead of her usual beribboned crown of braids, was pushed in her wheelchair by Rivera. In this, her last public appearance, she

LEFT: *Frida left her sickbed to protest the ouster of Guatemalan president Jacobo Arbenz Guzmán by the CIA, July 2, 1954, eleven days before her death. Diego is behind her; the painter Juan O'Gorman is to her right.*

BELOW: *At the rally protesting CIA involvement in Guatemala.*

made a heroic spectacle; holding a banner calling for peace, she found the energy to join in the crowd's cry: *"Gringos, asesinos, fuera!"* (Gringos, assassins, get out!) Home again, she confided to a friend, "I only want three things in life: to live with Diego, to continue painting and to belong to the Communist Party."[152]

When she succumbed eleven days later, her death was reported as being caused by pulmonary embolism, but, given her suicide attempts, many of Frida's friends believe that she killed herself. The last words in her journal would suggest as much: "I hope the exit is joyful—and I hope never to come back—Frida." The diary's last drawing is a black angel rising, surely the angel of death.

When Frida died, Rivera was like "a soul cut in two."[153] His great frog face sagged into folds of age and sorrow. He dug his nails into the palms of his clenched fists over and over again until they bled. In his autobiography, Rivera remembered, "July 13th, 1954, was the most tragic day of my life. I had lost my beloved Frida forever. . . . Too late now, I realized that the most wonderful part of my life had been my love for Frida."[154]

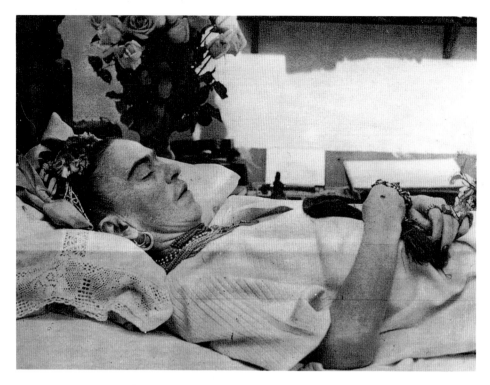

Frida lay in her four-poster bed dressed in a black Tehuana skirt and in her favorite *huipil* from Yalalag—the loose white overblouse with a lavender silk tassel that she wore in her *Self-Portrait with the Portrait of Dr. Farill.* Friends braided her hair with ribbons and flowers and adorned her with necklaces of silver, coral, and jade. Her hands, resting on her stomach, glittered with rings. Next to her remaining foot, with its bright red toenails, lay red flowers.

That evening Frida lay in state in the vestibule of the Palace of Fine Arts, while Rivera, friends, family, and notables from the worlds of art and politics, including former president Lázaro Cárdenas, formed honor guards around her coffin. Apparently with Rivera's permission, a young painter who had been Frida's student in the second half of the 1940s spread the red flag with a hammer and sickle over her coffin, causing a scandal that led to the dismissal of her old school friend Andrés Iduarte, who was director of the National Institute of Fine Arts at the time. Frida would have been amused by the furor created when Rivera refused to remove the flag and threatened to take his wife's coffin out onto the steps and keep vigil there. She had, after all, done everything in her power to help Rivera gain read-

Frida's casket being carried from the Palace of Fine Arts, Mexico City, where she lay in state. Rivera allowed one of her students to cover the coffin with a red Communist banner, causing a scandal, July 14, 1954.

Rivera and José Mancisidor carrying Frida's casket.

Frida's funeral procession. Diego, flanked by former president Lázaro Cárdenas (left), follows the hearse to the crematorium.

At the crematorium of the civil cemetery, the director of the National Institute of Fine Arts, Andrés Iduarte (to Rivera's right), giving a funeral oration.

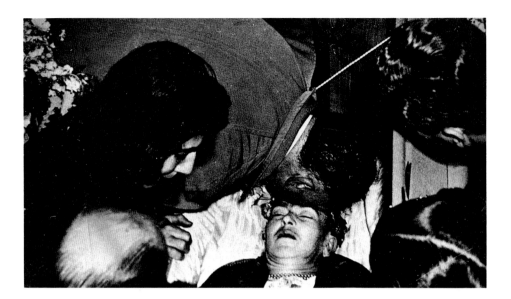

Rivera kissing Frida good-bye. His daughter Ruth is on his right.

mittance to the Communist Party. A few months later he was no longer a political exile. In his autobiography he said that after Frida's death "My only consolation now was my readmission into the Communist Party."[155]

At noon the next day a funeral procession of some five hundred mourners followed Frida's hearse down Avenida Juárez. At the crematorium of the Panteón Civil de Dolores her coffin was opened, and friends gathered around her as Andrés Iduarte delivered the funeral oration:

> Frida has died. Frida has died.
> The brilliant and self-willed creature who, in our day, lit up the classrooms of the National Preparatory School has died. . . . An extraordinary artist has died: alert spirit, generous heart, sensibility in living flesh, love of art even unto death, intimate of Mexico in vertigo and in grace. . . . Friend, sister of the people, great daughter of Mexico: you are still alive. . . . You live on.[156]

Frida's good friend the poet Carlos Pellicer read his sonnets to Frida: "You will always be alive on the earth,/you will always be a mutiny full of auroras,/the heroic flower of successive dawns."[157]

At quarter past one Rivera and various family members laid Frida on the automatic cart that would carry her to the crematory oven. Rivera bent to kiss her, and as she moved toward the fire, the crowd sang the "Internationale," the national anthem, and several ballads of farewell. As she entered the oven, friends recall, the intense heat made her sit up, and her hair formed an aureole around her head. Four hours later, when her ashes emerged from the oven, they retained for an instant her skeletal shape. Rivera pulled a sketchbook from his pocket and drew his wife one last time. Then he gathered her ashes into a red cloth and put them in a cedar box. It is said that, soon after she had been cremated, he ate some of her ashes in order to meld her being with his. He asked that, after his cremation, his ashes be mixed with Frida's, but his family chose a more august resting place for the great muralist, the Rotunda de los Hombres Ilustres.

Several years later, when Rivera gave Frida's Coyoacán home to the people of Mexico in order to perpetuate her memory, he stipulated that "a corner be set aside for me, alone, for whenever I felt the need to return to the atmosphere which recreated Frida's presence."[158] The museum recreates Frida's presence to such an extent that many visitors feel her spirit is alive there. When the Frida Kahlo Museum opened, a sack containing her ashes leaned against the headboard of her four-poster bed, and on top of it Frida's plaster death mask, draped in one of her rebozos, looked alive. This assemblage frightened visitors, so the ashes were moved to a pre-Columbian jar in the shape of a rotund, headless female. Cast in bronze and affixed to a marble base, the death mask no longer looks macabre, just dead. But the urn seems pregnant with life, just the kind of vitality that Frida saw in the pregnant clay idol in her painting *Four Inhabitants of Mexico:* "being dead," Frida said of this idol, "she has something alive inside."

In death Frida, too, is full of life. In recent years, she became first a myth and then a cult figure. In Mexico Frida is recognized as the country's greatest woman artist, and, in the opinion of many, Mexico's greatest artist. In 1984 the Mexican government decreed Frida Kahlo's work to be national patrimony, because it has "an unquestioned aesthetic value and has reached unanimous recognition within the national artistic community."[159] For women everywhere, and especially for women artists, Frida is an example of persevering strength. She painted against great odds: she worked in a macho culture and in the heyday of muralism, when a woman making small, highly personal easel paintings did not win much respect. She was not discouraged by the enormous fame and ferocious artistic drive of her husband—she neither competed with nor deferred to him. And

Frida and Diego,
c. 1954.

she kept on painting in spite of pain. To Mexican-Americans Frida is a political heroine; she demonstrated her love for *la raza* in her life and in her painting. To people who are ill, indeed to anyone oppressed by almost any sorrow, she offers hope. Her paintings are so powerful that people who look at them feel that Frida speaks directly and specifically to them. And, for all her anguish, Frida Kahlo's final gift is the preeminence of joy. During the last terrible months she found the strength to write in her journal:

> *I have achieved a lot.*
> *I will be able to walk*
> *I will be able to paint*
> *I love Diego more*
> *than I love myself.*
> *My will is great*
> *My will remains.*

Eight days before she died, she added a finishing touch to her last painting, a still life that pits the crimson pulp of chopped and sliced watermelon against the life/death duality of a half dark, half light sky. The painting both welcomes death and defies it with *alegría*. One last time Frida dipped her brush into red paint and inscribed her name and "Coyoacán 1954 Mexico" on the foremost slice. Then in large capital letters, she wrote the motto whose invocatory force makes both her art and her legend live: VIVA LA VIDA, she said, LONG LIVE LIFE.

Viva la vida, *1954.*

NOTES

1. André Breton, "Frida Kahlo de Rivera," in *Surrealism and Painting,* p. 144, reprinted from Frida Kahlo's exhibition brochure published by the Julien Levy Gallery in 1938.

2. Antonio Rodríguez, private interview, Mexico City, August 1977, and Antonio Rodríguez "Una Pintora Extraordinaria: La Vigorosa Obra de Frieda Kahlo Surge de su Propia Tragedia, con Fuerza y Personalidad Excepcionales," undated newspaper clipping, Antonio Rodríguez, personal archive, n.p.

3. Bertram D. Wolfe, "Rise of Another Rivera," *Vogue,* Nov. 1, 1938, p. 64.

4. Diego Rivera, "Frida Kahlo y el Arte Mexicano," *Bolitín del Seminario de Cultura Mexicana,* no. 2, Mexico City, Secretaría de Educacion Pública, Oct. 1943, p. 101. All translations from the original Spanish in letters, diaries, books, and articles are by the author.

5. Julien Levy, *Memoir of an Art Gallery* (New York: Putnam, 1977), p. 16.

6. *Time,* "Fashion Notes," May 3, 1948, pp. 33–34.

7. Frida Kahlo interviewed by Parker Lesley, Coyoacán, D.F., Mexico, May 27, 1939. Henceforth "Lesley, notes."

8. Peggy de Salle, private interview, Detroit, Jan. 1978.

9. Lesley, notes.

10. Dolores Alvarez Bravo, private interview, Mexico City, Sept. 1974.

11. Frida Kahlo's diary is on display in the Frida Kahlo Museum, Mexico City. I am grateful to Dolores Olmedo for giving me access to it.

12. Lesley, notes.

13. Diego Rivera, "Frida Kahlo y el Arte Mexicano."

14. Lesley, notes.

15. Lesley, notes.

16. Raquel Tibol, *Crónica, Testimonios y Aproximaciones,* p. 24; and Lesley, notes. The following quotation also comes from Lesley, notes.

17. Frida said that she painted the leaf after she had completed the nurse's breast, because she needed "to balance the breast. I invented it [the leaf] because I couldn't think of anything else." (Lesley, notes.) This is typical of the straightforwardness and lack of mystification with which she spoke of her art. Often her tone was nonchalant, as if she wanted to make her painting sound simpler and more naive than in fact it was. In terms of her painting procedure, a photograph taken about 1939 shows that in *My Nurse and I* Frida first painted her hair cut short like a boy's.

18. Tibol, *Crónica,* p. 24.

OPPOSITE: *At her worktable on the patio, c. 1950.*

19. Salomon Grimberg, "Frida Kahlos Einsamkeit," in *Frida Kahlo: Das Gesamtwerk,* p. 20. I am grateful to Dr. Salomon Grimberg for giving me the English text of this and other essays.

20. Frida Kahlo, "Retrato de Diego," *Novedades* (Mexico City), Supplement, "México en la Cultura," July 17, 1955, p. 5.

21. Tibol, *Crónica,* p. 23.

22. Felipe García Beraza, "La Obra Historica de Guillermo Kahlo," in *Homenaje a Guillermo Kahlo (1872-1941): Primer Fotógrafo Oficial del Patrimonio Cultural de Mexico,* exhibition catalogue published by El Instituto Mexicano Norteamericano de Relaciones Culturales, A.C., in August 1976, n.p.

23. María Luisa Kahlo, private interview, Mexico City, Nov. 1977.

24. Tibol, *Crónica,* pp. 26–27 and pp. 20–21, 26.

25. Ibid., p. 21.

26. María Luisa Kahlo, private interview.

27. Lucienne Bloch interviewed by Karen and David Crommie for their film *The Life and Death of Frida Kahlo,* 1968.

28. Emmy Lou Packard, private interview, San Francisco, Nov. 1978.

29. Linda Nochlin has observed that many women artists have had "strong or dominant" artist fathers to whom they are close. Linda Nochlin, "Why Have There Been No Great Women Artists?" in Thomas B. Hess and Elizabeth C. Baker, *Art and Sexual Politics* (New York: Macmillan, 1973), p. 30.

30. Tibol, *Crónica,* p. 26.

31. Raquel Tibol, *Frida Kahlo: Una Vida Abierta,* p. 17. Frida's medical record is vague. She said some doctors thought she had polio and others, "white tumor."

32. Lesley, notes.

33. Tibol, *Crónica,* p. 28.

34. Ella Wolfe, the widow of Rivera's biographer and a close friend of Frida's, told Salomon Grimberg that Frida said the artifacts belonged to Rivera and that she included them because they reminded her of him. Salomon Grimberg, "Vier Einwohner der Stadt Mexico," in *Frida Kahlo: Das Gesamtwerk,* p. 71.

35. Lesley, notes.

36. Ibid.

37. Ibid.

38. Wolfe, "Rise of Another Rivera," p. 131. *They Ask for Planes and Are Given Straw Wings* is lost but recorded in a photograph in the personal archive of Michel Petitjean, Paris. As in the self-portrait in *Four Inhabitants of Mexico,* this girl does not have joined eyebrows. Dressed in a Tehuana costume, she is perhaps the typical Indian child that Frida, in part, wanted to be.

39. Frida had love affairs with two of the Spanish refugees who she and Rivera helped after their arrival in Mexico.

40. Aurora Reyes, private interview, Mexico City, Nov. 1978.

41. Baltasar Dromundo, *Mi Calle de San Ildefonso,* Mexico City, Editorial Guarania, 1956, p. 46.

42. Andrés Iduarte, "Imagen de Frida Kahlo," clipping from a Caracas newspaper (Aug. 12, 1954), Isolda Kahlo archive, Mexico City.

43. Martha Zamora, *Frida: El Pincel de la Angustia*, p. 213.

44. Manuel González Ramírez, "Frida Kahlo," April 24, 1953, unidentified newspaper clipping, Isolda Kahlo archive.

45. Diego Rivera, *My Art, My Life,* pp. 128–29.

46. Bertram D. Wolfe, *The Fabulous Life of Diego Rivera*, p. 241.

47. Adelina Zendejas, interviewed by Karen and David Crommie for their film *The Life and Death of Frida Kahlo*, 1968.

48. Tibol, *Crónica,* p. 31.

49. Alejandro Gómez Arias has said that she was no longer a virgin at the time of the accident. According to him, the rod entered at the level of Frida's pelvic bone, and she pretended that it pierced her vagina in order to explain her not being a virgin. She also blamed her inability to have a child on the accident, but Gómez Arias thinks there may have been other reasons. Alejandro Gómez Arias, private interview, Mexico City, July 1977.

50. Tibol, *Crónica,* p. 32.

51. Ibid.

52. Frida Kahlo, letter to Alejandro Gómez Arias, quoted in Alejandro Gómez Arias, "Un Testimonio Sobre Frida Kahlo," in *Frida Kahlo,* Exposicíon Nacional de Homenaje, exhibition catalogue, Palacio de Bellas Artes, Instituto Nacional de Bellas Artes, Mexico City, 1977, n. p.

53. Andrés Henestrosa, private interview, Mexico City, March 1977.

54. Salomon Grimberg, unpublished letter to *The New York Times,* January 7, 1991.

55. Dr. Philip Sandblom, letter to *The New York Times,* Dec. 23, 1990, Arts and Leisure section, p. 4.

56. Quoted in a letter from Dr. Philip Sandblom to the author, March 2, 1991.

57. Juan O'Gorman and Lola Alvarez Bravo, interviewed by Karen and David Crommie, 1968.

58. Letter to Alejandro Gómez Arias, Sept. 29, 1926, Alejandro Gómez Arias's personal archive, Mexico City. I am grateful to Alejandro Gómez Arias for making Frida Kahlo's letters and his memories available to me.

59. Frida Kahlo, letter to Alejandro Gómez Arias.

60. A surgeon discovered that Frida had three vertebrae out of place. He prescribed a plaster cast that would keep her immobilized for a month and a special apparatus for her right foot.

61. Wolfe, "Rise of Another Rivera," p. 131.

62. A statement by Fernández about Frida's apprenticeship with him is on display along with some of Frida's first drawings in the Frida Kahlo Museum.

63. Bambi, "Frida Es una Mitád," *Excelsior* (Mexico City), June 13, 1954, p. 6.

64. Ibid.

65. Rivera, *My Art, My Life,* p. 170.

66. Ibid., p. 172.

67. Bambi, "Frida Es una Mitád."

68. Joseph Freeman, letter to Kenneth Durant, Sept. 30, 1929. Joseph Freeman Collection, Hoover Institution archive, Stanford University. I am grateful to Sarah Lowe for pointing out this letter to me.

69. Bambi, "Frida Es una Mitád."

70. Tibol, *Crónica,* p. 49.

71. Rafael Lozano, Mexico City dispatch to *Time,* Nov. 10, 1950.

72. Gisèle Freund, "Imagen de Frida Kahlo," *Novedades* (Mexico City), Supplement, "México en la Cultura," June 10, 1951, p. 1.

73. Paul Boatine, private interview, Detroit, Jan. 1978.

74. Rivera, "Frida Kahlo y el Arte Mexicano," p. 101, and private interview with an old friend of Frida's who wishes to remain anonymous.

75. Rosa María Oliver, "Frida la Unica y Verdadera Mitád de Diego," *Novedades* (Mexico City), Supplement, "México en la Cultura," Aug. 1959, p. 7.

76. Rivera, *My Art, My Life,* p. 242.

77. Carmen Phillips, private interview, Pipersville, Pennsylvania, Nov. 1979.

78. Frida Kahlo, "Retrato de Diego," p. 5.

79. See the film footage in the Hoover archive at Stanford University.

80. Breton, "Frida Kahlo de Rivera," p. 144.

81. Rafael Lozano, op. cit.

82. Bambi, "Frida Es una Mitád."

83. Frida Kahlo's letters to Dr. Leo Eloesser are in the personal archive of Joyce Campbell, Tacámbaro, Michoacán.

84. I am grateful to Salomon Grimberg for identifying this image for me.

85. Lesley, notes.

86. Antonio Rodríguez, "Frida Kahlo: Heroína del Dolor," *Novedades* (Mexico City), Supplement, "México en la Cultura," July 17, 1955, p. 1.

87. Tibol, *Crónica,* p. 50.

88. In his Chapingo murals (1926–27) Rivera depicted the body of a revolutionary buried beneath a thriving field of corn as a metaphor for the agrarian revolution.

89. Lucienne Bloch, private interview, San Francisco, Nov. 1978. I am grateful to Lucienne Bloch for sharing with me her memories and passages in her diary concerning Frida Kahlo.

90. Edgar P. Richardson, letter to the author, Jan. 30, 1978.

91. Letters to Dr. Leo Eloesser, Oct. 24 and Nov. 26, 1934.

92. Wolfe, *The Fabulous Life of Diego Rivera,* pp. 357–58.

93. Lesley, notes.

94. In 1934 the ends of the toes of her right foot were amputated. In 1935 and 1936 her foot was operated for sesamoids. Since 1931 she had also had a trophic ulcer on her right foot. This was healed in 1938 in New York.

95. Salomon Grimberg compares *Memory* to Saint Teresa of Avila's description of her Transverberation in "Memory: The Piercing of the Heart by the Arrow of Divine Love," in *Woman's Art Journal,* Fall/Winter 1990–91, pp. 3–6. Perhaps a more important model was the Virgin of Sorrows pierced by swords. Frida had many examples of the weeping Madonna in her collection of *retablos,* and she depicted the Mater Dolorosa in *My Birth.*

96. Breton, "Frida Kahlo de Rivera," p. 144.

97. "Bomb Beribboned," *Time,* Nov. 14, 1939, p. 29.

98. W. P., *Art News,* Nov. 12, 1938, p. 13.

99. Frida Kahlo, letter (written in English) to Nickolas Muray, personal archive of Mimi Muray, Alta, Utah. All letters to Muray come from this source. I am indebted to Mimi Muray for letting me read Kahlo's letters to her father.

100. Frida Kahlo, letter to Ella and Bertram D. Wolfe, March 17, 1939, Bertram D. Wolfe archive, Hoover Institution, Stanford University. I am grateful to Ella Wolfe for giving me copies of Kahlo's letters and for sharing with me her memories of Frida.

101. L. P. Foucaud, "L'Exposition de Frida Kahlo," *La Flèche,* March 1939. Clipping in the Frida Kahlo archive, Frida Kahlo Museum. Translation by the author.

102. As early as 1932 Frida played the Surrealist game *cadavre exquis:* drawing highly scatological figures to which each player contributes a section of the body without seeing what the other players have drawn. There is no question that she and Rivera kept themselves informed about art developments in Europe.

103. This and the following quotation come from Wolfe, "Rise of Another Rivera," p. 64.

104. *Time,* Oct. 30, 1939, p. 44.

105. *El Universal,* Oct. 19, 1939, clipping in Bertram D. Wolfe archive.

106. Rivera, *My Art, My Life,* p. 226.

107. Frida Kahlo, letter to Nickolas Muray, Oct. 13, 1939.

108. MacKinley Helm, *Modern Mexican Painters* (New York: Dover, 1968), pp. 167–68.

109. Rivera, "Frida Kahlo y el Arte Mexicano."

110. Alejandro Gómez Arias, "Un Testimonio Sobre Frida Kahlo."

111. A 1941 photograph by Bernard Silverstein shows Frida in her living room with the Judas figure that served as a model for the Judas in *The Wounded Table.* Painted on the bib of the papier-mâché Judas's overalls is a skull and crossbones that underscores the creature's dangerousness. In her painting, Frida transformed the Judas head into a round head somewhat reminiscent of Diego's. She added joined eyebrows like her own, and she gave the Judas a wounded chest like hers in a 1949 painting, *The Love Embrace of the Universe, the Earth (Mexico), Diego, Me, and Mr. Xolotl.*

112. The quotation is from Rivera, *My Art, My Life,* p. 226.

113. Salomon Grimberg, "Frida Kahlos Einsamkeit," p. 74.

114. There are two curious details in the depiction of the skeleton: between the ribs and the top of the pelvis is a round shape with a red center. It could be the lumbosacral disc tipped upward, but Frida might well have intended it to look like a wound. The skeleton appears to be bleeding from what looks like a vagina—perhaps another expression of Frida's sense of herself as a wounded sexual being and her association of sex with pain.

115. Clare Boothe Luce, private interview, New York, Nov. 1978.

116. The idea of wearing Christ's crown of thorns as a necklace has a tradition in Mexican colonial art, as seen, for example, in the great stone atrial cross from the Capilla de los Indios in the Basilica de Guadalupe, Mexico City, which Frida must have known. The sixteenth-century cross shows Christ wearing one crown of thorns on his head and another hanging as a pectoral, or necklace.

117. Helga Prignitz-Poda, "Wissenschaft und Pflanzen, Liebe, Tod und Teufel," in *Frida Kahlo: Das Gesamtwerk*, p. 43.

118. Salomon Grimberg suggests that the cat means the threat of death. He says that a popular Mexican belief places the image of death over the shoulder of a person who is about to die. See Grimberg's note on Frida's 1954 *Self-Portrait with the Image of Diego on My Breast and María on My Brow* in *Frida Kahlo: Das Gesamtwerk*, p. 263.

119. Dr. Leo Eloesser, letter to Frida Kahlo, Frida Kahlo archive.

120. Frida Kahlo, undated letter to Sigmund Firestone, postmarked Nov. 1, 1940. Kahlo's letters to Firestone are in the personal archive of Mr. and Mrs. Philip M. Liebschutz, Rochester, New York.

121. Emmy Lou Packard, private interview.

122. Rivera, *My Art, My Life,* p. 242. The following quotation is from the same source.

123. Wolfe, *The Fabulous Life of Diego Rivera,* p. 364.

124. Rivera, *My Art, My Life,* p. 245.

125. Undated newspaper clipping, Rivera file, San Francisco Art Institute.

126. A photograph of Frida painting *Self-Portrait as a Tehuana,* which Bernard Silverstein took in 1941 indicates that this portrait was worked on over a period of two years. Also in 1941 Silverstein took a photograph of Frida wearing the Tehuana headdress. A photograph of Frida sitting in front of the still unfinished *Self-Portrait as a Tehuana* (reproduced in *Frida Kahlo: Das Gesamtwerk*) was taken by Florence Arquin almost certainly in 1943 (according to Florence Arquin's husband, Samuel Williams, who says Arquin began to travel to Mexico in 1942, but became a close friend of the Riveras in 1943). That Frida left *Self-Portrait as a Tehuana* unfinished for so long suggests that its subject— her longing for Diego—might have been too painful a reminder to the remarried Frida, of the year in which she and Rivera were divorced.

127. Frida Kahlo, "The Birth of Moses," *Tin-Tan* 1 (Summer–Fall, 1975), p. 5.

128. *Diego and I* was painted as a gift for Florence Arquin. When Arquin saw the original sketch for the painting in the summer of 1948, Frida had depicted herself wearing a Tehuana headdress. When the finished painting arrived in Chicago in July 1949, Frida's loose hair and her expression of despair were a surprised. Arguin and her husband, Samuel A. Williams. (Samuel A. Williams, in conversation with the author, Feb. 1991.)

129. Frida Kahlo, "Retrato de Diego," p. 5. The following quotation is from the same essay.

130. Ibid.

131. *Frida Kahlo: Das Gesamtwerk,* p. 158.

132. Antonio Rodríguez, private interview. Salomon Grimberg feels that *The Little Deer* reveals Kahlo's preoccupation with transformation and reincarnation. (Salomon Grimberg, *Frida Kahlo,* exhibition catalogue, The Meadows Museum, Southern Methodist University, Dallas, 1989, pp. 37–38.)

133. *Frida Kahlo: Das Gesamtwerk,* p. 257, reproduces a drawing from the Aztec Codex Vaticanus A, which shows a man surrounded by the various symbols that stand for different parts of the body. The head of a deer is juxtaposed with the man's right foot.

134. I am grateful for this insight to Terese Bergfors and Ana María Rojas, who shared their thoughts about *The Little Deer* in a letter to the author in Oct. 1987.

135. Frida Kahlo, letter to Eduardo Morillo Safa, Oct. 11, 1946, Mariana Morillo Safa personal archive, Mexico City. Morillo Safa was Frida's chief patron and the purchaser of *Tree of Hope.* Mariana Morillo Safa generously shared with me Kahlo's correspondence with her father and her own memories of Frida.

136. According to Grimberg (op. cit., p. 38), a Spanish refugee painter who was Frida's lover in 1946 taught her this song when she went to New York for the spinal fusion and expressed to him her fears about her deteriorating health. In return, she gave her lover a botanical print of a tree whose verso she inscribed with words of love.

137. Frida Kahlo, letter to Eduardo Morillo Safa, op. cit.

138. Frida appears to have been caught in the Munchausen syndrome, which impels patients to want to have operations. Dr. Leo Eloesser thought most of Frida's operations were unnecessary. Joyce Campbell, private interview, Tacámbaro, Mexico, July 1977.

139. Dr. Guillermo Velasco y Polo, private interview, Tepoztlán, Mexico, Oct., 1977.

140. Elena Vásquez Gómez, private interview, Mexico City, Aug. 1977.

141. Dr. Velasco y Polo, private interview.

142. Lozano, dispatch to *Time,* Nov. 1950.

143. Ibid.

144. Bambi, "Un Remedio de Lupe Marín," *Excelsior* (Mexico City), June 16, 1954, p. 3.

145. Lozano, dispatch.

146. Dr. Velasco y Polo, private interview.

147. Lozano, dispatch.

148. Ibid.

149. Andrés Henestrosa, private interview, Mexico City, March 1977.

150. Antonio Rodríguez, private interview.

151. Rivera, *My Art, My Life,* p. 284.

152. J. O., "Frida Kahlo, Una Vida de Martiro," July 22, 1954, newspaper clipping, Isolda Kahlo archive.

153. Rosa Castro, private interview, Mexico City, Nov. 1977. Corliss Lamont, an American whose portrait Rivera was painting at the time when Frida died, offered another view of Rivera's reaction to Frida's death. He told his nephew Lansing Lamont that when Frida died, Rivera did not seem overly distraught. Lansing Lamont recalled that Rivera "continued having Corliss sit for him, but he made one small change in the portrait. Rivera returned from his wife's funeral service bearing the lilies that adorned her casket. And these he inserted into the portrait of Corliss as background color." (Letter from Lansing Lamont to the author, Jan. 13, 1983.)

154. Rivera, *My Art, My Life,* pp. 285, 287.

155. Ibid., p. 286.

156. Iduarte, "Imagen de Frida Kahlo."

157. The Pellicer poem is one of three he wrote for Frida in 1953.

158. Rivera, *My Art, My Life,* pp. 285–86.

159. "Patrimonio de la Nacion, la Obra de Kahlo," *Uno Mas Uno,* July 19, 1984, p. 15.

LIST OF ILLUSTRATIONS

WORKS OF ART

All the works of Frida Kahlo are reproduced by the authorization of the Instituto Nacional de Bellas Artes, Mexico City.

Page

2   *Self-Portrait as a Tehuana,* 1943. Oil on Masonite, 29⅞″ × 24″. Private collection, Mexico City. Photograph by Raúl Salinas.

5   *Self-Portrait with Monkey,* 1938. Oil on Masonite, 16″ × 12″. Collection of the Albright-Knox Art Gallery, Buffalo, New York.

8   *My Birth,* 1932. Oil on metal, 12½″ × 14″. Private collection, United States.

11   *My Nurse and I,* 1937. Oil on metal, 11¾″ × 13¾″. Collection of Dolores Olmedo Foundation, Mexico City. Photograph by Raúl Salinas.

15   *Doña Rosita Morillo,* 1944. Oil on canvas, mounted on Masonite, 30½″ × 28½″. Collection of Dolores Olmedo Foundation, Mexico City. Photograph by Jorge Contreras Chacel.

16   Sketch for *My Grandparents, My Parents, and I,* 1936. Pencil on paper, 12⅛″ × 13⅜″. Courtesy of Christie's.

17   *My Grandparents, My Parents, and I,* 1936. Oil and tempera on metal panel, 12⅛″ × 13⅝″. Collection of the Museum of Modern Art, New York. Gift of Allan Roos, M.D., and B. Mathieu Roos.

20   *Portrait of Don Guillermo Kahlo,* 1951. Oil on Masonite, 23.8″ × 18.3″. Collection of the Frida Kahlo Museum, Mexico City. Photograph by Raúl Salinas.

25   *Four Inhabitants of Mexico,* 1938. Oil on wood panel, 12¼″ × 18¾″. Private collection, California.

27   *Girl with Death Mask,* 1938. Oil on metal, 7.8″ × 5.8″. Private collection, Monterrey, Mexico. Courtesy of Christie's.

28   *They Ask for Planes and Are Given Straw Wings,* 1938. Collection unknown.

32   Letter to Alejandro Gómez Arias, 1926. *(top)* Private collection, Mexico City. "Here I'm Sending You My Picture," c. 1922. *(bottom)* Childhood drawing. Private collection, Mexico City.

FRIDA KAHLO

2 3 8

34   *Retablo.* Private collection, United States. Photograph by Hayden Herrera.

35   *The Accident,* 1926. Pencil on paper, 7.8″ × 10.6″. Collection of Juan Coronel, Cuernavaca, Mexico.

40   *La Adelita, Pancho Villa, and Frida,* c. 1927. *(left)* Oil on canvas, 25⅝″ × 17¾″. Collection of the Instituto Tlaxcalteca de Cultura, Tlaxcala, Mexico.

The Cachuchas, 1927. *(right)* Oil on canvas, 25⅝″ × 17¾″. Collection of the Instituto Tlaxcalteca de Cultura, Tlaxcala, Mexico.

41   *Portrait of Adriana,* 1927. *(left)* Oil on canvas, 41.7″ × 29.1″. Collection unknown.

Portrait of Miguel N. Lira, 1927. *(right)* Oil on canvas, 39″ × 26.6″ Collection of the Instituto Tlaxcalteca de Cultura, Tlaxcala, Mexico.

42   *Portrait of Alicia Galant,* 1927. *(top)* Oil on canvas, 42.1″ × 36.8″. Collection of Dolores Olmedo Foundation, Mexico City.

43   *Self-Portrait,* 1926. Oil on canvas, 31″ × 23″. Private collection, Mexico City. Photograph by Rafael Doniz.

44   *Portrait of Cristina Kahlo,* 1928. Oil on wood, 38.9″ × 32″. Private collection. Courtesy of Sotheby's.

47   *Insurrection,* mural by Diego Rivera, 1928. Ministry of Education.

49   *Self-Portrait,* 1929. Oil on Masonite, 31¼″ × 27½″. Collection of Antony Bryan. Photograph by Raúl Salinas.

50   *Indian Woman Nude,* c. 1929. *(left)* Oil on canvas. Collection unknown.

Portrait of a Girl with a Ribbon Around Her Waist, c. 1929. *(right)* Oil on canvas. Collection unknown.

52   *Portrait of Virginia (Niña),* 1929. Oil on Masonite, 33″ × 26.8″. Collection of Dolores Olmedo Foundation, Mexico City. Photograph by Jorge Contreras Chacel.

53   *Two Women,* 1929. Oil on canvas, 27⅜″ × 21″. Private collection, United States. Courtesy of Mary-Anne Martin/Fine Arts, New York.

54   *The Bus,* 1929. *(top)* Oil on canvas, 10¼″ × 22″. Collection of Dolores Olmedo Foundation, Mexico City. Photograph by Raúl Salinas.

Frida, lithograph by Diego Rivera, 1930. *(bottom)* Collection of Dolores Olmedo Foundation, Mexico City.

55   *Portrait of Lupe Marín,* c. 1930. *(left)* Oil on canvas, dimensions unknown. Collection unknown.

Portrait of a Woman in White, c. 1930. *(right)* Oil on canvas, 46.8″ × 31.8″. Private collection, Berlin, Germany.

56 *Self-Portrait,* 1930. Oil on canvas, 26″ × 22″. Private collection, Boston, Massachusetts. Photograph by Raúl Salinas.

59 *Self-Portrait (Dedicated to Leon Trotsky),* 1937. Oil on Masonite, 30″ × 24″. Collection of the National Museum of Women in the Arts, Washington, D.C. Gift of the Honorable Clare Boothe Luce.

60 *Frida and Diego Rivera,* 1931. Oil on canvas, 39¹⁄₈″ × 31″. San Francisco Museum of Modern Art, Albert M. Bender Collection, gift of Albert M. Bender.

61 *Girl in a Red Dress,* by José María Estrada, active 1830–1860. *(lower right)* Oil on canvas, 16¹⁄₂″ × 12³⁄₈″. Museo Nacional de Arte, Mexico City.

64 *Portrait of Mrs. Jean Wight,* 1931. Oil on canvas, 24.9″ × 18.1″. Private collection, Mr. and Mrs. John Berggruen, San Francisco, California.

65 *Portrait of Lady Cristina Hastings,* 1931. *(left)* Pencil on paper, 19″ × 12¹⁄₄″. Collection of Dolores Olmedo Foundation, Mexico City. *Portrait of Dr. Leo Eloesser,* 1931. *(right)* Oil on Masonite, 33¹⁄₂″ × 23¹⁄₂″. Collection of the University of California, San Francisco, School of Medicine.

67 *Frida Kahlo and Diego Rivera,* 1930. *(center)* Pencil and ink on paper, 11.4″ × 8.5″. Iconography Collection, Harry Ransom Humanities Research Center, University of Texas, Austin.

68 *Nude of Eva Frederick,* 1931. *(left)* Pencil on paper, 24.4″ × 18.8″. Collection of Dolores Olmedo Foundation, Mexico City. Photograph by Raúl Salinas. *Portrait of Eva Frederick,* 1931. *(right)* Oil on canvas, 24³⁄₄″ × 18¹⁄₂″. Collection of Dolores Olmedo Foundation, Mexico City. Photograph by Jorge Contreras Chacel.

70 *Frida and the Caesarean Operation,* c. 1932. Oil on canvas, 28.7″ × 24.4″. Collection of the Frida Kahlo Museum, Mexico City.

71 *Henry Ford Hospital,* 1932. *(top)* Oil on metal, 12¹⁄₄″ × 15¹⁄₂″. Collection of Dolores Olmedo Foundation, Mexico City. Photograph by Raúl Salinas.

72 *Self-Portrait, 9 July 1932,* 1932. Pencil on paper, 8″ × 5.1″. Collection of Juan Coronel, Cuernavaca, Mexico.

73 *Henry Ford Hospital,* 1932. Pencil on paper, 5.5″ × 8.2″. Collection of Juan Coronel, Cuernavaca, Mexico.

FRIDA KAHLO

240

74 *Retablo,* 1937. *(top)* Collection of Hayden Herrera. Photograph by Jim Kalett.
Self-Portrait Dreaming, 1932. *(bottom)* Pencil on paper, 10.6″ × 7.8″. Collection of Juan Coronel, Cuernavaca, Mexico.

76 *Me and My Doll,* 1937. Oil on metal, 15¾″ × 12½″. Private collection, Mexico City. Photograph by Raúl Salinas.

77 *Frida and the Miscarriage,* 1932. Lithograph, 12½″ × 9¼″. Collection of Dolores Olmedo Foundation, Mexico City. Photograph courtesy of Mary-Anne Martin/Fine Arts, New York.

78 Painting by anonymous folk artist. Collection of the Frida Kahlo Museum, Mexico City. Photograph by Raúl Salinas.

79 *The Deceased Dimas,* 1937. Oil on Masonite, 18⅞″ × 12⅜″. Collection of Dolores Olmedo Foundation, Mexico City. Photograph by Raúl Salinas.

80 *Itzcuintli Dog with Me,* 1938. Oil on canvas, 11″ × 8″. Private collection, Dallas, Texas.

82 *Self-Portrait with Monkeys,* 1943. Oil on canvas, 32⅛″ × 4¾″. Private collection, Mexico City. Photograph by Raúl Salinas.

83 *Self-Portrait with Monkey,* 1945. Oil on Masonite, 23.6″ × 16.7″. Collection of the Estate of Robert Brady, Cuernavaca, Mexico.

84 *Luther Burbank,* 1931. Pencil on paper, 11.9″ × 8.4″. Collection of Juan Coronel, Cuernavaca, Mexico.

85 *Luther Burbank,* 1931. Oil on Masonite, 34½″ × 24½″. Collection of Dolores Olmedo Foundation, Mexico City. Photograph by Raúl Salinas.

86 *Still Life,* 1942. Oil on metal, 24.8″ diameter. Collection of the Frida Kahlo Museum, Mexico City. Photograph by Raúl Salinas.

87 *Fruits of the Earth,* 1938. Oil on Masonite, 13.6″ × 23.6″. Collection of the Banco Nacional de Mexico, Fomento Cultural Banamex, Mexico City. Photograph by Jorge Contreras Chacel.

88 *Tunas (Still Life with Prickly Pear Fruit),* 1938. *(top)* Oil on tin, 7¾″ × 9¾″. The Robert Holmes à Court Collection, Perth, Australia. Courtesy of Mary-Anne Martin/Fine Arts, New York.
Pitahayas, 1938. *(bottom)* Oil on metal, 10″ × 14″. Collection of the Madison Art Center, Madison, Wisconsin.

89   *Xochitl, Flower of Life,* 1938.
     Oil on metal, 7″ × 3¾″.
     Collection of Dr. Rodolfo
     Gómez, Mexico City.

90   *Flower of Life,* 1944. Oil on
     Masonite, 11½″ × 9″.
     Collection of Dolores
     Olmedo Foundation,
     Mexico City. Photograph
     by Jorge Contreras
     Chacel.

91   *Sun and Life,* 1947. *(left)* Oil
     on Masonite, 15¾″ ×
     19½″. Private collection.
     Courtesy of Galleria
     Arvil, Mexico City.
     Photograph by Raúl
     Salinas.
     Moses, 1945. *(right)* Oil on
     Masonite, 37″ × 20″.
     Private collection,
     Houston, Texas.
     Photograph by Raúl
     Salinas.

92–93 *Roots,* 1943. Oil on
     metal, 11¾″ ×
     14½″. Private collection,
     Houston, Texas.
     Photograph by Raúl
     Salinas.

94   *Showcase in Detroit,* 1932.
     Oil on metal, 12¼″ ×
     15″. The Robert Holmes
     à Court Collection, Perth,
     Australia. Photograph by
     Raúl Salinas.

97   *Self-Portrait on the Border
     Line Between Mexico and
     the United States,* 1932.
     Oil on metal, 12½″ ×
     13¾″. Collection of Mr.
     and Mrs. Manuel Reyero,
     New York. Photograph by
     Jacques Rutter.

100 *My Dress Hangs There,* 1933.
     Oil and collage on
     Masonite, 18″ × 19¾″.
     Estate of Dr. Leo
     Eloesser. Courtesy of
     Hoover Gallery, San
     Francisco.

101 Mural by Diego Rivera,
     1934. *(bottom)* Palace of
     Fine Arts. Photograph by
     Raúl Salinas.
     View of New York, 1933.
     (lower right) Pencil and
     ink on paper, 10.6″ ×
     8″. Private collection.

102 *Self-Portrait "Very Ugly,"*
     1933. Fresco panel,
     27²/₅″ × 22¹/₅″.
     Private collection, Dallas,
     Texas.

104 Two "exquisite corpses,"
     1933. Pencil on paper,
     8.4″ × 5.3″. *(left)* Private
     collection, Dallas, Texas,
     and *(right)* private
     collection, California.

105 *Self-Portrait,* 1933. *(left)* Oil
     on metal, 13½″ × 11½″.
     Private collection, Mexico
     City. Photograph by Raúl
     Salinas.

107 Detail of mural *Mexico
     Today and Tomorrow* by
     Diego Rivera, 1934.
     National Palace, Mexico
     City.

108 *All-Seeing Eye,* 1934. Pencil
     on paper, 8.2″ × 12″.
     Collection of Juan
     Coronel, Cuernavaca,
     Mexico.

109   *Self-Portrait with Curly Hair,*
        1935. Oil on wood panel,
        7⅝″ × 5¾″. Private
        collection, California.
        Photograph by Hayden
        Herrera.

110   *A Few Small Nips,* 1935. Oil
        on metal, 15″ × 19″.
        Collection of Dolores
        Olmedo Foundation,
        Mexico City. Photograph
        by Raúl Salinas.

111   José Guadelupe Posada, *A
        Victim of Francisco
        Guerrero, "El Chalequero,"*
        1890. *(left)* Engraving, 5″
        × 7″.
        Sketch for *A Few Small Nips,*
        1935. *(right)* Pencil on
        paper. Collection of the
        Frida Kahlo Museum,
        Mexico City.

113   *Memory,* 1937. Oil on metal,
        15¾″ × 11″. Private
        collection, Paris.
        Courtesy of Mary-Anne
        Martin/Fine Arts, New
        York.

114   *Remembrance of an Open
        Wound,* 1938. Oil.
        Destroyed by fire.
        Photograph courtesy of
        Raquel Tibol.

115   *Study for Remembrance of an
        Open Wound,* 1938. *(left)*
        Pencil and ink on paper,
        11½″ × 7¾″. Private
        collection, Washington,
        D.C.
        *Self-Portrait with Bandaged
        Foot,* c. 1938. *(center)*
        Pencil on paper, 11.4″ ×
        8″. Collection of María
        Luisa Proenza, Mexico
        City. Photograph by
        Rafael Doniz.

        Self-Portrait Drawing,
        c. 1937. *(right)* Pencil and
        colored pencil on tracing
        paper, 11.6″ × 8.2″.
        Private collection, Dallas,
        Texas.

116   *Self-Portrait,* c. 1938. *(lower
        left)* Oil on wood, 1.6″ ×
        1.5″. Private collection,
        New York.

120   *I Belong to My Owner,* 1937.
        (left) Oil. Collection
        unknown. Photograph
        courtesy of Stanton
        Catlin.
        Portrait of Alberto Misrachi,
        1937. *(right)* Oil on metal,
        13.5″ × 10.6″. Collection
        of Ana Misrachi, Mexico
        City.

121   *Portrait of Diego Rivera,*
        1937. Oil on wood, 18.1″
        × 12.5″. Private
        collection, Mexico City.
        Photograph by Jorge
        Contreras Chacel.

124   *The Airplane Crash,* 1938.
        Oil. Collection unknown.
        Photograph courtesy of
        CENIDIAP.

125   *The Frame,* c. 1938. *(left)* Oil
        on metal with glass,
        11½″ × 8½″. Collection
        of the Musée National
        d'Art Moderne, Centre
        Georges Pompidou, Paris.

126   *What the Water Gave Me,*
        1938. Oil on canvas, 38″
        × 30″. Collection of
        Isidore Ducasse Fine
        Arts, New York.
        Photograph by Raúl
        Salinas.

127   *Two Nudes in a Forest,* 1939.
        Oil on sheet metal, 9⅞″
        × 11⅞″. Collection of
        Mary-Anne Martin/Fine
        Arts, New York.

128 *Fantasy*, 1944. *(top left)*
     Pencil and colored pencil
     on paper, 9.4″ × 6.2″.
     Collection of Dolores
     Olmedo Foundation,
     Mexico City.
     Roots, c. 1946. *(top right)*
     Pencil and ink on paper,
     8.5″ × 11.2″. Private
     collection, New York.
     Karma II, c. 1946. *(bottom)*
     Pencil and ink on paper,
     8.5″ × 11.1″. Private
     collection, New York.

129 *Karma I*, c. 1946. Sepia on
     paper, 7.2″ × 8.5″.
     Private collection, New
     York.

130 Diary pages. *(top and
     bottom)* Collection of the
     Frida Kahlo Museum,
     Mexico City. Photographs
     by Hayden Herrera.

132 *El verdadero vacilón* (The
     True Tease), c. 1946.
     Pencil and ink on paper,
     8.4″ × 10.7″. Private
     collection, New York.

137 *The Two Fridas*, 1939. Oil on
     canvas, 67″ × 67″.
     Collection of the Museo
     de Arte Moderno, Mexico
     City. Photograph by
     Jorge Contreras Chacel.

138 *The Wounded Table*, 1940.
     (bottom) Oil on canvas,
     47.8″ × 96.5″. Collection
     unknown. Photograph
     courtesy of Salomon
     Grimberg.

140 *The Suicide of Dorothy Hale*,
     1939. Oil on Masonite,
     23¼″ × 19″. Collection
     of the Phoenix Art
     Museum, Phoenix,
     Arizona.

141 *The Dream*, 1940. *(bottom)*
     Oil on canvas,
     29¼″ × 38¾″. Private
     collection, New York.

143 *Self-Portrait*, 1940. Oil on
     canvas, 24½″ ×
     18¾″. Iconography
     Collection, Harry
     Ransom Humanities
     Research Center,
     University of Texas,
     Austin.

145 *Self-Portrait*, 1940. Oil on
     Masonite, 23½″ ×
     15¾″. Private collection,
     United States. Courtesy of
     Mary-Anne Martin/Fine
     Arts, New York.

146 *Self-Portrait*, 1940. Oil on
     Masonite, 24″ × 17″.
     Private collection, United
     States.

148 *Fulang-Chang and I*, 1937.
     Oil on composition
     board, 15¾″ × 11″.
     Collection of the Museum
     of Modern Art, New York.
     Gift of Mary Sklar.

149 *Self-Portrait with Monkey*,
     1940. Oil on Masonite,
     21″ × 16¾″.
     Private collection, United
     States.

150 *Self-Portrait with Cropped
     Hair*, 1940. Oil on canvas,
     15¾″ × 11″. Collection
     of the Museum of Modern
     Art, New York. Gift of
     Edgar Kaufman, Jr.

154 Detail of mural by Diego
     Rivera. City College of
     San Francisco.

156 *Self-Portrait*, 1941. Oil on
     canvas, 14.9″ × 10.6″.
     Private collection, Mexico
     City.

158 *Self-Portrait with Bonito,* 1941. Oil on canvas, 21.6″ × 17.1″. Private collection, United States. Photograph courtesy of Salomon Grimberg.

159 *Self-Portrait with Braid,* 1941. Oil on Masonite, 20″ × 15¼″. Private collection, Mexico City. Photograph by Raúl Salinas.

160 *Portrait of Marucha Lavin,* 1942. *(center)* Oil on copper, 25.5″ diameter. Collection of Eugenia Lavin, Mexico City. Photograph by Jorge Contreras Chacel.

161 *Portrait of Lucha María, a Girl from Tehuacán,* 1942. *(top)* Oil on Masonite, 21.4″ × 16.9″. Private collection, Mexico City.
Portrait of Lupita Morillo Safa, 1944. *(left)* Oil on Masonite, 22″ × 19¾″. Private collection. Courtesy of Galeria Arvil, Mexico City.
Portrait of Natasha Gelman, 1943. *(right)* Oil on canvas, 11.4″ × 9″. Private collection, Mexico City.

162 *Me and My Parrots,* 1941. Oil on canvas, 32″ × 24½″. Private collection, New Orleans, Louisiana.

163 *The Flower Basket,* 1941. *(top)* Oil on copper, 25.3″ diameter. Private collection. Courtesy of Mary-Anne Martin/Fine Arts, New York.

164 *The Bride Frightened at Seeing Life Opened,* 1943. Oil on canvas, 24.8″ × 32″. Private collection, Mexico City.

165 *Self-Portrait with Monkey and Parrot,* 1942. Oil on Masonite, 21″ × 17″. Collection of the IBM Corporation, Armonk, New York.

166 *Thinking About Death,* 1943. Oil on canvas mounted on Masonite, 17¾″ × 14½″. Collection of Dolores Olmedo Foundation, Mexico City. Photograph by Raúl Salinas.

168 *Self-Portrait,* 1948. Oil on Masonite, 19″ × 15½″. Private collection, Mexico City. Photograph by Raúl Salinas.

169 *Diego and Frida 1929–1944,* 1944. *(left)* Oil on wood, image .9″ × 2.9″, frame 10.2″ × 7.2″. Collection of Manuel Arango, Mexico City. Photograph by Jorge Contreras Chacel.
Birthday note. *(right)* Ink on paper. Collection of the Frida Kahlo Museum, Mexico City.

172 *Diego and I,* 1949. Oil on Masonite, 11⅝″ × 8¹³⁄₁₆″. Collection of Mary-Anne Martin/Fine Arts, New York.

174 *The Love Embrace of the Universe, the Earth (Mexico), Diego, Me, and Señor Xolotl,* 1949. Oil on canvas, 27½″ × 23⅞″. Private collection, Mexico City. Photograph by Jorge Contreras Chacel. Courtesy of Centro Cultural Arte Contemporaneo, Mexico City.

181 *The Broken Column*, 1944. Oil on Masonite, 15³/₄″ × 12¹/₄″. Collection of Dolores Olmedo Foundation, Mexico City. Photograph by Raúl Salinas.

182 *The Chick*, 1945. Oil on Masonite, 11″ × 8.6″. Collection of Dolores Olmedo Foundation, Mexico City.

184 *Self-Portrait with Small Monkey*, 1945. Oil on Masonite, 22″ × 16¹/₄″. Collection of Dolores Olmedo Foundation, Mexico City. Photograph by Raúl Salinas.

185 *The Mask*, 1945. Oil on Masonite, 15.8″ × 11.8″. Collection of Dolores Olmedo Foundation, Mexico City.

186 *Without Hope*, 1945. Oil on canvas mounted on Masonite, 11″ × 14¹/₄″. Collection of Dolores Olmedo Foundation, Mexico City. Photograph by Jorge Contreras Chacel.

187 *Magnolias*, 1945. Oil on Masonite, 16.14″ × 22.4″. Collection of Balbina Azcarraga, Mexico City. Photograph by Hayden Herrera.

189 *The Little Deer*, 1946. Oil on Masonite, 8⁷/₈″ × 11⁷/₈″. Collection of Mrs. Carolyn Farb, Houston, Texas. Courtesy of Mary-Anne Martin/Fine Arts, New York.

190 *Ruin*, 1947. Pencil on paper, 6¹/₂″ × 9″. Collection of the Frida Kahlo Museum, Mexico City.

192 *Tree of Hope*, 1946. Oil on Masonite, 22″ × 16″. Collection of Isidore Ducasse Fine Arts, New York.

193 Detail of mural by Diego Rivera for the Hotel del Prado, 1947–1948. Currently in Mexico City.

195 *Self-Portrait with Loose Hair*, 1947. Oil on Masonite, 24″ × 17³/₄″. Private collection, Des Moines, Iowa.

199 *My Family*, c. 1950–1951. Oil on Masonite, 16.1″ × 23.2″. Collection of the Frida Kahlo Museum, Mexico City.

200 *Self-Portrait with the Portrait of Doctor Farill*, 1951. Oil on Masonite, 16¹/₂″ × 19³/₄″. Private collection, Mexico City. Photograph by Rafael Doniz.

202 *The Circle*, c. 1951. *(top)* Oil on sheet metal, 5.9″ diameter. Collection of Dolores Olmedo Foundation, Mexico City. Photograph by Raúl Salinas.

203 *Still Life with Parrot*, 1951. Oil on canvas, 10″ × 11″. Iconography Collection, Harry Ransom Humanities Research Center, University of Texas, Austin.

204 *Fruit of Life*, 1954. Oil on Masonite, 17.7″ × 24.4″. Private collection, Mexico City.

FRIDA
KAHLO
2 4 6

205 *Still Life with Legend,* c. 1953. *(top)* Oil on Masonite, 15¼″ × 25½″. Private collection, Mexico City.
Still Life, 1951. *(bottom)* Oil on Masonite, 10¾″ × 14″. Collection of Dr. Samuel Fastlich.

206 *Coconuts,* 1951. *(top)* Oil on Masonite, 10″ × 13.7″. Collection of the Museo de Arte Moderno, Mexico City.
Still Life with Parrot and Flag, 1951. *(bottom)* Oil on Masonite, 11″ × 15.7″. Collection of Díaz Ordaz, Mexico.

207 *Naturaleza viva,* 1952. *(top)* Oil on canvas. Private collection, Monterrey, Mexico.

214 *Marxism Will Give Health to the Sick,* 1954. Oil on Masonite, 30″ × 24″. Collection of the Frida Kahlo Museum, Mexico City. Photograph by Raúl Salinas.

216 Diary page 1953. Collection of the Frida Kahlo Museum, Mexico City. Photograph by José Verde.

217 Diary pages, 1953. *(top and bottom)* Collection of the Frida Kahlo Museum, Mexico City. Photographs by Hayden Herrera.

227 *Viva la vida,* 1954. Oil on Masonite, 23⅓″ × 20″. Collection of the Frida Kahlo Museum, Mexico City. Photograph by Raúl Salinas.

DOCUMENTARY PHOTOGRAPHS

Page

6 Courtesy of Isolda Kahlo.

9 Courtesy of Isolda Kahlo.

10 *(top)* Aplite speckled with garnets, 8 inches. Dumbarton Oaks Research Library and Collections, Washington, D.C.
(bottom) Photograph by Guillermo Kahlo. Courtesy of Isolda Kahlo.

13 *(left)* Photograph by Fritz Henle. Courtesy of Photo Researchers, Inc.
(right) Photograph by Guillermo Kahlo. Courtesy of Isolda Kahlo.

14 Photograph by Guillermo Kahlo. Courtesy of Isolda Kahlo.

16 *(left)* Courtesy of Isolda Kahlo.
(far right) Courtesy of Isolda Kahlo.
(right) Courtesy of Isolda Kahlo.

18 Courtesy of Isolda Kahlo.

21 *(left)* Photograph by Gisèle Freund. Courtesy of Photo Researchers, Inc.

22 Photograph by Lola Alvarez Bravo. Courtesy of Salomon Grimberg.

26 Photograph by Guillermo Kahlo. Courtesy of Isolda Kahlo.

29 Photograph by Guillermo Kahlo.

30 *(left)* Courtesy of Salomon Grimberg.
(right) Courtesy of Isolda Kahlo.

33 Photographer unknown. Courtesy of *Excelsior.*

39 Photograph by Guillermo Kahlo. Courtesy of Isolda Kahlo.

42 *(right)* Photograph by
Guillermo Kahlo.
Courtesy of Isolda Kahlo.

45 Photograph by Guillermo
Kahlo. Courtesy of
Alejandro Gomez Arias.

46 Photographer unknown.
Courtesy of Isolda Kahlo.

47 Photographer unknown.

48 Photograph courtesy of
Mexican Folkways, New
York Public Library.

51 Photograph by Paul Juley.
Courtesy of Salomon
Grimberg.

57 *(left)* Photographers
unknown. Courtesy of
publisher of *Saint Cineme*
by Herman Weinbes.
(right) Courtesy of the
Rockefeller Archive
Center.

58 *(top left)* Courtesy of AP/
Wide World Photos.
(lower left) Courtesy of
Excelsior.
(right) *Life* magazine, 1937.

61 *(left)* Photograph by Paul
Juley. Courtesy of the
National Museum of
American Art,
Smithsonian Institution.

62 *(left)* Photograph by Edward
Weston. Copyright © 1981
by Arizona Board of
Regents, Center for
Creative Photography.
(right) Photograph by Paul
Juley. Courtesy of the
National Museum of
American Art,
Smithsonian Institution.

63 Photograph by Edward
Weston. Copyright © 1981
by Arizona Board of
Regents, Center for
Creative Photography.

66 Photo by Imogen
Cunningham. Courtesy of
the Imogen Cunningham
Trust.

67 *(top left)* Courtesy of AP/
Wide World Photos.
(top right) Photograph by
Paul Juley. Courtesy of
the National Museum of
American Art,
Smithsonian Institution.

69 *(left)* Courtesy of Detroit
Institute of Arts.
(right) Photographer
unknown.

71 *(bottom)* Courtesy of
Excelsior.

78 *(lower left)* Photograph by
Mario Salmi. Courtesy of
Galería de Arte
Mexicano.

81 Photograph by Fritz Henle.
Courtesy of Photo
Researchers, Inc.

95 *(left)* Photograph by
Lucienne Bloch. Courtesy
of Lucienne Bloch.
(top right) Courtesy of
Detroit Institute of Arts.

96 Photographer unknown.

98 Photograph by Lucienne
Bloch. Courtesy of
Lucienne Bloch.

99 Photograph by Lucienne
Bloch. Courtesy of
Lucienne Bloch.

101 *(top right)* Courtesy of AP/
Wide World Photos.

103 *(top)* Photograph by
Lucienne Bloch. Courtesy
of Lucienne Bloch.
(bottom) Photograph by
Lucienne Bloch. Courtesy
of Lucienne Bloch.

105 *(right)* Photographer
unknown.

106 *(left)* Photographer
unknown.
(center)
(top right) Photograph
courtesy of Isolda Kahlo.
(lower right) Courtesy of
Isolda Kahlo.

FRIDA KAHLO
247

FRIDA
KAHLO
—■—
2 4 8

112 (left) Courtesy of AP/Wide
       World Photos.
     (right) Photograph by
       Lucienne Bloch. Courtesy
       of Lucienne Bloch.
116 (top) Courtesy of Jean Van
       Heijenoort.
117 (left) Photograph by
       Nickolas Muray. Courtesy
       of Salomon Grimberg.
     (top right) Photograph by
       Elinor Mayer.
     (lower right) Photograph by
       Julien Levy. Courtesy of
       Julien Levy.
118 (top) Courtesy of Raquel
       Tibol.
     (bottom) Photograph by
       Nickolas Muray. Courtesy
       of Mimi Muray.
119 (top) Courtesy of Jean Van
       Heijenoort.
     (lower right) Photograph by
       Nickolas Muray. Courtesy
       of George Eastman
       House.
122 Courtesy of Excelsior.
123 Photograph by Dora Maar.
       Courtesy of Mark
       Kelman.
125 (right) Photograph by
       Nickolas Muray. Courtesy
       of George Eastman
       House.
133 Courtesy of AP/Wide World
       Photos.
134 (left) Photographer
       unknown.
     (right) Courtesy of AP/Wide
       World Photos.
135 Photograph by Nickolas
       Muray. Courtesy of
       George Eastman House.
136 Photograph by Fritz Henle.
       Courtesy of Photo
       Researchers, Inc.
138 (top left) Photograph by
       Bernard G. Silberstein.
       Courtesy of Bernard G.
       Silberstein.

141 (top right) Photograph by
       Bernard G. Silberstein.
       Courtesy of Bernard G.
       Silberstein.
153 Courtesy of AP/Wide World
       Photos.
155 (left) Courtesy of AP/Wide
       World Photos.
     (right) Photograph by
       Emmy Lou Packard.
       Courtesy of Emmy Lou
       Packard.
157 (top) Photograph by Raúl
       Salinas.
     (lower right) Photograph by
       Juan Gúzman.
160 (lower left) Courtesy of
       Excelsior.
163 (lower left) Photograph by
       Nickolas Muray. Courtesy
       of George Eastman
       House.
167 (left) Photograph by
       Bernard G. Silberstein.
       Courtesy of Bernard G.
       Silberstein.
     (right) Photograph by
       Bernard G. Silberstein.
       Courtesy of Bernard G.
       Silberstein.
170 Photograph by Gisèle
       Freund. Courtesy of
       Photo Researchers, Inc.
171 (left) Photograph by Lola
       Alvarez Bravo. Courtesy
       of Salomon Grimberg.
     (right) Photograph by Mario
       Salmi. Courtesy of
       Salomon Grimberg.
173 (bottom) Photograph from a
       Mexican newspaper
       clipping.
     (top right) Courtesy of AP/
       Wide World Photos.
     (lower right) Photograph by
       Mario Salmi. Courtesy of
       Galería de Arte
       Mexicano.
175 (left) Photograph by
       Bernard G. Silberstein.
       Courtesy of Bernard G.
       Silberstein.

(right) Photograph by Bernard G. Silberstein. Courtesy of Bernard G. Silberstein.

176 (top) Photograph by Juan Gúzman. Courtesy of CENIDIAP-INBA, Mexico.
(bottom) Photograph by Florence Arquin. Courtesy of Samuel A. Williams and Carol J. Williams.

177 Photograph by Guillermo Zamora. Courtesy of CENIDIAP-INBA, Mexico.

179 (top left) Photographer unknown.
(top right) Courtesy of Fanny Rabel.
(bottom) Photograph by Juan Gúzman. Courtesy of the Rockefeller Archive.

180 Photograph by Florence Arquin. Courtesy of Samuel A. Williams and Carol J. Williams.

188 Photograph by Nickolas Muray. Courtesy of George Eastman House.

194 (top) Courtesy of Isolda Kahlo.
(lower left) Photograph from a newspaper clipping.

196 (left) Photograph by Juan Gúzman. Courtesy of Juan Gúzman.
(top right) Photograph by Juan Gúzman. Courtesy of Juan Gúzman.
(bottom right) Photograph by Juan Gúzman. Courtesy of Juan Gúzman.

197 Photograph by Juan Gúzman. Courtesy of Juan Gúzman.

198 Photograph by Juan Gúzman. Courtesy of Juan Gúzman.

201 Photograph by Gisèle Freund. Courtesy of Photo Researchers, Inc.

202 (lower left) Photograph by Bernice Kolko.

207 (bottom) Photograph by Antonio Rodríguez. Courtesy of Antonio Rodríguez.

208 (left) Courtesy of Excelsior.
(right) Photograph by Bernice Kolko. Courtesy of Salomon Grimberg.

209 Photograph by Bernice Kolko.

210 (lower left) Photograph by Hermanos Mayos.
(right) Courtesy of Excelsior.

211 Courtesy of CENIDIAP-INBA, Mexico.

212 Courtesy of CENIDIAP-INBA, Mexico.

213 (top) Courtesy of CENIDIAP-INBA, Mexico.
(bottom) Photograph by Raúl Salinas.

218 Photograph by Lola Alvarez Bravo. Courtesy of Salomon Grimberg.

219 (top) Courtesy of Excelsior.
(lower right) Courtesy of Excelsior.

220 Photograph by Lola Alvarez Bravo. Courtesy of Salomon Grimberg.

221 (top) Courtesy of Excelsior.
(bottom) Courtesy of Excelsior.

222 (top) Courtesy of Excelsior.
(bottom) Courtesy of Excelsior.

223 (bottom) Courtesy of Excelsior.

225 Photograph from a newspaper clipping.

228 Photograph by Florence Arquin. Courtesy of Samuel A. Williams and Carol J. Williams.

SELECTED BIBLIOGRAPHY

Adelaide Festival of Arts, Inc. *The Art of Frida Kahlo*. Exhibition catalogue. Adelaide, South Australia: Adelaide Festival of Arts, Inc., 1990. Essays by Teresa del Conde and Charles Merewether.

Breton, André. *Surrealism and Painting*. Translated by Simon Watson Taylor. New York: Harper & Row, 1972.

Carter, Angela. *Frida Kahlo*. London: Redstone Press, 1989.

Dallas Museum of Art. *Images of Mexico: The Contribution of Mexico to 20th Century Art*. Exhibition catalogue. Dallas: Dallas Museum of Art, 1988. Essays by various scholars.

Del Conde, Teresa. *Vida de Frida Kahlo*. Mexico City: Secretaría de la Presidencia, Departamento Editorial, 1976.

Flores Guerrero, Raul. *Cinco Pintores Mexicanos*. Mexico City: Universidad Nacional Autonoma de Mexico, 1957.

Fundación Cultural Televisa, A.C., Centro Cultural/Arte Contemporaneo. *Women in Mexico*. Bilingual exhibition catalogue for exhibition shown first at the National Academy of Design, New York, before traveling to Mexico. Mexico City: Fundación Cultural Televisa, A.C., 1990. Essays by Linda Nochlin and Edward J. Sullivan.

García, Rupert. *Frida Kahlo: A Bibliography*. Berkeley, Calif.: Chicano Studies Library Publications Unit, University of California, 1983.

Heijenoort, Jean van. *With Trotsky in Exile: From Prinkipo to Coyoacan*. Cambridge, Mass., and London: Harvard University Press, 1978.

Helm, MacKinley. *Modern Mexican Painters*. New York: Dover, 1968.

Herrera, Hayden. *Frida: A Biography of Frida Kahlo*. New York: Harper & Row, 1983.

——. *Frida Kahlo: Her Life, Her Art*. Ann Arbor, Mich.: University Microfilms, 1981.

Instituto Nacional de Bellas Artes. *Diego Rivera: Exposicion Nacional de Homenaje*. Exhibition catalogue. Mexico City: Instituto Nacional de Bellas Artes, 1977.

——. *Frida Kahlo: Exposicion Nacional de Homenaje*. Exhibition catalogue. Mexico City: Instituto Nacional de Bellas Artes, 1977. Essays by Alejandro Gómez Arias and Teresa del Conde.

——. *Frida Kahlo Acompanada de Siete Pintoras*. Exhibition catalogue. Mexico City: Instituto Nacional de Bellas Artes, 1967.

Meadows Museum, Southern Methodist University. *Frida Kahlo*. Exhibition catalogue. Dallas: Meadows Museum, Southern Methodist University, 1989. Essay by Salomon Grimberg.

2 5 2

Metropolitan Museum of Art. *Mexico Splendors of Thirty Centuries*. Exhibition catalogue. New York: Metropolitan Museum of Art, and Boston: Bulfinch Press, 1990. Entries on Frida Kahlo by Hayden Herrera.

Ministry of Culture, Spain. *Frida Kahlo*. Exhibition catalogue. Sala Pablo Ruíz Picasso. Madrid, 1985. Essays by various scholars.

Museum of Contemporary Art. *Frida Kahlo*. Exhibition catalogue. Chicago: Museum of Contemporary Art, 1978. Essay by Hayden Herrera.

Organizing Committee of the Games of the XIX Olympiad. *The Frida Kahlo Museum*. Museum catalogue with texts by Lola Olmedo de Olvera, Diego Rivera, and Juan O'Gorman. Mexico City: Organizing Committee of the Games of the XIX Olympiad, 1968.

Prignitz-Poda, Helga; Grimberg, Salomon; and Kettenmann, Andrea. *Frida Kahlo: Das Gesamtwerk*. Frankfurt: Verlag Neue Kritik, 1988.

Rivera, Diego, with March, Gladys. *My Art, My Life: An Autobiography*. New York: Citadel, 1960.

Rodríguez Prampolini, Ida. *El Surrealismo y el Arte Fantastico de Mexico*. Mexico City: Instituto de Investigaciones Esteticas, Universidad Nacional Autonoma de Mexico, 1969.

Seibu Museum of Art. *Frida Kahlo*. Exhibition catalogue. Shiga, Japan: Seibu Museum of Art, 1989. Essays by Teresa del Conde and Hayden Herrera.

Technical Committee of the Diego Rivera Trust. *Museo Frida Kahlo*. Museum catalogue. Mexico City: Technical Committee of the Diego Rivera Trust, 1958. Essays by Carlos Pellicer and Diego Rivera.

Tibol, Raquel. *Frida Kahlo*. Translated by Helga Prignitz-Poda. Frankfurt: Verlag Neue Kritik, 1980.

——. *Frida Kahlo: Cronica, Testimonios y Aroximaciones*. Mexico City: Editorial de Cultura Popular, 1977.

——. *Frida Kahlo: Una Vida Abierta*. Mexico City: Editorial Oasis, 1983.

Whitechapel Art Gallery. *Frida Kahlo and Tina Modotti*. Exhibition catalogue. London: Whitechapel Art Gallery, 1982. Essay by Laura Mulvey and Peter Wollen.

Wolfe, Bertram D. *The Fabulous Life of Diego Rivera*. New York: Stein and Day, 1963.

Zamora, Martha. *Frida Kahlo: El Pincel de la Angustia*. Mexico City, 1987 (self-published).

——. *Frida Kahlo: The Brush of Anguish*. Abridgment and translation of Martha Zamora's *Frida Kahlo: El Pincel de la Angustia* by Marilyn Sode Smith. San Francisco: Chronicle Books, 1990.

For more complete bibliographical references see Rupert García, *Frida Kahlo: A Bibliography*; Hayden Herrera, *Frida: A Biography of Frida Kahlo*; and Helga Prignitz-Poda, Salomon Grimberg, and Andrea Kettenmann, *Frida Kahlo: Das Gesamtwerk*.

INDEX

NOTE: Page numbers in italics refer to illustrations and information in captions.

Accident, The, 35
Adelita, Pancho Villa, and Frida, 40, 41
Aguirre, Ignacio, 108
Airplane Crash, The, 26
All-Seeing Eye, 108
Alvarez Bravo, Lola, 9
Alvarez Bravo, Manuel, 119
Arbenz, Jacopo, 218
Arias, Alehandro Gómez, 32–35, 36, 42, 48, 138
    Frida's letters to, 32, *32,* 37, 38–39, 42–45, 48, 191
Art News, 116
Atl, Dr., *210*
Ávila Camacho, Manuel, 86

Baker, Josephine, *211*
Ballad of the Proletarian Revolution, 47
Bender, Albert, 62
Berceuse, La, 14
Best-Maugard, Adolfo, 42
"Bird," *131*
Bloch, Lucienne, 19, 94, *104,* 106
"Blue House," *4–6, 7, 14, 106,* 132, *176*
Botticelli, Sandro, 41
Boytler, Arcady, 188
Braque, Georges, 185
Breton, André, 3, 58–60, 116–*19, 116, 118, 119, 123,* 124–25
Breton, Jacqueline, *118*
Bride Frightened at Seeing Life Opened, The, 164
British Hospital, Mexico City, 194
Broken Column, The, 180–83, *181*
Bronzino, 41
Bus, The, 54, 55

Cachuchas, The, 40, 41
Campos, Isabel, *29*
Cárdenas, Lázaro, 220, 222
Cardoza, Lya, *118*
Cardoza y Aragón, Luis, *118*
Caso, Antonio, 30
Charlot, Jean, 57
Chávez, Carlos, 67
Chick, The, 182
Circle, The, 183, 202

Coconuts, 206
Covarrubias, Miguel, *118, 179*
Covarrubias, Rosa, *118, 179*
Creation, 32, 33
Cubism, 101, 185

Deceased Dimas, The, 78, 79
Detroit Institute of Arts, 69, *69, 71,* 95
Díaz, Porfirio, 18, 48
Diego and Frida, 1929–1944, 169, *169*
Diego and I, 172, 173
Doña Rosita Morillo, 14, 15
"Dove Made a Mistake, The," 217
Dream, The, 141–42, *141,* 147
Duchamp, Marcel, 119, *123*
Durant, Kenneth, 48

Eisenstein, Sergei, *57*
Eleanora di Toledo, 41
Eloesser, Dr. Leo, 36, *57, 65,* 69, 144, 153, 155, 182
Estrada, Arturo, *179*
Estrada, José María, 61
"Exquisite Corpses" drawings, *104*

Fantasy, 128
Farell, Carmen, *210*
Farill, Dr. Juan, *200,* 201, *201*
Faure, Elie, *57*
"Feet, What Do I Need Them For If I Have Wings to Fly," *216*
Félix, María, 57, 173, *173*
Fernández, Fernando, 41
Few Small Nips, A, 109–12, *110, 111*
Firestone, Sigmund, 147, 153
Flèche, La, 122
Flower Basket, The, 157–63, *163*
Flower of Life, 89, 89
Foucaud, L. P., 122–24
Four Inhabitants of Mexico, 23–24, *25,* 224
Frame, The, 122, *125*
Freeman, Joseph, 48
Freud, Sigmund, 89
Frida, 54
Frida and Diego Rivera, 1931, *60,* 61–62
Frida and the Miscarriage, 75, 77
Frida and the Caesarian Operation, 70
Frida Kahlo and Diego Rivera, 67
Frida Kahlo Museum, 6, *6,* 139, 224
    paintings in, 78, *78*

"Frida Kahlo's Loneliness," 13–14
Fruit of Life, 204, 208
Fruits of the Earth, 86, *87*
Fulang-Chang, *173*
Fulang-Chang and I, 148, 151

Galería Arte Contemporaneo, 211
García Busto, Arturo, *179*
Garza, Dr. Roberto, *210*
Gauguin, Paul, 48
Girl with Death Mask, 26, *27*
Goddard, Paulette, 57, *134,* 151, *154,* 163
Golden Gate International Exposition,
        Rivera mural for, 152, 154–55, *154*
Goya, Francisco José de, 198
Goya Attended by Dr. Arrieta, 198
Grimberg, Dr. Salomon, 14, 35–36

Hale, Dorothy, 141
Hammer, Mrs. William C., *67*
Hansen, Reba, *116*
Hastings, Lord and Mrs., *96*
Henestrosa, Andrés, 36
Henry Ford Hospital, 70–75, *71, 73, 125,* 147
"Horrendo 'ojosauro,' El," *130*
Horsepower, 67
Hospital for Special Surgery, 187–88
Hotel del Prado, 193

"I Am Disintegration," 217
I Belong to My Owner, 120
Iduarte, Andrés, 30–31, 220, 222, 223
Indian Woman Nude, 50, *50*
Insurrection, 47
Itzcuintli Dog with Me, 80, 81

Julien Levy Gallery, 116, *117*

Kahlo, Adriana (sister), 39
    photographs of, *39*
    portrait of, *41*
Kahlo, Antonio (nephew), 78, *106,* 139
Kahlo, Cristina (sister), 9, 18, *107*
    affair with Rivera, 106, 112
    birth, 12, 13
    photographs of, *6, 29, 39, 106*
    portrait of, *44,* 45
Kahlo, Frida
    art and doll collections, 6, *136, 170*
    birth, 7, *8,* 9
    bisexuality, 127, 191
    bus accident, 31, 34–38, 55
    as childless, 69, 75, 127
    costumes of, 6–7, 38, 48, 152
    death, 4, 219
    education, 7, 29–31
funeral, 220–24, *221–23*
health, 45, 47–48, 134, *135,* 152–53, 157
    amputation of leg, 37, 215–16
    following accident, 36, 38–40
    foot problems, 24

in mid-1940s, 180–94
    from 1950 to death in 1953, 194–219
    polio, 7, 19, 26–29, 37, 194
homes, *106, 157, 177, 213*
    Blue House, 4–6, 7, *14, 106,* 132, *176*
imaginary friends, 29, 45
as invalid, 3, 6, 41, 201
miscarriages, 9, 67–78, 94, 187
mother's death, 9
as painter, 40–219
    after accident, 40–45
    Cubism and, 101, 185
    exhibitions, 116–24, *210,* 211
    influences on, 41–42, 48, 50, 55, 61, 73,
        86, 185
    primitivism and, 75, 183
    self-portraits, *see names of individual
        paintings*
    Surrealism and, 86, 116, 124–29
    techniques, 19
    use of color, 144–47
personality, 31–32, 96–98, 136–38
pets, *80,* 81, 139, 142, *162, 178, 188,* 191
photographs of, *10, 22, 51, 63, 66, 78, 95,
        96, 98, 99, 105, 106, 112, 116, 117, 123,
        125, 136, 141, 160, 163, 167, 170, 171,
        173, 175, 179, 180*
    funeral, *221–23*
    in last years, *196, 198, 202, 207–13, 218–
        20, 228*
    with pets, *81, 122, 188*
    with Rivera, *47, 48, 61, 62, 67, 69, 71,
        95, 101, 103, 106, 112, 116, 118, 119,
        122, 133, 153, 155, 167, 194, 197, 223,
        225*
    as youth, *16, 26, 29, 30, 32, 39, 42, 45*
politics and, 47, *121,* 211–15, 218–19, *219*
relationship with father, 18–21, 194
relationship with mother, 18
religion and, 18, 144
Rivera and, 20, 46–135, 151–78, 194, *213,*
        216, 218–19
    divorce, 7, 132–35, 139
    early relationship, 32, 46–48
    Frida's paintings of Diego, 47, *60,* 61–
        62, *67, 172*
    infidelities, 57–58, 106–8, 112, 119, *119,*
        132, *134,* 151, 163, 173, 175, 190–91,
        218
    marriage, 7, 48, *48*
    photographs, *see* Kahlo, Frida,
        photographs of
    remarriage, 7, 153–55, *155*
    Rivera's paintings for Frida, 47, 54, *107,*
        154–55, *193, 212*
self-portraits, *see titles of individual
        paintings*
suicide attempts, 218, 219

Kahlo, Guillermo (father), 18–22, 36, 47–48
  death, 157
  described, 18
  epilepsy, 19, 21, 39
  Frida's portrait of, 20, 21–23
  as photographer, 18, 21, 22, 39
  photographs of, *16, 18, 21*
  self-portrait, *18*
Kahlo, Isolda, 78, *106*, 139
Kahlo, Matilde Calderón de (mother), 48
  death, 9
  illness of, 14, 39
  marriage, 18
  photographs of, *6, 13, 16, 39*
Kahlo, Matilde (sister), 36
Karma I, 129
Karma II, 128

Lenin, V. I., 98
Liberation of a Peon, The, 62
Little Deer, The, 188–91, *189*
Louvre, 122
*Love Embrace of the Universe, the Earth
    (Mexico), Diego, Me, and Señor Xolotl,
    The,* 174, 175–78, *176*
Luce, Clare Boothe, 139
Luther Burbank, 84–86, *84, 85*

Magnolias, 187
Mancisidor, José, *221*
Mariana, 78
Marin, Lupe, 32, *105, 118*
Marx, Karl, 212, 215
Marxism Will Give Health to the Sick, 212–
    15, *214*
Mask, The, 185, *185*
"Masked Dancers," *131*
Me and My Doll, 75, *76*
Me and My Parrots, 162
Memory, 26, 112–14, *112, 113*
"Memory," 31
"Mexican Autobiography," 211
Mexican Revolution, 7
Mexico Today and Tomorrow, 107
"Mexique," 119, *123*
Michel, Cocha, *210*
Miró, Joan, 122
Modigliani, Amedeo, 42
Modotti, Tina, 46, 47, 86
Moses, 89–91, *91, 213*
Moses and Monotheism (Freud), 89
Muray, Nickolas, *118,* 119, 134–35, 138, 142,
    151, *163*
My Birth, 8, 9–10, *111*
My Dress Hangs There, 98–105, *100,* 215
My Family, 197–98, *99*
My Grandparents, My Parents, and I, 14–18,
    17
  sketch for, *16*
My Nurse and I, 10–13, *11*

Nandino, Elias, 135
National Agricultural School at Chapingo,
    86
National Institute of Fine Arts, 30, *220, 222*
National Preparatory School, 7, 29–30
Naturelza viva, 207, 208
New Workers' School, *103*
New York Times, The, 37
Nicolas, Vidal, *198*
*Nightmare of War and the Dream Peace,
    The, 211,* 212
Niña, 50, 52
Noguchi, Isamu, 57–58, *108,* 141
Nude of Eva Frederick, 68

Orozco, José Clemente, 30, *213*

Paalen (artist), 122
Paine, Frances Flynn, 57, *67*
Palace of Fine Arts, 211, *220, 221*
Peláez, Antonio, *210*
Pellicer, Carlos, 223
Picasso, Pablo, 57, 122
Pierre Colle Gallery, 119
Pitahayas, 61, 86
Portrait of Adriana, 41
*Portrait of a Girl with a Ribbon Around Her
    Waist, 50*
Portrait of Alberto Misrachi, 121
Portrait of Alicia Galant, 42, 42
Portrait of a Woman in White, 55
Portrait of Cristina Kahlo, 44, 45
"Portrait of Diego," 175, 178
Portrait of Diego Rivera, 121
Portrait of Dr. Leo Eloesser, 65
Portrait of Don Guillermo Kahlo, 20, 21–23
  Frida painting, *21*
Portrait of Eva Frederick, 68
Portrait of Lady Christina Hastings, 65
*Portrait of Lucha Maria, a Girl from
    Tehuacán, 161*
Portrait of Lupe Martin, 55
Portrait of Lupita Morillo Safa, 161
Portrait of Marucha Lavin, 160
Portrait of Miguel N. Lira, 41
Portrait of Mrs. Jean Wight, 64
Portrait of Natasha Gelman, 161
"Portrait of Neferúnico, Founder of
    Madness," *130*
Portrait of Virginia (Niña), 50, 52
Posada, José Guadalupe, 109, *111,* 152, *193*

Rabel, Fanny, *179*
Remembrance of an Open Wound, 114–15,
    115
Retablo, 74
Reyes, Aurora, 26

Rivera, Diego, 3, 94, 101
    attempts on Trotsky's life and, *134, 152*
    death, 224
    Frida and, *see* Kahlo, Frida, Rivera and
    health, *58*
    home of, 6
    murals, 7, 47, 55, 106
        Ballad of the Proletarian Revolution, 47
        at Detroit Institute of Arts, 69, *69, 71*
        for Golden Gate International
            Exposition, 152, 154–55, *154*
        Hotel de Prado, *193*
        Insurrection, 47
        Liberation of a Peon, 62
        Mexico Today and Tomorrow, 107
        at National Preparatory School, 30, 32,
            33
        at New Workers' School, *103*
        Night of the Rich, 55
        Rockefeller Center, 12, 98–101, *101*
    photographs of, *57, 62, 173, 175, 208, 221,*
        222
        with Frida, *47, 48, 61, 62, 67, 69, 71, 95,*
            101, 103, 133, 153, 155, 167, 194, 197,
            223, 225
    physical appearance, 7, 14, 42
    as womanizer, *see* Kahlo, Frida, Rivera
        and
Rivera, Ruth, *223*
Rockefeller, Nelson, 98, *179*
Rolando, Rosa, *118*
Roots (1943), 91, *92–93*
Roots (1946), *128*
Rotunda de los Hombres Ilustres, 224
Rousseau, Henri, 50
Ruin, 190, 191

Safa, Eduardo Morillo, 14, 193
Saint Luke's Hospital, San Francisco, 153
Sandblom, Dr. Philip, 37
Schachtman, Max, *58*
Schiaparelli, Elsa, 7
Self-Portrait (1926), 3, 42–45, *43*
Self-Portrait (1929), 48–50, *49*
Self-Portrait (1930), 56
Self-Portrait (1933), *105*
Self-Portrait (1940) (three paintings), 142–
    47, *143, 145, 146*
Self-Portrait (1941), *156*
Self-Portrait (1948), *168,* 169–71
*Self-Portrait as a Tehuana (Diego in My
    Thoughts), 2,* 163–67, *167*
Self-Portrait (Dedicated to Leon Trotsky), 58,
    59

Self-Portrait Drawing, 115
Self-Portrait Dreaming, 74
Self-Portrait (miniature), *116*
Self-Portrait, 9 July 1932, 72
*Self-Portrait on the Border Line Between
    Mexico and the United States,* 94–98,
    97
Self-Portrait "Very Ugly," 102
Self-Portrait with Bandaged Foot, 115
Self-Portrait with Bonito, 157, 158
Self-Portrait with Braid, 157, 159
Self-Portrait with Cropped Hair, 147, *150,*
    151–52
Self-Portrait with Curly Hair, 109, *109*
Self-Portrait with Loose Hair, 195
Self-Portrait with Monkey (1938), *5*
Self-Portrait with Monkey (1940), *149,* 151
Self-Portrait with Monkey (1945), *83*
Self-Portrait with Monkey and Parrot, 165
Self-Portrait with Monkeys, 82
Self-Portrait with Small Monkey, 183–85, *184*
Self-Portrait with the Portrait of Dr. Farill,
    198–202, *200, 201*
Showcase in Detroit, 94
Siquieros, David Alfaro, 30
Sklar, Mary, 151
Spanish Civil War, 26
Stackpole, Ginette, 67
Stackpole, Ralph, 67
Still Life (1942), *86*
Still Life (1951), *205*
Still Life with Legend, 205
Still Life with Parrot, 203
Still Life with Parrot and Flag, 206
Stockholm Peace Petition, 197
Suicide of Dorothy Hale, The, 139–41, *140*
Sun and Life, 89, *90*
Surrealism, 86, 116, 122, 124–29

Tanguy, Yves, 122
TASS, 48
*They Ask for Planes and Are Given Straw
    Wings,* 26–29, *28*
Thinking About Death, 166, 167
Time, 116, 211
Tlazolteolt, goddess, Aztec sculpture of, 10,
    10
Torres Bodet, Jaime, *213*
Tree of Hope, 10, 191–93, *210*
Trotsky, Leon, 58, *58, 116, 119,* 151
    attempts on life of, *134, 154*
Trotsky, Natalia, 58, *116, 119*
Tunas (Still Life with Prickly Pear Fruit), 86,
    88

Two Fridas, The, 10, 29, 135–38, *136, 137,*
    152
Two Nudes in a Forest, 127, *127*
Two Women, 50, *53*

Universal Ilustrado, 31

Vallarta, Manuel Sandoval, *213*
van Gogh, Vincent, 14, 147
Van Heijenoort, Jean, *116, 119*
Vasconcelos, José, 30
Veraza, Alberto, *39*
Veraza, Carlos, *39*
Verdadero vacilón, El (The True Tease), *132*
View of New York, 101
Viva la vida, 227

West, Mae, 101
What the Water Gave Me, 117, 125–29, *126*
Wills, Helen, 62
Wilson, Dr. Philip, 187–88, 191
Without Hope, 185–87, *186*
Wolfe, Bertram D., 26, 106–107
Wolfe, Ella, 107
Wounded Table, The, 24–25, 138–39, *138,*
    151
Wright, Mrs., *95*

Xochitl, Flower and Life, 88, 89

Young Communist League, 47

Fashion Institute of Design & Merchandising
Resource & Research Center
55 Stockton St., 5th Floor
San Francisco, CA 94108-5805

SAN FRANCISCO
a certain style

BY DIANE DORRANS SAEKS

PHOTOGRAPHS BY JOHN VAUGHAN

FOREWORD BY HERB CAEN

SAN FRANCISCO *a certain style*

CHRONICLE BOOKS

SAN FRANCISCO

Copyright © 1989, 1999 by Diane Dorrans Saeks and the John Vaughan Estate.

All rights reserved. No part of this book may be reproduced in any
form without written permission from the publisher.

Library of Congress Cataloging-in-Publication Data:

Saeks, Diane Dorrans.
San Francisco: A Certain Style/Diane Dorrans Saeks;
Photography by John Vaughan.
     204 p.   25 x 25 cm.
     Includes index.
     ISBN 0-8118-2234-6
     1. Interior decoration—California—San Francisco—History—
20th century.
     2. Interior architecture—California—San Francisco—History—
20th century.
     I. Vaughan, John, 1952– . II. Title

NK2004.S24 1989   89-17299
728'.09794'61—dc20   CIP

The author and photographer gratefully acknowledge the editors
of *Architectural Digest*, *Metropolitan Home*, *Home*, *House Beautiful*,
and *Victoria* for use of photographs previously published in those
magazines.

The photographer thanks Claire Marie for the flowers at the Rosekrans
residence. For years of processing his film, he also thanks Faulkner
Color Lab.

Printed in Hong Kong

Book design: Laura Lamar
Cover design: Design M/W

Distributed in Canada by Raincoast Books
8680 Cambie Street
Vancouver, British Columbia V6P 6M9

10 9 8 7 6 5 4 3 2 1

Chronicle Books
85 Second Street
San Francisco, California 94105

www.chroniclebooks.com

Previous page: **Whitney
Warren's legendary house on
Telegraph Hill, empty
save for a taste of the dramatic
architectural details and
antiques that formerly graced
the rooms.
Architect: Gardner Daily.**

Table of Contents

Acknowledgements 7
Foreword by Herb Caen 8
Introduction 16

1 GRAND STYLE

Introduction 23
Filoli, Woodside 26
Rosekrans House, Pacific Heights 31
Anthony Hail House, Russian Hill 37
Elaine McKeon House, Hillsborough 43

2 THE DESIGNERS

Introduction 49
John Dickinson Firehouse, Pacific Heights 53
Charles Pfister Apartment, Nob Hill 56
Gary Hutton Studio, The Mission 59
Tedrick and Bennett Cottage, Russian Hill 60
Jois and Irving Belfield Apartment, Nob Hill 63
Chuck Winslow Cottage, Lower Pacific Heights 65
William Whiteside Apartment, Alta Plaza 69
Ron Mann Studio, Potrero Hill 71
Leavitt and Weaver Apartment, Russian Hill 75
Scott Lamb Apartment, Broadway 76
Jeffrey Walker Apartment, Buena Vista Park 79

3 THE COLLECTORS

Introduction 83
Robert Hutchinson Apartment, Sutter Street 87
Byron Meyer House, Russian Hill 93

Mary Keesling House, Russian Hill 97
Eileen Michael House, Russian Hill 98
Glen Smith Apartment, Fillmore Street 103

4 UNIQUE STYLE

Introduction 107
Allen and Grant House, Berkeley Hills 110
Elsa Cameron House, Fairfax 115
Robert Steffy House, Russian Hill 118
David Peugh Apartment, Western Addition 122
Chuck Winslow Apartment, Potrero Hill 124
Mendelsohn House, Richmond District 128
A Shaker-Style House, Cow Hollow 134
Diane Burn Nursery, Pacific Heights 138
Thomas Bennett Apartment, Russian Hill 141
Jan Dutton House, Fairfax 143
A Family House, Tiburon 145
Chuck Williams Cottage, Nob Hill 151
Frederick Hill Apartment, Lafayette Park 152
An Artist's House, Berkeley 155
Gleeson and Jeanrenaud House, Potrero Hill 158

5 VICTORIANA

Introduction 165
Wetzel House, Alexander Valley 166
Toby Levy Redesign, Russian Hill 170
Ralph Du Casse House, Pacific Heights 172
Peter and Judy Severson House, Marin County 176
Steve Silver House, Sonoma 183

SAN FRANCISCO CATALOGUE:

Design and Style Resources 194

Photographs on following pages:
Fogscape (page 6): Sutro Tower sails through incoming fog, viewed from architect Darwin McCredie's garden. His renovated attic apartment is visible within.
Cityscape (pages 10-11): The spires of the City from Potrero Hill. Controversial new structures have changed the skyline forever but handsome old downtown buildings of character and strength still stand as reminders of an elegant past.
Roofscape (pages 12-13): Cow Hollow and Pacific Heights from Charlotte Swig's sunny terrace.
Tablescape (pages 14-15): Arts patrons John and Dodie Rosekrans surround themselves with art, flowers, and objects to please the senses. Designer Michael Taylor's ploy: Fill their smoking room with large-scale sculpture, opulent chairs, curious minerals to make it appear dramatically larger.

Acknowledgements

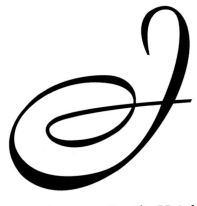

ohn and I had the very best time choosing, photographing, and writing about the houses of San Francisco. We wish to acknowledge all of the San Francisco designers and architects whose ideas are lavished on the rooms in these pages. Our warmest thanks, too, to the owners of the houses—from Nob Hill to the Mission and over to Pacific Heights, from the Alexander Valley to Hillsborough. ❡ To Herb Caen, San Francisco chronicler, thanks for a picture-perfect foreword. ❡ To Dorothy Kalins, Carol Helms, Ben Lloyd, Steven Wagner, Barbara Graustark, Arlene Hirst, Newell Turner, and all our wonderful friends at *Metropolitan Home*—cheers and thanks for being the best. ❡ Heartfelt thanks to Paige Rense, Editor-in-Chief of *Architectural Digest,* for her many years of generosity and support. ❡ Andree Putman has encouraged us in this book from the very beginning. Our grateful thanks and respect. ❡ Warm thanks to Margaret Kennedy, Executive Editor of *House Beautiful.* ❡ Thanks to Russell McMasters and Robert Steffy for inspiration, generosity, and warm friendship. Maria Gresham and Perry Klehbahn have been the very finest assistants. ❡ To Nion McEvoy, David Barich, Jack Jensen, Annie Barrows, and the staff at Chronicle Books—our appreciation for enthusiasm and openness to our ideas. ❡ Fred Hill has been a wonderful agent. ❡ To our editor, Terry Ryan, thanks for the best encouragement and humor, and for the keen editing eye. ❡ To Ron Mann and Steven Mann, Geraldine Paton, and Gwyneth Dorrans for always being there. ❡ And an especially warm round of applause to our book designer, Laura Lamar. Her caffè lattes at the light box, Max, merry laughter, and the Mac made light work and marvelous layouts.

Diane Dorrans Saeks
John Vaughan

To my son, Justin, with love.

In fond memory of John Dickinson, friend and mentor.

D.D.S.

To Mom and Dad.

J.E.V.

Foreword

*J*unky houses at the end of junky alleys, secret gardens behind blank-faced mansions that turn a cold shoulder to the world, flower-like Southeast Asian children playing innocently in the Tenderloin, a cable car inching crookedly down Washington toward Powell, where the view opens suddenly to Bay-Bridge'd magnificence. ¶ It's a City, all right, a nervous place built on jitters and fidgets and filled-in land. It could go any minute, slipping and sliding into the enigmatic bay. A lot of it is gone already—the city of forgotten people who led fabulous lives in houses built for the ages disappeared long ago. Myths and legends have died, with nobody left to remember. Ghostly dance music in the marble halls of ancient hotels, Cape Jasmine gardenias turning brown, faded photos of people from another time, smiling around a supper club table, each with a cigarette in one hand, a glass of rotgut in the other. The dashing, debonair royalty of another San Francisco with their Stutz Bearcats and plus fours and white teeth in faces forever tanned. They had style and money to burn, and their snobby manners were impeccable, old boy. ¶ I wander around the city, rubbing shoulders with ghosts, trying to find the pieces. Up to Twin Peaks, where a giant statue of St. Francis by Beniamino Bufano was planned and forgotten; but once there was a giant Christmas tree every December. Past Red Rock in the Sunset, where the young Saroyan sat and looked out at the shining sea. Out to the Cliff House, a shadow of the magnificence that Mayor Adolph Sutro gazed down on from his garden-girt mansion on the bluffs. "In San Francisco," Saroyan once said in an excess of ebullience, "even the ugly is beautiful," and I know what he meant as I drive past the odd little houses on the silent streets of the outer avenues, a study in photo-realism, every block different but alike. Clement, Irving, Balboa, the heartland of the city, the stores and restaurants marching into infinity. ¶ If you can avert your eyes from certain difficult realities, the city is looking good, fat, prosperous, and preposterously glamorous. Van Ness aglow with operas and ballets and symphonies and parties. The days are short and the nights are long, always the perfect proportions for a city that has played hard from birth. The merry-go-round spins even faster, and "Laughin' Sal" cackles madly, the uninvited guest at the never-ending banquet of Baghdad-by-the-Bay.

. . . Herb Caen

When he's not at the "Loyal Royal" writing his popular six-days-a-week column for the *San Francisco Chronicle*, Herb Caen may be at home in his comfortable Nob Hill apartment, *above and opposite.* **Interior design: Billy Gaylord with Andrew Lau.**

Introduction

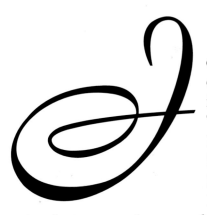

John Dickinson, who design professionals consider one of the most original and influential American designers, was my first inspiration for this book. ❡ In the late sixties, well before High Tech, Dickinson designed a steel-pipe four-poster bed for artist Ralph Du Casse, wrapped it with walls of charcoal-and-white herringbone tweed, and covered it luxuriously with pure camel-hair originally intended for menswear. ❡ In Dr. Leo Keoshian's Peninsula house, sumptuous but spare furniture of Dickinson's design was showcased in creamy white rooms. *Faux primitif* animal-footed tables and chairs, glossy white epoxyed tables, a grand stainless-steel bath standing alone in the center of an all-white bathroom are pure Dickinson. ❡ In 1980, I started work on a book about John's designs. I'd been writing about interior design and fashion since my first year at university, but this was to be my real education. At nine every Sunday morning, I'd arrive at John's Washington Street firehouse, with its brass name plates and white-canvas-duck-curtained portiere. Climbing the stairs worn to a beautiful patina by decades of firemen, I'd hear bouncy Cole Porter from John's Steinway. Throwing open the ten-foot-high white-lacquered doors at the top of the stairs, I would see John across the room playing the piano in his starched white Sulka pajamas. Sun streaming through brass-bound window shutters turned his white hair into a halo. He was always smiling. ❡ This sky-lit living room (shown on page 50) was so dramatic in size and in its particular pieces that a visit was never mundane. There was Dickinson's collection of African figures mounted in groups on white plinths. At first glance, they looked like delicately carved ivory figures or bizarre porcelain effigies. In fact, I discovered, they were "airport art" bought at a local import house and lacquered white by the designer himself. Sofas were upholstered in white Naugahyde bound with expensive wool cord tied as carelessly as twine. He loved this paradox, which Andree Putman dubbed "rich and poor." And there were always blueprints and drawings push-pinned to the walls, maybe a new prototype, fabric swatches, gifts in Tiffany boxes, books and magazines to intrigue the visitor. ❡ In John's realm, under the gaze of two enormous fiberglass phrenology heads, you were on stage and wanted to be your best. I'd approach the piano very slowly so that John would keep playing. The moment was magic, and we'd start a

In John Dickinson's firehouse bedroom stands a 15-foot-high four-poster of hand-carved *faux* bamboo with a black fitted cover. Redwood wainscotting was stripped and given coats of varnish to emphasize the grain, and to give the nostalgic air of an old railroad station waiting room, said the designer. Walls are covered in horsehair-textured black vinyl. Double french doors open to a sheltered balcony overlooking a brick-paved garden, its symmetry emphasized by neat squares of clipped boxwood bushes.

morning of interviewing and reviewing in an up-tempo mood. ❧ Other Sundays, John would hold court in his magnificent four-poster bed—hand-carved and painted to look like bamboo, and covered with a black woven cashmere throw. The walls of his bedroom were black "horsehair," offset with redwood wainscotting and a pair of hand-painted chests. ❧ John was opinionated, witty, and very down-to-earth. "Prettiness has nothing to do with style," he said. "If you're stripping down rooms and editing, as I do, there's no place for it. Logic precludes prettiness." "A color scheme is a questionable device on which to base a room's design," he noted. ❧ John Dickinson died in 1982, and the book project was set aside. When I took it up again, I decided to expand its scope and make it a tribute to all the designers of San Francisco. ❧ I asked John Vaughan, the brightest and best young photographer of interiors, to join me on the project. We ran through all our lists and photographs, reviewed hundreds of houses and apartments, and with great care chose our favorites. Not for one moment did we plan a scientifically mapped tome that included every architect, designer, or hill. Still, the finest work is represented here. We've covered the City and places City people escape to on weekends. ❧ After reading these pages, you'll have a sense of wonderful lives lived to the fullest in remarkable settings. Passions of San Franciscans— from art collections and art deco furniture to gardens and pets—are all here. Perhaps most exciting and revealing is the design talent we discovered on film. Gary Hutton's synthesis of Victoriana with today's simplicity, Michael Taylor's grandeur, Jan Dutton's ethereal laces, and Ami Magill's murals in Diane Burn's nursery are a revelation. ❧ Robert Hutchinson's sculpted walls are his setting for Indian baskets, clay bowls, European paintings, and an extraordinary orchid collection. ❧ John and Dodie Rosekrans were two of Michael Taylor's best clients, and their interiors reflect that ideal collaboration between informed, curious clients and their designer. Standing on a bluff overlooking the San Francisco Bay, their house would be remarkable anywhere. ❧ These pages also reveal worldliness and a preference for comfort over pompousness or pretension. These rooms were not designed to speed the owners' way up the social ladder, to suggest centuries of ancestors, or to affix the designer's name forever to the furniture. ❧ Anthony Hail's refined rooms could be in London or Paris, but most interiors on these pages could exist only here. Quintessentially Californian, Ron Mann's designs seem to spring from the earth. Using massive Douglas fir slabs, cast stone, sand-cast bronze, wrought iron, and very direct forms, he creates designs and rooms that are at once surprising and very comforting in their sophistication and simplicity. The pages of this book celebrate this search for individuality. ❧ Just as John Dickinson taught me to see design from a new perspective, I want these pages to give a new view of San Francisco. Behind the closed doors and curtained windows are some glorious rooms.

Diane Dorrans Saeks
San Francisco, June, 1989

Opposite: Ron Mann's vibrant interior designs are fully realized, comfortable rooms. Here in a Montara oceanside house, a no-color, no-pattern bedroom scheme gains drama from overscale furniture, a floor of recycled douglas fir planks with concrete grouting, and Mann's sure-footed multi-level floor plan. Firewood stacked outside the window stays as summer sculpture. Angleback wicker chairs designed by Ivy Rosequist for Wicker Wicker Wicker. Papier-mâché whale sculpture by Steven Mann.

Grand Style

An occasional minor earthquake or rumbling temblor shakes the calm of the City and reminds residents of a more precarious time when an earthquake and fire destroyed its heart. Otherwise, San Francisco seems to have been standing on these hills forever—or at least longer than a mere 140 years or so. ¶ Grand mansions and patrician palazzi edging the bluffs of Pacific Heights and circling Lafayette Park give the distinct impression that they set up residence centuries ago. Solid fortunes made from sugar, gold, railroads, and real-estate speculation provided these grandstand positions, their proud profiles, and the classic Mediterranean-and European-influenced architecture. ¶ In fact, in 1776, the San Francisco Bay that greeted Lieutenant Colonel Juan Bautista de Anza and his band of Spanish settlers was sandy, wind-swept, and wild, with few trees to provide shelter. The rocky hills and headlands beyond the north tower of the Golden Gate Bridge today give some idea of the terrain. Few new settlers arrived on this hardship post in the 60 years following the establishment of the Presidio and the mission. ¶ Around 1835, an Englishman, William A. Richardson, built a house in what is now Portsmouth Square, and the village of Yerba Buena began. A straggly collection of pueblos, huts, tents, and tacked-together shacks huddled around a cove and provided shelter for those first San Franciscans. California was proclaimed part of the United States by treaty in 1846, and soon the land to the north and south of Market Street was surveyed, and rough streets and paths crisscrossed the hills. Fortune seekers arrived. The Gold Rush was on. ¶ City lots in those days may have been sold for as little as $90. But with later speculation, an acre could increase in value from $500 to $20,000 in just a decade. ¶ In the 1850s and 1860s, the fanciest part of town was Rincon Hill. Andrew Hallidie's invention, the cable car, tamed steep Nob Hill in 1873 and gave instant status to the area. As more lines were added, Russian Hill became a desirable address. ¶ In the years between 1870 and 1906, as the City boomed, thousands of houses, most of them Victorian-style, were built. San Francisco extended west from grand Nob Hill, east from South Park, and south beyond the Mission. Grand boulevards like Van Ness Avenue and Dolores Avenue were lined with impressive mansions. Handsome houses in well-tended gardens stood in solitary splendor in Pacific Heights with grand vistas of the Bay.

After extensive refurbishing directed by interior designer Anthony Hail, the main residence of Filoli is now open to the public for viewing. To recreate the interiors as they looked in the twenties, Hail gathered together furniture and paintings bequeathed by Lurline Roth, one of the estate's residents, and special pieces loaned from the Getty Museum, the California Palace of the Legion of Honor, and the M.H. de Young Memorial Museum. *Previous pages:* The ballroom at Filoli with murals painted in 1925 by Ernest Peixotto, a well-known illustrator. The chandelier was said to once hang in the Hall of Mirrors at Versailles. Crystal sconces have amethyst drops.
Opposite: The refurbished Filoli dining room has Chippendale-style chairs and an eighteenth-century Dutch cabinet. Filoli, a half-hour drive south of San Francisco, may be visited by advance reservation (415-364-2880).

Then came the Great Earthquake and Fire and the end of ostentatious turreted castles, mansions, and fanciful chalets on Nob Hill and Russian Hill. The grandes dames on the heights were spared, and the trauma was soon over. Spirits revived, and after briefly sheltering in Golden Gate Park, residents returned and rebuilt, this time with fire-proof steel frames. ¶ Undaunted by the thought of another quake (even today, few people really worry about fault-lines or tremors), San Franciscans swiftly built *beaux arts* mansions, neo-classical manor houses, Dutch Colonial mansions, grandly curlicued apartment buildings, and handsome Spanish Colonial Revival-style dwellings to house the wealthy and would-be's alike. ¶ Walking tours along outer Broadway, up and down Pierce and Steiner, Vallejo and Green streets, around Alta Plaza and the Presidio Wall show many turn-of-the-century mansions still occupying favored status. There are houses by Willis Polk—even a beauty built by Joseph Strauss, the structural engineer for the Golden Gate Bridge. The mild weather in San Francisco is kind to their splendor; owners care for them diligently and trim the pretty topiaries and evergreen trees. ¶ Not surprisingly, San Francisco's mansions are now million-dollar babies. No doubt their original go-getter owners would be very pleased.

Filoli's French Room has elaborate French chairs uphol-stered with Aubusson tapestries, on Aubusson carpets. Flowers from the Filoli gardens fill the rooms, which were designed for entertainment on a grand scale. (Fans of "Dynasty" may recognize Filoli. The television series' pilot was filmed there, and stock footage of the 654-acre property occasionally appears.)

FILOLI, WOODSIDE

Many of California's top architects and designers have worked on the buildings and interiors of Filoli. Willis Polk desgined the 43-room house. The highly acclaimed gardens were originally designed by Isabella Worn.

We can thank Mr. and Mrs. William Bowers Bourn II, San Francisco architect Willis Polk, and an enormous fortune gained from gold and spring water for Filoli, the elegant 654-acre estate 30 miles south of San Francisco. Named for a credo admired by owner Bourn—FIght for a just cause, LOve your fellow man, LIve a good life—Filoli was built between 1915 and 1917 and offers glimpses of California life on a grand scale. ¶ Polk had designed the Bourn's brick townhouse (still standing on Webster Street, between Broadway and Pacific Avenue) and in 1915 began work on their Woodside country estate. ¶ On watershed lands to the south of Crystal Lake, he sited the mansion among a magnificent stand of live oak trees. Bruce Porter, known for his stained-glass windows and murals, planned the Italian/French-style gardens, which were planted by Isabella Worn. ¶ The exteriors of the house are often called modified Georgian in style, but the inventive Polk brought together several other architectural traditions. The interiors are primarily English-and French-influenced, while the tile roof is in the Spanish tradition. ¶ The interiors contain 43 rooms and a total of about 43,000 square feet, including servants'

For many years, Filoli has been known for its superbly planted gardens, but the residence stood empty. First-floor rooms, including the French room, the ballroom, and library, are now furnished as they were when the Bourn family were residents. The Filoli estate is 30 miles south of San Francisco.

quarters and a ballroom. ¶ Long, wide hallways provide easy circulation to all rooms. Beautifully proportioned rooms with 17-foot ceilings, glorious wood-panelled walls, wood-burning fireplaces, and lovely views of the gardens from the windows create visions of a grand California country life. ¶ The massive ormolu-decorated fireplace and magnificent murals in the ballroom depicting the Lakes of Killarney and the Bourn's Irish estate are of particular interest. A study of the floors throughout the first floor reveals acacia koa wood in the study, quarter-sawn oak parquetry in the grand ballroom, and walnut laid in a herringbone design in the library. ¶ After a tour of the house, visitors can spend hours walking through the Walled Garden, the Sunken Garden, the Rose Garden, the Yew Allee, with its espaliered apple and pear trees, and the Woodland Garden with its marble plaque, inscribed *Festina Lente* (Make Haste Slowly), an excellent motto for enjoying Filoli and its gardens. ¶ The gardens and interiors of Filoli are open to the public between February and November by advance reservation. Filoli is a property of the National Trust for Historic Preservation in the United States. Telephone (415) 364-2880 for information and reservations.

ROSEKRANS HOUSE, PACIFIC HEIGHTS

A quartet of opulent gilded armchairs stands in the extraordinary Rosekrans living room. California-born designer Michael Taylor had a remarkable understanding of furniture scale and placement. He planned a large, comfortable sofa, a seemingly artless juxtaposition of refined and earthy materials, plus chairs to cluster for party conversations. From the arched windows, views across the Bay to the Marin Headlands. Bronze figure by Italian sculptor Emilio Greco.

Early in the century, when ornate High-Victorian architecture was in full bloom in San Francisco, Mr. and Mrs. Andrew Welch had the wit and imagination to hire architect/classicist Willis Jefferson Polk to design their new Pacific Heights mansion. ¶ For inspiration, the cosmopolitan couple and the worldly Polk turned to a Spanish Renaissance palace, the lyrical Casa de Zaporta in Saragossa. As in Spain, the exterior is understated, the interior quite theatrical and grand. Entry to the 1917 mansion is through a dramatic two-story atrium, intricately carved with sandstone columns, balconies, and friezes, all closely replicating the original. ¶ After Mrs. Welch willed the mansion to the archdiocese of San Francisco, it was beautifully maintained as the Archbishop's Palace for 40 years. ¶ When John and Dodie Rosekrans bought the house in 1979, they covered the soaring atrium with a greenhouse roof to halt erosion of the sandstone carvings and to provide a year-round room for entertaining. Giant palms enhance this exotic courtyard. ¶ The couple brought in a friend, interior designer Michael Taylor, to furnish the grand rooms. Choosing chairs, tables, and sofas and art of character and bold scale, Taylor has

imbued the mansion with style and comfort. Here, as in his favorite clients' houses, the designer is at his best, creating rooms of cosmopolitan charm and eclectic individuality far from the pared-down "California Look" he helped popularize. ❡ Here, an eighteenth-century Samarkand rug provides a geometric counterpoint to a quartet of gilded armchairs. A contemporary Italian sculpture is juxtaposed with an extraordinary 12-panel coromandel screen. African village sculpture stands beside contemporary California sculpture. ❡ "While a room should be beautiful, it should not be too perfect," said Taylor. "Perfection in every detail usually makes a room studied, formal, rather dull, and even forbidding." ❡ The set of four over-scale, scroll-armed, gilded armchairs (just one is an eighteenth-century original) were upholstered in rich golden silk. Eight straight-backed English hall chairs are placed around a new travertine-topped dining table, Taylor's own design. ❡ In the smoking room, walls are covered in pale-gold grass cloth, a subtle backdrop for the extraordinary collection of sculptures, quartz crystals, carvings, and plants. The room is also a show-case for a Senufo bird carving and prehistoric stone objects on a travertine table.

From the open-air terrace of this Willis Polk house, visitors can enjoy a view of two other wonders of San Francisco—the Palace of Fine Arts, *above*, originally designed by Polk's teacher, Bernard Maybeck, and the Golden Gate Bridge. In the superbly proportioned bedroom, with intricately carved pilasters, the draped Majorcan bed is as beautifully finished as a couture gown.

California design at its
cosmopolitan best, *opposite,* in
the Rosekrans bedroom. The
atrium/entry was faithfully
modeled after a courtyard of a
Spanish Renaissance palace, the
Casa de Zaporta in Saragossa.
Left: urns and busts displayed
before the fine view.

In the quietness and luxe of interior designer Anthony Hail's Russian Hill sitting room, it would be easy to imagine that he lives somewhere in Belgravia or in a very chic Paris *arrondissement* overlooking a private park. San Francisco rush hour may be in full throttle, but Hail's rooms offer few clues of a bustling city outside. ¶ Along the enfilade of his rooms, through lacquered double doors, are glimpses of museum-quality antiques, seventeenth-century Esfahan carpets, with impressionist light filtering through the windows. The house, a Victorian first renovated by architect Julia Morgan in 1916, was completely remodeled by Hail to improve the rooms' proportions. ¶ "Soon after we moved into this house, I realized that I didn't have one stick of furniture, not one decorative object, that is new. Actually my taste runs to furniture of the late eighteenth century. I don't seem to keep anything later than 1800. Maybe I should appreciate modern things more," mused the handsome Hail, a Tennessee native who started collecting antiques right out of Harvard. ¶ His taste runs to the classical, the refined, the subtle. And while anything Louis XVI (*late Louis Seize*) is automatically a favorite, he's

The house owned by Anthony Hail and his business partner, Charles Posey, stands on one of the few flat blocks of Russian Hill. From a small, elegant entry, stairs lead to the sitting room, which has windows on three sides.

One of Anthony Hail's heroines is Edith Wharton, whose opinionated 1897 book, *The Decoration of Houses,* is often seen as the coming of age of American architecture and the beginning of interior design as we know it today. She would certainly approve of the balance, symmetry, appropriateness, and luxury of Hail's house.

also very partial to low-key Northern European antiques. In his bedroom sits a Danish Louis XVI mechanical architect's table, one of his favorite pieces. ❡ "Living and working with antiques is my whole life, the main focus of everything I do," said Hail, a fixture of the San Francisco decorating and social scene since he arrived from New York in 1955. ❡ Still, Hail is no great respecter of borders. With his acquisitions, he brings to his rooms French chairs, Chinese lacquer tables, English bookcases, Russian chandeliers, Swedish prints, and Persian rugs, mixed with American know-how.

Hail's striped bedroom, *opposite,* displays the luxury of beautiful light, and his thoughtful placement of favorite drawings and furniture. *Below:* a gentleman's bathroom.

"I see each room as a lifetime proposition. The way I work is never instant decorating. First, and most important, I do as much as I can to get the architecture right, to make a wonderful background for antiques and people. Then I find a few beautiful antiques— rugs, vases, lamp bases, bookcases," said Hail, explaining his approach. ¶ "I find I am working with fewer antiques than I used to. No one can afford a whole room of antiques any more. The point is that you can start with antiques from your family and add to them over the years. Reproductions can be very beautiful. I line them all and have them smell quite wonderful. And I usually do plain curtains—that way you don't get tired of looking at them, and they don't overpower the room," he said. ¶ "I always remind my clients, 'Remember, this is not a museum you're creating.' You must have table tops that can take drinks, plus sturdy chairs that men can sit in. Fabrics must wear well, and not be so precious that friends are afraid to relax," said the pragmatic Hail. ¶ "None of my own house is just for display, and I insist that clients use all of their rooms. You must live with your antiques. I sit in these chairs. I bring out my best china every day." ¶ Don't Spare the Horses is his motto. "Beauty and pleasure are givens, but rooms must be usable, not fragile or intimidating, "Hail said.

In Hillsborough—a fast 30-minute drive south into the Peninsula—stands one of the most remarkable residences in California. Built 20 years ago of stone quarried in Sonoma County, the house is the result of a collaboration between owners George and Elaine McKeon, architect Angus MacSweeny, and interior designer Michael Taylor. ¶ MacSweeney drew up the original plans. When he died midway into the project, the McKeons hired interior designer Michael Taylor at the suggestion of their friend Dodie Rosekrans (see page 31). ¶ It was Taylor who designed the extraordinary oak-beamed ceiling in the living room and stained it a pale sand-beige. Over five years, he added over-scale sofas upholstered in linen velvet and an extraordinary collection of furnishings and antiques. ¶ "Michael thought the finest furniture was created in the eighteenth century, so we found French, English, Chinese, and Venetian pieces from that period. He's known for inspiring the "California Look," but he used antiques with great flair. They had to be the finest quality and unusual," said Elaine McKeon, president of the board of trustees, San Francisco Museum of Modern Art.

Michael Taylor would walk into this 52' x 26' living room and tell the owner it was the most comfortable room he had ever designed. The oak panelling formerly graced the Great Hall of Moreton Paddocks, Warwickshire, England. A rare George I (ca. 1720) cabriole-legged stool of walnut and parcel gilt with a silk seat stands in the center of the grand room.

A pair of Queen Anne mirrors hangs above Taylor-designed "rock pile" console tables. Oak shutters with a "linen-fold" design were distressed to appear old.

For her remarkable five-acre property with its 67 California oaks, Elaine McKeon first hired landscape architect Thomas Church to design and plan the landscape. He laid out the patios, pool, and shady loggia, and had all the trees (including stone pines) trimmed. After Church died, landscape architect Garrett Eckbo completed and revised the garden. Every March, gardeners plant 50 flats of impatiens around the giant California live oaks. In the sunny Peninsula climate, the flowers flourish until November. Classic roses like Peace, Queen Elizabeth, First Prize, and Tropicana are among McKeon's favorites. *Opposite:* Teak furniture invites year-round gatherings of family and friends.

Oak panelling in the entrance hall was formerly at home in the Old Rectory, Amersham, Buckinghamshire. Taylor's keen eye discovered an English console table in the manner of William Kent (1760) and topped it with an elaborately carved gilt-wood George II mirror. In the center of the marble-tiled hall is a fine Elizabethan oak refectory table (ca.1590).

The Designers

San Francisco has been blessed with a remarkably talented group of interior designers who find their inspiration in the gracious beauty of the region and around the world. They're highly individual and experimental, pulling out all stops for both adventurous and old-line clients. ❡ In a city where almost everyone comes from "somewhere else," no single look, trend, or style predominates. Some designers have made an art of strict minimalism, while others call on a fine band of local craftsmen to lacquer, incise, *faux* paint, sew, and stencil their designs to a fare-thee-well. ❡ Certainly, traditional rooms are most popular, but in young California it's hard to take period rooms too seriously. So designers mix countries-of-origin and periods, create instant heirlooms, juxtapose fine and folk antiques, contrast new materials with ancient stones and minerals. In rooms with good bones, thanks to exemplary architecture, they hang California artists' paintings and showcase contemporary crafts. They design comfortable viewing pavilions for glorious vistas. And they fashion urbane rooms illuminated with San Francisco's clear light and warmed by the California sun. ❡ For certain clients, designers may offer opulence, but as John Dickinson noted, a designer's life is not all deluxe. "Tacky things with grand things, mundane with exotic things give rooms vitality," he said. Dickinson also loved novelty in his rooms, but noted that a room based on amusing ideas would not be a laugh. ❡ San Francisco's designers revere the past and design's finest moments, but history does not weigh heavily on their shoulders. It's a rare house that was built before the turn of the century—the twentieth century. Designers in San Francisco can start anew each day. ❡ "When I've got my creativity going, that's when I'm most alive and conscious. When I'm solving design problems, rethinking an old design, I really feel life around me," said designer Ron Mann, who credits nature as his true source of inspiration. ❡ Designers use Chinese and Japanese antiques in a contemporary setting, happily work with luscious silks and romantic chintzes, as well as plain cotton canvas. Lighthearted, sun-struck colors wear well when the temperature seldom dips below 50 degrees or soars to 75 degrees. Never concerned with providing respite from a harsh climate, designers have carte blanche to dream. ❡ Labels and pretension don't belong here. Rather, each designer goes his or her own way, reinventing as they go along.

In John Dickinson's Victorian firehouse, the sky-lit ceiling and walls are as the designer found them, a mottled topaz. In the hallway, a dresser of *faux ivoire* handpainted by Dickinson. An imposing pair of heads between shuttered windows was acquired from a sale at the Old Spaghetti Factory (a former North Beach landmark) and refinished. *Overleaf:* Dickinson creates his own room patterns with a highly disciplined no-color scheme that emphasizes the outlines of the plaster tables and curvy Victorian chairs in changing light from the south-facing windows. The pair of paintings is by Ralph Du Casse (see his house on page 172).

The highly recognizable "California Look"—paled-down creamy colors and haute-casual overstuffed upholstery in light-filled rooms accessorized with elements of nature—is beloved in a city that likes barefoot ease presented with sophistication. ¶ Design stars like Michael Taylor (originally from Modesto) and the late John Dickinson (raised in Berkeley) have become admired internationally. Both have profoundly influenced today's designers. Missouri-born Mann has a free-spirited approach that encourages his followers to bring nature indoors—to use timbers, stone, and weather-worn rocks as part of a highly polished interior. ¶ Chuck Winslow, originally from the East Coast, likes to juxtapose contemporary art and an international cast of antique furniture. "The combination can be a marvelous visual surprise. Looking for the less obvious combination is the key," said Winslow. ¶ Performing their own neat balancing act on the edge of the Pacific Ocean, San Francisco's designers introduce the world to new possibilities.

An 1893 firehouse with brass name plates and a white canvas-curtained portiere was the remarkable residence and office for designer John Dickinson for 15 years until he died in 1982. ¶ Certainly the finest example of his work, it was also his design laboratory. There was magic, elegance, and mystery in his rooms. Where fire engines once stood, Dickinson parked his black-lacquered vintage Jaguar, its flanks ornamented with natural woven cane. Guests walked up a narrow flight of redwood stairs, worn by the boots of firemen and his many friends to a gray patina. At the top, an oversized white-enamelled door swung open to reveal one enormous sky-lit room (formerly the firemen's dormitory) that served John both as living room and studio. ¶ Dickinson said, "The walls are just as I found them—cracked old plaster, but the color of smoky topaz. I had them washed and touched up a bit, and painted the old dado white. The partitioning walls for the new kitchen and dressing room are new, but look old, thanks to a great *trompe l'oeil* job by Carole Lansdown." ¶ "The fireplace took a year to execute," recalled Dickinson. "It's nickel-plated steel and brass with moldings that match the dados. They're both the same distance from the floor, a fine point no one cares about but me." ¶ Later would come John's plaster tables, white

Standing on two white-lacquered plinths and displayed in an oak cabinet were John's attenuated white-lacquered carved African figures, a brilliant use of "airport art." To infer that he bought them en route to Mombasa or Zanzibar would be romantic. In fact, John gathered the collection at Cost Plus for a few dollars but spent considerably more getting the finest lacquer job.

Naugahyde-upholstered sofas, ten Victorian chairs upholstered in taupe leather and piped in white, an art nouveau table of grand proportions, plus a pair of carnival heads on columns that also housed speakers and storage. ¶ Just before John died, his last table made its appearance alongside his sofas. It was a design that pleased him very much—a wood table carved and lacquered to look like a cube with a bulky horse blanket thrown over it. The table's solid shape, he said, would be just right in a room where there were already enough furniture legs. ¶ In all his work, designer John Dickinson was unintentionally a trend-setter. Using mens-wear tweeds, camelhair, and gray flannels for upholstery, wall-coverings, and luxurious lap robes had his imprimatur first. Plain, honest materials—like unbleached canvas, woven wools, unstained wood, leather with piping, gray industrial carpet—were enhanced by the gleam of steel and brass and lots of sparkling white paint. And often he intro-duced something a little unsettling—carved or real bleached bones, a pencil drawing of a skull, bird claws. "Taste is a word I avoid," he once said. "'Good' or 'bad,' it's all so nebulous. The more you're dealing solely with taste in a room, the more you're on shaky ground. Give me vulgarity any time. I find it has great vitality."

Accessories that made walk-on appearances in John Dickinson's firehouse at various times included a shell basket filled with white conch shells; architectural models; an African tribal stool and headrests; Italian alabaster fruit; ceramic phrenology heads; a white bowl of onyx eggs; a flat, white stoneware dish of perfectly oval gray river stones; a collection of crystal and brass eggs, bleached coral branches, ship sextants, brass firehose nozzles, carved fruitwood bones, along with his standard white ironware ashtrays and stacks of books. Still, his rooms were clearly not about mere styling. "I don't put my stamp on a room by styling—doing things like plumping cushions with a knife-chop or fluffing up the curtains. Then design becomes ephemeral," Dickinson said. "Basic construction of a room should be where good design comes from; otherwise, it is not really style."

The Designers **55**

CHARLES PFISTER APARTMENT, NOB HILL

Full-height casement windows fill the rooms with light. Classic canvas-covered sofas and chairs in the salon were designed by Charles Pfister for Knoll and make the perfect accompaniment to his gilded *fauteuils,* granite-topped tripod tables, and extraordinary plants.

I think the location of my apartment, right at the summit of Nob Hill, is nonpareil. It overlooks Huntington Park and the historic Pacific Union Club. And the exterior and interior of the 1927 building have a great sense of proportion and scale. I find it just as glamorous and urbane as could be," said architect/designer Charles Pfister, whose clients nevertheless often call him away to London, Tokyo, The Hague, and New York. ¶ "I've lived here for five years, and the furnishings are still changing. Things come and go, and I don't think of it as 'finished.' I know I'll add more treasures, or retire an old favorite. This is the way it is now but not necessarily forever." ¶ When he first moved into these grand rooms, Pfister opted for a paled-down background. Mirrors on the walls further enlarge the apparent size of his rooms. Restoring his apartment in the spirit, style, and character of the original, he saw no reason to alter the interior architecture. ¶ Diffused northern light emphasizes the appealing pallor of the rooms.

The only real color in these powder-pale rooms comes from a handsome early nineteenth-century French needlepoint rug in the salon. Pfister had his Thonet deco dining chairs (bought at auction from the historic old Palace Hotel) finished in a subtle bronze lacquer. Floors were deliberately left bare.

Night and day create very different moods here. Early morning sun fills the rooms with cheer and brightly illuminates every crisp corner. Nighttime, with lights dimmed, the space expands, and Hutton's setting is as glamorous as a thirties private club.

A friend of mine said my studio reminded him of a dentist's office in Los Angeles in the fifties," said interior designer Gary Hutton. His Mission District apartment/studio is located in a one-story building built for light industry in 1946. Still, with its exposed concrete walls, concrete floor, steel-framed wrap-around windows, exposed-beam ceilings, and clean lines, it was the perfect setting for Hutton. He had been looking for a building where he could set up office and use the rooms as a lab for new designs. ❡ Patterns of sunlight streak through the apartment—actually one large room with an office, a kitchen, and a new sky-lit bathroom. ❡ Walls were painted white, the floor sealed and stained black. Metal shades on the high windows look forties period-perfect, but they're actually new. "I wanted to keep the design fresh and crisp with lots of texture. The scheme had to make sense with the architecture and its period. Chintz wouldn't exactly do it," said the designer. ❡ He set up a dining/conference room in one sunny corner, a comfortable sitting room with high-backed linen-upholstered sofas in another corner. ❡ A pair of geometric-patterned thirties Turkish rugs, found by chance in an antique store, look as if they were recently designed by Hutton himself.

In the sitting area are three cigarette tables that look like antique bronzes. They were designed by Gary Hutton using a lacquered gold-leaf finish on fiberglass. "It's a complicated and extravagant finish, but I had to mute the gold effect because it's too luxe for an industrial building," said Hutton. While he keeps accessories and *objets* to a carefully edited minimum, Hutton continues to add turn-of-the-century Rookwood pottery, paintings of rural scenes by American artists, and handcrafted glass. In fact, nothing in this scheme is set forever, as Hutton continues to experiment, observe, learn, and design. New chairs and tables will doubtless come and go, making brief appearances before moving on to clients and friends. With the black-and-white scheme, open plan, and Hutton's endless appreciation of the classic and the new, the studio will soon look completely different. Hutton's stylish apartment owes everything to his go-for-it approach and nothing to the once-historic-but-now-changing neighborhood. Always experimenting, Hutton plays with scale, new materials, different furniture arrangements, and lighting.

TEDRICK AND BENNETT COTTAGE, RUSSIAN HILL

The French military scene on the nine-foot screen along one wall of their living room presents a diverting tableau. "Our French screen gives the room dimension and an extra 'outdoor' view, a different window on the world," said designer Michael Tedrick. He and Tom Bennett are also fond of natural-fiber textiles in subtle, faded colors. Here, they've chosen a luxurious woven raw silk for simple curtains, plus nubby tweeds and long-staple cotton for upholstery, throws, and pillows. Passionate collectors, the two have gathered diverse but harmonious antiques.

A tiny, charming cottage is not exactly what you expect to find on grand Russian Hill, but tucked away in quiet lanes and along zigzag pathways are some of the City's most prized locations. ¶ A few years ago, interior design partners Michael Tedrick and Thomas Bennett were lucky enough to discover this sunny two-bedroom cottage. Its sheltered brick-paved garden terrace, bay views, and privacy add to its cachet. The cottage is part of a William Wurster-designed complex built in the thirties. ¶ Tedrick and Bennett have used the rooms as their laboratory, ignoring formula decorating in favor of their own mix of international antiques, muted colors, and textural fabrics. Their seemingly artless approach brings together a striking eight-panel Napoleonic wallpaper screen, a Directoire chest of drawers, a pair of Welsh jockey benches, a French zinc table with a Brazilian blue-granite top, plus new pine tables by Tony Cowan of Cottage Tables. Quirky Japanese antique fabrics, baskets, and pottery bring their own character. ¶ "We like to be surrounded with the things we love," they said. "We appreciate the hands-on craft and inherent beauty of each piece." ¶ Still, their interests range widely, and their rooms evolve slowly and thoughtfully. Chances are, in a few years, this same view will be completely different.

In a famous Nob Hill apartment building (ca. 1912), Jois Belfield worked with her favorite palette. Her rooms have a feeling of pared-down luxury with rich silks, textured linens, a white wool carpet, handpainted bronze canvas, and natural canvas.

JOIS AND IRVING BELFIELD APARTMENT, NOB HILL

The elaborate moldings in her four-bedroom apartment reminded designer Jois Belfield of an iced wedding cake. ❡ "I painted the walls a 'clotted cream' color so that they wouldn't look too stuffy. It's a more interesting tone than pure white because it changes with the season and the time of day. In the morning, the rooms look crisp. In afternoon light, the 'thick cream' color looks pale golden. There's something about the light in San Francisco that makes this exact tone work wonderfully," she said. ❡ For contrast, Belfield chose bronze tables and the dash of pink silk on pillows. ❡ So that the living room wouldn't look too "sweet" or "prissy," she stacked oak firewood next to the fireplace. "The room needs that roughness," said Belfield.

"In a building of this grand style and age, you'd expect silk draperies on the windows. Instead, I did plain white canvas draped casually," she said.

In this 1906 cottage, museum-caliber antiques live happily with contemporary classics like architect Warren Platner's wire-rod tables. ¶ Interior designer Chuck Winslow is a master at creating pretty rooms with character, comfort, and vitality. In his design schemes, neoclassical chairs, Chinese antiques, romantic chintzes, provocative contemporary paintings, imaginative tabletop collections, humble cottons, extravagant silks and gilding, fine craftsmanship, and comfortable-as-an-old-shoe furniture come together in rooms of great charm and authority. ¶ "My dream decorating has a look that's all very offhand," said the designer, "but, of course, it takes attention to detail, scale, and quality to make that work." ¶ There's a reverence for the past, but it's given snap with offbeat colors and contemporary art. Nothing "matches" in the conventional sense, but everything works together to

All rooms in Chuck Winslow's cottage work hard. "My rooms change from day to day, season to season," said the designer. *Above:* pine bookshelves frame the marble fireplace surround. Pink walls, pink pigskin suede, a fat sofa upholstered in linen, and sisal carpet create a gentle, relaxed mood. *Opposite:* a painting by Delia Doherty in the entry hall.

In the salon, crystal candlesticks, Warren Platner's sixties wire-rod tables, an antique dhurrie, and Italian chairs with turquoise pillows. Dog-lover Winslow also displays his growing collection of *papier-mâché* and folk art hounds.

create a room you've never seen before. The designer adds the backbone of East Coast formality to informal, California-cool country houses, and his irreverence for grandeur to urbane apartments. ¶ "Rooms should always look as if they happened over years, updated spontaneously with new paintings and unusual furniture," said Winslow. "They should show signs of life, echoes of human voices, and hands-on history. ¶ The designer uses tabletops and walls as his canvas, composing eye-pleasing tablescapes with favorite sculptures, small-scale paintings, glorious flowers, crystal candlesticks, and stacks of art books. Still, his rooms never feel cluttered. ¶ "I move things around all the time. Nothing stays in the same place for very long; otherwise, you lose the joy and surprise of seeing it," said Winslow.

WILLIAM WHITESIDE APARTMENT, ALTA PLAZA

C hic California comfort thrives under the sure hand of interior designer William Whiteside in his studio apartment overlooking Alta Plaza. Luxurious materials—glove leather, raw silk—and a well-edited collection of art and objects provide pleasures for the hand and the eye. The sisal carpet was a practical, low-key choice. ¶ The imposing scale of the Italianate mantelpiece and a Japanese *tansu* (chest), and three overstuffed, leather-covered chairs and ottomans all seem to amplify the studio space. ¶ Throughout, Whiteside combined rugged textures and rough surfaces to rein in the opulence. His deft mix of East and West— Chinese chairs, the hefty and highly detailed *tansu*, classic moldings, exotic flowers, and soothing colors—is often a feature of San Francisco interiors.

In William Whiteside's beautifully appointed sunny studio, three Japanese millstones are displayed on the massive mantel. Fat down-filled club chairs and cushy ottomans provide a versatile seating plan for fireside suppers, early morning newspaper reading, and foggy-day musing. The studio is on the first floor of a shingled townhouse designed by Willis Polk.

Starting with a very umpromising block-walled sky-lit loft short on architectural interest and free of interior walls, designer Ron Mann created a studio of dramatic simplicity. Furnished with his own furniture and accessories, the loft changes with the season and the designer's whim, with new items making their appearance as they roll from his drawing board. ¶ "I've now come to a place in my life where I'm living out my design fantasies," said Mann, whose métier is usually a natural material like weathered wood, pale stone, verdigris'd bronze, undyed canvas or white plaster in a paled-down color scheme. ¶ "The open space of this studio gave me such a wonderful freedom to experiment and try new ideas. I've painted the floor, added platforms to delineate a sitting area and an office. Since I've always got new designs brewing, it's a wonderful way to test

To warm up a concrete floor, Missouri-born Ron Mann handpainted and tooled this instant white "rug." Curvy cotton-duck upholstered sofa, and stone chest of drawers are his own designs. Chair from Wicker Wicker Wicker.

Designer Ron Mann's bold new quilt, artfully crafted in woven strips of pure white padded cotton, drapes his new sleeping platform. "Headboard" is an antique Majorcan screen. Wicker chair by Ivy Rosequist.

them, look at them in all possible lights, try them on for size, and get to know them," he said. ¶ There's real comfort, sensuality, and rough-hewn charm in his designs, with none of the trappings and pretensions that often accompany today's interiors. He pays homage to the rocks and noble timbers of California with his tables, lamps, and chairs, but this is no simple-minded, back-to-nature love affair. ¶ The Mendocino and Big Sur coasts offer up driftwood logs, and Mann's travels to Majorca and Mexico yield new designs of sophistication and grace prized by cognoscenti around the world.

Ron Mann loves to surround himself with his newest designs. Here, a Spring roomscape includes a Portuguese cupboard filled with variations of his sandcast bronze shadow vases and plates. Cor-Ten steel candleholders on the driftwood table are also his designs.

In Craig Leavitt and Stephen Weaver's Russian Hill apartment, it's very much Louis-meets-Leavitt-and-Weaver. This talented pair of designers nonchalantly mixed fine French furniture, New Guinea wood carvings, a Parisian park chair, their own over-scale "Javelin" lamps with huge parchment shades, and an eclectic collection of luxurious fabrics. Needlepoint pillows (stitched with aphorisms by a friend with a tart tongue) and rich memorabilia are counterpoints in the monochromatic scheme. ¶ These elegant, witty rooms, with their pale northern light, are proof positive that designers often do their best work for themselves with no client running interference. ¶ "We like to let the rooms happen rather than work with a floor plan," said Weaver. "In a sense, we don't make a big effort. We love rooms that look a little worn. Fading and wear give rooms a reso-nance and comfort we like." ¶ Tone-on-tone textured plaster walls, luxurious wool fabrics, and leather upholstery offer tactile pleasures. ¶ "If the design of accessories and furniture is top-quality," said Leavitt, "it will all work. We like simple proportions with rich details." ¶ "We edit carefully. We're always tempted to gather all our favorite things around us," noted Weaver.

Craig Leavitt and Stephen Weaver mix their own dramatic furniture designs with favorite antiques. In the living room of their Russian Hill apartment, Weaver's painting of Leavitt's 12 favorite rooms hangs on a raked plaster wall. "Arrowhead" granite-topped table and "Javelin" lamp are their own designs, *opposite*. The designers brought together a suede-upholstered Italian chair, a New Guinea story-board carving, and their own silver-leaf "Lightning Rod" table in the apartment foyer, *near left*.

SCOTT LAMB APARTMENT, BROADWAY

Sacramento native Scott Lamb grew up drawing and painting and dreaming of wonderful rooms. "When I was a design student, my scrapbook was filled with photographs of English rooms and English-style houses. The English, particularly in their country houses, have such a feeling for comfort. Unlike most American designers, they appreciate a slight shabbiness and signs of age. For them, the brand-new rooms that haunt our design magazines are reason for grave doubt and suspicion," said Lamb. "I'm looking for a quality of design that lasts. I don't like faddish furniture or trendy design. This translates for me to French, English, and American antiques, Chinese porcelains, fine upholstery, silks, linens, and cottons in soft colors. Then I always add something eccentric and over-scale." ¶ For his Broadway apartment, Lamb first painted the walls a warm canteloupe color. In his ongoing design, an over-scale sofa, topped with down-filled pillows, plus a pair of chintz-covered chairs anchor the room. Ever-changing tabletop collections include museum-quality sculpture and inexpensive personal favorites, like handpainted porcelain vegetables and alabaster fruit.

"I plan rooms that will get even better as they settle in. They should look softer and friendlier with time. Pillows, preferably down-filled, should not be too stiff. Rooms are for living and reading and for entertaining friends. They should not look like stage sets. I'd never design a room using antiques exclusively. It would look like a museum," said interior designer Scott Lamb.

After first improving the interior architecture of the sunny rooms, Lamb put together his apartment scheme with pretty, muted tones like peach, moss green, pale coral, and cream. Into this setting, he brought the snap of Japanese tables, Chinese porcelains, the delicate tracery of gilt sconces, handpainted screens, and somewhat over-the-top quilted silk curtains on the windows to muffle sound.

Before he flew off to New York to become Director of Creative Services for Polo/Ralph Lauren, designer Jeffrey Walker lived in this sunny, white apartment on the edge of Buena Vista Park. Walker's creamy monochromatic scheme—with its stylized, sculptural furniture, natural canvas upholstery (by Sam Yazzolino), and well-edited objects—confidently pays homage to his mentor, San Francisco designer John Dickinson. ❡ The curvy white-lacquered table (after Jean-Michel Frank), a "Stonehenge" fiberglass lamp, and framed furniture drawings are all by John Dickinson. ❡ Ironstone bowls and platters, gleaming stripped floors, and simple white-on-white upholstery were all Dickinson inspirations. Still, Walker here gives Dickinson's pristine scheme a bold new spin with a spindly Flos lamp next to the mantel, geometric mirrors, and a *faux*-finished stage-set chair of rather grand proportions to take away the room's edginess. An elaborate white-lacquered capital, used here as a table, is a typical Walker tongue-in-cheek touch. It's a fiberglass cast intended for store display. Fat cushions invite guests to sit in the window and take in the view toward the Bay.

John Dickinson once said that all white tones—creamy white, gray-white, and white-white—live happily together. Jeffrey Walker's interior proves that all white is all right. Framed table design drawings and lamp, *above*, by John Dickinson.

Designer Jeffrey Walker muted the mood in his bedroom with a subtle dappled *faux*-marble wall finish, low-slung Roman shades in natural cotton duck, and pale cotton bedcoverings. The custom-designed, over-scale platform bed and matching side-tables are painted matte white. Walker included his techie work desk, task lamps, and upholstered armchair as part of the room, not clumsy intruders. Witty touches here include a French theatrical column that's actually a store display fake, and a white ironstone bowl of natural sponges. Framed architectural drawings were booty from a Venetian holiday. A master of visual effects, Jeffrey Walker used color and scale deftly in his bedroom/studio to create a restful refuge.

The Collectors

 like to live surrounded by my collections," said designer Robert Hutchinson. "My decorating goal in this apartment is to present favorite things I've gathered over the years in a way that is free and open." Hutchinson first came to San Francisco from Louisiana more than 25 years ago to study with famed art and design teacher, Rudolph Schaeffer. (Michael Taylor and Charles Pfister also studied with Schaeffer, mentor until he died at age 102 for many of the City's finest artists and designers.) ¶ Highlights of Hutchinson's 30 years of collecting include Mexican and Egyptian masks, Asian burial jars, stone bowls and implements, and African ceremonial masks and stools. ¶ A museum-quality sculpted greenstone Maori weapon is set on a low shelf in Hutchinson's bedroom. A dramatic king's mask of carved wood from Cameroon stands guard beside his white-linen-covered bed. "Every piece I own has meaning to me. I move them about, walk around them, look at them from all directions, and display them all with great care and appreciation," said the designer. ¶ Byron Meyer has the same high regard for his paintings and sculpture. Favorite pieces are shuttled from room to room, edited, and sometimes moved out altogether after years of enjoyment and then much introspection. Since our photographs of Meyer's bold collection (page 93) were taken, his Guston and Hudsons and Arnesons have been joined by a small transcendental painting by Ross Bleckner and a graphic painting by Sean Scully. "It's always hard parting with a painting I've loved for years. But I have only so much wall space. I can lend out paintings for shows, but if this collection is going to grow and stay fresh, something has to go," said Meyer, a major supporter of Northern California artists. ¶ Not all collections start in an art gallery or antique store. Some come from the natural world. Like Ron Mann, Hutchinson finds dramatic rocks on his travels and brings them home. "I get a great deal of pleasure using natural objects. Recently I set an over-scale bamboo tray on a granite table and filled it with river rocks that looked like Henry Moore sculptures. The stones were beautiful. All I had to do was give them a presentation." ¶ Ron Mann will return from a hike along the rocky Montara shore with spherical speckled rocks that look as if they came from an art studio, or with pale turquoise beach glass. He sets them on weathered wood tables or in newly cast bronze bowls. "Not everything in a room has to be precious," he said.

In designer/collector Robert Hutchinson's city office, favorites are displayed on "floating" shelves. Among his international cast of characters: a Columbian burial jar, Thai terra-cotta heads, coil vessels, Mayan creatures in stone, an Indian seed vessel with a coiled snake, a carved African mask, an Ivory Coast tribal bed, a Korean carved granite pot, and a 200 B.C. Greek road marker.

In Robert Hutchinson's apartment, *opposite,* Mezcala-style stone masks (100 B.C. - 300 A.D.) from Guerrero, Mexico, mounted on the wall and lit by candles. *Center:* Robert Hutchinson (with Michael Carr) "Nicoya" chair, a new three-legged design in wood with hand-finished openwork. *Above:* the front door with textured plaster panels and a gold leaf finish by Michael Carr.

John Dickinson warned against filling rooms with art bought for investment. "Always buy paintings for the pure pleasure. If you must buy art for investment, keep it in a bank vault where it belongs," he growled. ¶ Designer Eleanor Ford also cautions against collecting simply to impress. "It's better to have one fine piece of art than a lot of itsy-bitsy things," she said. "Collections are lovely, but they must be good and well-edited." ¶ Designer Chuck Winslow's interiors (page 124) always have the added spark of contemporary art. "Living with my art collection is like having my best friends around all the time," said Winslow, who has been collecting the works of Billy Sullivan, Robin Bruch, and Stephen Mueller. "I like the visual surprise of a Manuel Neri plaster figure standing beside a pair of Directoire chairs, or a vibrant Tom Holland construction over a Louis XVI fireplace. It's a more personal statement," said the designer, who might also set a beautiful but inexpensive auction find on a precious antique Chinese table. "Contemporary art is one of the few precious things we can still afford to collect," he said. "I always advise clients to buy the very best they can afford. And it's better to purchase a first-rate lithograph than a third-rate painting. Photography can be the beginning of a fine collection for many young people." ¶ Architecture, remarkable paintings and sculpture, and the carefully chosen furniture were the stars, never the bibelots, of Michael Taylor's beautiful rooms. "When in doubt about a room, take out," the great collector (and editor) said. "If a room is in trouble, it's often because there's too much in it. If you can't see the room for the clutter, edit."

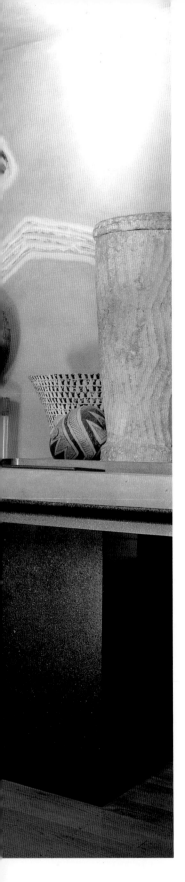

When designer Robert Hutchinson bought his two-story storefront property, he discovered it had been built in 1912 with bricks salvaged from the devastation of the 1906 Earthquake. "I set up my studio downstairs and proceeded to renovate upstairs, recreating the rooms for my own pleasure and redecorating all the surfaces," he said. ¶ He spent hours hand-shaping walls out of mud and color and sticks, creating sensuous curves, sculpted shelves, and generous open spaces for his furniture. "It was two years of dabbing and painting and 'ruining' my house, slapping colors up there like some primitive man in his hut. It was my one and only chance to have fun and accomplish something that no client would ever let me do," Hutchinson recalled. ¶ Wall finishes are layers of clay painted with multiple washes to give a centuries-old look. ¶ "As my collections of European arts and crafts—and then African and Asian and South American artifacts—developed, my rooms changed.

Hutchinson's apartment is a lively gallery of his diverse collections. From *left,* a Bob Brady figure, a Stephen De Staebler clay vessel, and Indian mask. African vessels stand on a lignum vitae table top set on a carved Plexiglass base. Hand-painted colors and sticks on the wall are for texture, line, and humor, said the designer. *Above:* a detail of the bathroom with an Aztec figure.

Hutchinson sees his Sutter Street apartment as a laboratory for his ideas. Here, he can use and observe his designs, refine them, edit them, and enjoy each one. ¶ A smooth chunk of lignum vitae tops a Hutchinson-designed curved Lucite base. A great slab of granite stands on a sculpted wood base. A large-scale drafting table is supported by a hand-formed base that looks like slabs of terra cotta. A steel daybed covered with superb Navaho rugs stands in one corner of his office-study accompanied by a remarkable tabletop grouping of ash-gray burial jars, primordial stones, and delicate Indian clay bowls. On a wall nearby, Hutchinson brought a gallery-caliber display to life by creating the illusion that precious Indian bowls are tipping off shelves or falling from a ledge. In fact, they're well-supported by concealed metal supports built into the shelves. Still, his conceit does make visitors look twice at this shapely clay collection. ¶ Here in his apartment, he opened up rooms, created a stair bannister

Hutchinson's collections take over his kitchen, too. A grouping of Indian stone mortars, Central American figures, and river rocks beneath copper pots. In his orchid house, Chinese storage jars, a Mayan salt grinder. "I collect orchids because the flowers are breathtaking but they come from simple, sculptural plants," he said. Favorite orchids: *Brassavolas.*

from smoothly sculpted tree branches, and painted his bathroom walls with a watery wash the color of verdigris. Almost every fixture—door handles, drawer pulls, faucets, shelves, and tabletops—has been designed or hand-sculpted by Hutchinson himself. ¶ He can relax in a sunny roof terrace, cook for company in his spacious kitchen, tend his orchid collection in a sheltered greenhouse, or sculpt a cushy chair to pull up beside the fire, with its remarkable hand-plastered geometric surround. ¶ In his apartment, the designer can introduce his new hand-carved tables and chairs, new ideas for shelves and lighting, critiquing them for weeks before approving them for clients. ¶ Inevitably, since he has so many, prized objects will be retired to a storage room, and others will be brought out to be displayed and appreciated again on tables and shelves. Guided by Hutchinson's free spirit, these rooms will continue to soar.

"I designed the bedroom with all the comforts I could plan in close quarters," said Hutchinson. Beside the bed, a king's mask from Cameroon and a Dogon figure. *Center:* an English japanned red lacquer chest-on-chest. Black lacquer table, chair, and bed are Hutchinson's designs.

When San Francisco Museum of Modern Art trustee Byron Meyer purchased his elegant townhouse atop Russian Hill, the first phone call he made was to interior designer Michael Taylor. Taylor, who once said that the best decoration results from "weeding out," paid a visit. Thus, in 1974, began a year-long design collaboration to rid the 1931 house of its cut-pile carpet, fussy detail, and heavy velvet draperies, and to provide Meyer with the perfect background for his busy life and a first-rate art collection.
¶ Taylor wanted the rooms to have a timeless, international look. First, he pared down and polished the interior architecture, opening doors to create vistas from room to room and cleaning out extraneous moldings, fuss, and trim. ¶ Hardwood floors were left bare or covered with no-nonsense sisal. Sand-textured paints in muted taupe were laid on walls with a trowel to create an authentic antique look. ¶ The same nubby fabric—raw silk with the look of inexpensive burlap—was used in the living room and Meyer's luxurious bedroom. Taylor's signature fossil-stone was used for occasional tables, and for Meyer's remarkable custom-made dining table.

Opposite: A Gilbert & George work on paper, *Rest,* hangs on one wall of the dining room. The table, with stone pedestals, was designed by Michael Taylor. *Art Patron Disguised as Local Artisan* by Robert Arneson is a tongue-in-chic tribute to Meyer. A Dale Chihuly glass sculpture glows in the center of the oak table beneath an oxidized bronze, *Cone Boy,* by Tom Otterness, *left.*

"My art collection keeps changing because I like to get the newest works by my favorite artists, plus new works by young artists with staying power," said Meyer. ❡ His collection started with paintings by Bay Area figurative painters and now encompasses paintings and sculpture by all major California artists, including Richard Diebenkorn, Robert Arneson, Sam Francis, Ed Ruscha, Billy Al Bengston, Wayne Thiebaud, and Peter Voulkos. "Over the 30 years I've been collecting, I also keep coming back to Paul Wonner, Elmer Bischoff, and Robert Hudson, who were my teachers at night classes at the San Francisco Art Institute. I had to develop my eye, and I learned so much from them," said Meyer. ❡ Collecting Philip Guston in the seventies turned Meyer around and made him search for challenging paintings. Now his collection covers wide territory—from Robert Arneson's sly sculptures to Eric Fischl's sexually charged canvases. He's looking with interest at Man Ray and Joel-Peter Witkin photographs, and exploring the possibilities of video art. ❡ "I really appreciate the luxury of having my favorite paintings around me," admitted Meyer. "They're all here, and I never have to worry that the guard might say, 'I'm sorry, we're closing.'"

Colors of walls and fabrics were muted to emphasise Meyer's carefully curated collection. At *left*, Robert Hudson's painted steel sculpture stands near a window in the living room. Other major works include a Sam Francis painting, *Facing Oil*, Roy De Forest's witty canvas atop the sofa, and a standing bronze by A.R. Penck on the mantel.

MARY KEESLING HOUSE, RUSSIAN HILL

The charming but self-effacing lettuce-green exterior of one of the last Victorian houses on Russian Hill gives no hint that the interior contains dramatic John Dickinson-designed rooms with style that Queen Victoria could never have imagined. Nor are there any remaining hints that the house was formerly owned by actress Ina Claire, whose Hollywood-glamorous interior scheme included acres of ruby red carpet and swags of blue silks. ❧ First built in 1861 for a lawyer and his family, the house has spacious rooms of elegant proportions, rosy terra cotta walls, restored Victorian moldings, and a highly personal collection of contemporary ceramics, paintings, and mixed media works by noted California artists. ❧ "When I first started collecting seriously in the late fifties, San Francisco artists who are now internationally recognized were just on the way up. I've bought paintings over the years only by artists I believe in. I'm not interested in being *au courant* or in constantly turning over my collections," said the owner, who noted that her house was not an easy one in which to hang large paintings. Big canvases tend to stay put and anchor a changing display of smaller pieces.

John Dickinson's white-lacquered "Stonehenge" tables and a canvas-upholstered sofa serve as dramatic counterpoints to elaborate lacquered Chinese chests, boudoir chairs, a Biedermeier game table, and a superb lacquered and gilded Queen Anne secretaire. The designer planned the rooms with places to sit with friends, with a book, or beside windows, so that the owners can enjoy green views of their garden and the Art Institute tower through the trees. Among Keesling's collection: ceramics by Rudy Autio, Robert Shaw, and Robert Arneson, and paintings by Frank Lobdell (above sofa), Richard Diebenkorn, Robert Hudson, and Nathan Oliveira.

A white ceramic plate by
Pablo Picasso was a gift from
Michael Taylor.

I studied drawing with Wayne Thiebaud as a college student, and the first piece I collected was his hand-colored etching of a slice of cake," said Eileen Michael, a patron of the San Francisco Museum of Modern Art. Today, her favorite may be a Manuel Neri plaster figure, or a Roy De Forest oil, but a setting created by Michael Taylor forms the elegant background. ❡ When she first decided to buy her circa 1886 house, it was (like most houses of the Victorian era) dark and uninspiring, with poky rooms but a fine location. ❡ In quick order, she brought in designer Michael Taylor, a family friend, who first had the back wall knocked down and french doors installed. ❡ "Michael Taylor worked in the most inspiring, enthusiastic way. He always had lots of ideas, and he changed them constantly as the room slowly came together. He was a total perfectionist," said Michael. ❡ For her upstairs bedroom, Taylor spent days getting the creamy white color right. ❡ "He'd have the paint applied, then change it the slightest gradation. He'd go home, then come back the next day and perhaps change it again. I'd marvel at his work. It's beautiful in the most subtle way," she said.

One living room wall was enveloped with mirror to increase its apparent size. Taylor-designed chairs and a large melon-shaped ottoman were upholstered with natural-colored linen velvet trimmed with his signature Bouillon cord fringe.

Eileen Michael's bedroom/sitting room was one of the last designs executed by Michael Taylor. Afternoon light pours into the room through Taylor's trademark plantation shutters. In contrast to the large-scale four-poster draped in quilted white linen, Taylor brought together a pair of Diego Giacometti stools, a Michael Taylor-designed travertine table, and an ornate gilt chair upholstered in chartreuse silk. Pablo Picasso lithograph, 1947, *Tete de Jeune Fille* (a portrait of Francoise Gilot). Architect: Sandy Walker.

"Michael always said that the bedroom was the most important room in the house," said Eileen Michael. "He thought you should sit up in bed and feel wonderful." ❡ For her, Taylor designed a quilted-linen-draped bed that's a room within a room. Beside it, he placed two elegant but functional bedside tables with drawers and shelves for books and a telephone, along with fine reading lights. "Michael said that you should be able to go upstairs to your room, light the fire, read in a very comfortable chair, and put your feet up on a table that you couldn't scratch," she recalled. ❡ She appreciated his dedication all the more because the highly successful designer had probably never designed rooms as small as those in her first house. "He brought a lot of large furniture in, but the house never looked cluttered. Michael Taylor was such a talent and so wonderful to work with. But you always had to let him go with his ideas. He did lose his enthusiasm if you tried to tell him what to do."

L iving above the store surrounded by his favorite things is the happy lot of antique dealer/interior designer Glen Smith. In 1980, Smith and his G.W. Smith Galleries were pioneers in the Fillmore Street neighborhood that is now bustling with chic restaurants. Making his move from Palm Beach, Smith purchased a pre-Earthquake storefront building with a Japanese fish market at street level and a photography studio upstairs. Still, the spacious second floor had high ceilings and original mantelpieces of cast iron and marbleized enamel that had made the journey from New York around The Horn, and Smith moved in, making few changes. ❡ Today, the upstairs apartment looks as if Smith inherited it from his own travel-mad, antique-collecting family. ❡ In his front parlor, Smith clearly kept many of his best antique pieces for himself. "I've always been fascinated with neoclassical antiquities. That's what I buy for myself," said Smith. "Even when I go to Bali, the pieces I buy have an affinity with Etruscan ceremonial sculpture." ❡ This is neoclassicism that crosses borders. Four Italian Directoire chairs and a fine pair of Biedermeier gondole chairs were upholstered anew in San Francisco, using black cotton printed with a design taken from Greek pottery. Irish, English, French, Italian and American, Indonesian and Greek—even Eskimo—pieces are

Beneath a nineteenth-century neoclassic Swedish mirror, antique dealer Glen Smith displays a crystal obelisk, a first-century Roman head, and a Regency theatrical helmet of tole on an Italian Adam-style marble-topped console table.

A *faux* tortoise table displays an orrery. Four seventeenth-century marble plaques of Roman emperors hang on the wall. The carved wood girandole is of the Adam period. French bronze lamps have Corinthian column bases.

represented and given new life (and company) in this collection. The black-lacquered floor is covered with a pair of Aubusson carpets, their lovely colors further faded by the bright California sunshine. Still, his precious things are made to be used, and his chairs are comfortable as well as remarkable. "I love the purity and simplicity of classic lines. It's not muddled like rococo," said Smith. ¶ He insists that the look and feel of wonderful rooms is a result of thoughtfully arranged furniture. "I place comfortable chairs in groups for conversation, objects on large tables to please the eye, smaller tables beside chairs to hold drinks or books, and desks with good chairs in my bedroom, where I do all my work," he said. ¶ In odd corners of his treasure-filled apartment, he stood vitrines filled with collections of eighteenth-and nineteenth-century tobacco containers, scrimshaw, Indonesian miniatures. On the walls of his study hang colorful framed gouaches of the erupting Vesuvius, as seen by an international cast of painters. ¶ "This is my life. I've devoted my whole life to finding and collecting. But I only buy things I like. That's my rule. To me, it doesn't matter whether they're antique or contemporary if there's perfection in the design. Still, I notice I hardly ever buy anything modern," chuckled Smith.

A pair of 1780 English plaster figures stands on plinths beside a dramatic pair of Ionic columns that originally stood in an Irish country house. Green silk-upholstered Regency gentleman's reading chair by Thomas Hope is inlaid with ebony.

Unique Style

Fashion designers Jeanne Allen and Marc Grant can sit outside on the terrace of their hexagonal house in the Berkeley Hills (opposite) and gaze past gnarled pine trees to the San Francisco Bay. Directly below their house is the Campanile on the campus of the University of California. Across the dazzling Bay, beyond Treasure Island, the distant Golden Gate Bridge is stretched between the Presidio and the Marin headlands like a cobweb. ❡ The couple can watch white fog sweep over the Sausalito hills, blot out the bridge, and swirl past the Sutro Tower to shroud the chock-a-block City. ❡ Over in Marin County, a neat twenties house (page 145) is the perfect vantage point for eyeing bobbing boats, a quiet cove, and San Francisco shining like the Emerald City in the clear blue light. ❡ In Cow Hollow (a now-chic preserve named for dairy farms there in the last century), a fashion company executive and his wife enjoy privacy-with-Bay-views in their sunny updated house. ❡ In Pacific Heights, from the windows of a handsome Italianate Victorian (page 138) that may have been built as early as 1865, the view east takes in the City glowing in the morning sun. ❡ On Russian Hill, designer Thomas Bennett can take tea beside the fire (page 141) and watch gray pines buck and sway as the summer fog makes a mad dash down Hyde Street. From his bay window, he might catch a glimpse of the toy-like cable car speeding along its shiny tracks. ❡ San Franciscans have the best of all worlds. They live in one of the most beautiful city settings in the world, in sun-filled houses and apartments within a ten-or twenty-minute drive from glorious Golden Gate Park, museums, the Marina, Sausalito, the walking trails of Marin or the East Bay parks. On weekends they can escape to the quietness and comfort of a hilltop flat to observe the life on the Bay from a distance, or take to the water on a sailboard, yacht, or ferry boat. ❡ San Francisco is a city of friendly neighborhoods, each with its own character and indigenous specialty goods. Residents may shop for freshly roasted coffee, crusty breads, or antipasti in North Beach, then walk a few blocks to Chinatown for bok choy, fresh noodles, branches of colorful spring blossoms, or watercress. ❡ From his apartment above Fillmore Street, David Peugh (page 122) can stroll up the hill as far as Jackson Street to find antiques, Italian footwear, chocolate

Opposite: **Despite windows and glass doors on all sides of Jeanne Allen and Marc Grant's house to take in the panorama, the wide overhang allows direct sunlight only at sunrise and sunset. The polished oak floor and a redwood plywood ceiling seem to soak up light and keep the mood inside the rooms somewhat muted.** *Overleaf:* **With oaks and redwoods to provide privacy, Allen and Grant have left the windows bare. Evenings, the lights of the City glow in the distance.**

truffles, Sicilian sausages, used books, hip sunglasses, sushi, vintage clothing, doughnuts, pizza-by-the-slice, and freshly brewed coffee—morning jet fuel for the locals. For respite, he can take in a movie at the Clay theater or meet a friend for lunch at a sunny cafe. ¶ Food is San Francisco's obsession. Stores on every block purvey salad greens, organically grown fruit, ice cream, French pastries, sourdough bread, nine-grain sandwiches, fresh juices. California's bounty is there for everyone to taste. ¶ Friday nights, Elsa Cameron stocks up in the City before driving north into Marin County. Once up there on her sunny perch (page 115), she likes to settle in and cook for friends. Her house in the hills of Marin is so hard to find that she will rendezvous with guests in Fairfax before leading a convoy up the narrow switchback roads to her aerie. On Sunday, she heads back to the City as the setting sun turns the Bay to molten gold. ¶ All this beauty, and houses of character for respite. Who would ever want to leave?

ALLEN AND GRANT HOUSE, BERKELEY HILLS

Nestled in the Berkeley Hills with fine views over San Francisco Bay stands a remarkable 1,200 square-foot hexagonal house designed by Frank Lloyd Wright. The house, owned by San Francisco fashion designers Jeanne Allen and Marc Grant, was originally designed in 1938 as a Malibu beach house but was never built. ¶ Forty years later, a Wright devotee bought the plans from the Frank Lloyd Wright Foundation and proceeded to build the house under the proviso that every detail of the interior and exterior would be faithfully reproduced. At that time, it was the only Wright plan constructed posthumously. ¶ Allen and Grant, feeling the pinch in a decorative but tiny Russian Hill apartment, first heard about the house from one of the carpenters working on it, but never dreamed that they would one day own it. ¶ They observed the construction from a distance as the solid, earthquake-proof foundations were secured on pilings and beams atop 400,000 pounds of gravel. Forty thousand bricks were custom-made—and rejected because the color and size were wrong. Rugs Wright had specified were woven in China. ¶ Soon after the house was completed, they heard from their carpenter friend that it was for sale, with two asking prices—one with furnishings, one without. ¶ Allen and Grant

One early change the couple made was to turn the tiny "bedroom" cubicles (Wright considered sleeping a passive exercise not requiring precious space) into efficient offices where the two often work on weekends. Daytime sofas in the living room unfold into futon beds that can be set up before the fireplace, in a sheltered corner, even on the decks, *opposite,* for summer snoozing. *Left:* Jeanne Allen is a superb chef and loves to cook cracked crab and salads for friends. Since she and Grant spend months each year in Japan designing their fabrics, sushi is another favorite.

On summer days, Allen and Grant throw open doors and windows and barbeque on the deck, *opposite.* In winter, or in foggy August when afternoons are California cool, they bring out sketch books and pens and design their fabrics and fashions before the flickering fire.

Not surprisingly, over the years Allen and Grant have grown to appreciate Frank Lloyd Wright. While they don't regret shipping off those hexagonal stools and museum-quality rugs, they now find themselves on the Wright house-tour circuit—and more intrigued than ever by the Wright mystique.

originally intended to forgo the furnishings, but after lengthy negotiations with the house-proud sellers, they bought the lot. ¶ Since the couple couldn't see living in this enchanted pavilion with Wright's curiously dated color scheme—orange, Easter-basket purple, acid yellow, and lime green—they packed the furnishings and donated them to London's Victoria and Albert museum. ¶ While Allen and Grant admit that "the house looks its best empty," they set about furnishing it with the things they love—Japanese antiques, flea-market finds, family heirlooms, Oriental carpets. Their own easy-to-live-with collage of colors was inspired by tones in Japanese woodblock prints—glossy blacks, rust, gold, gray, warm brown, and navy blue—which complement the raw natural woods particularly well. Many of the tweeds and printed cottons they've used for upholstery are quilted—a signature of their Jeanne Marc fashion collections. ¶ Since Jeanne Allen and Marc Grant travel on business for five or six months a year—much of it in Japan—they find their peaceful house on its quiet hillside street particularly welcoming. The serene setting, along with Wright's obvious admiration for things Japanese throughout the design, smooth the transition from an Osaka apartment to California.

Weekdays, art curator Elsa Cameron lives in a bright yellow Victorian cottage in the Castro, purchased for a song in the sixties. Weekends, she packs her bags and makes a 35-minute dash north to her Fairfax retreat. ¶ With its open-door welcome, sunny colors, crowd-around dining tables, sink-in chairs, and dance-floor-sized deck, the house is like a year-round summer holiday. Furniture with the look of family hand-me-downs are mostly flea-market (even sidewalk) finds, repaired and repainted. ¶ Still, when Cameron first found it, the 1912 summer house suffered from decades of ill-advised renovation and debris from a disastrous storm. For Cameron, who saw the potential and the spectacular views toward Mount Tamalpais, it was love at first sight. ¶ With designer Michael Cyckevic, she recreated her summer cottage with inspiration from Monet's Giverny and the colors of Tuscan afternoons. Open windows and lacy curtains frame her world-class view of the green slopes of Mount Tamalpais.

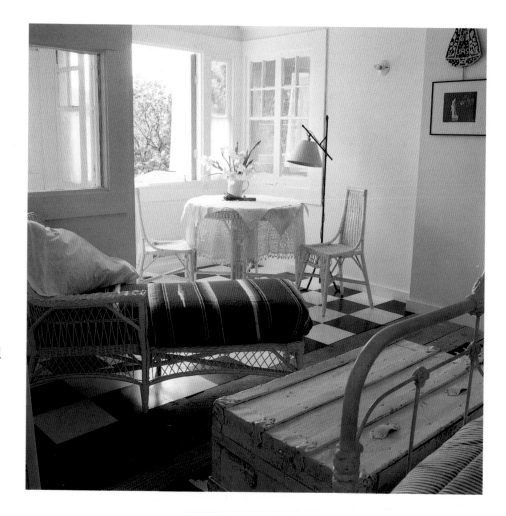

Upstairs in her light-filled, all-white bedroom, Elsa Cameron brought together a restored wrought-iron bed, and old steamer trunk, wicker chairs, and other unusual pieces to create a room that looks as if it has been there since the house was first built.

Treasures brought home from
Mexico add color and zest to
Elsa Cameron's sunny rooms.
The eclectic finds that fill every
shelf and tabletop are like her
extended family.

Signs of wear only add to
the value of Cameron's wicker
and willow chairs. "I like things
that look as if they had a
life before I discovered them,"
said Cameron.

ROBERT STEFFY HOUSE, RUSSIAN HILL

The living room looks west to the hills of the Presidio. "I'm very lucky because it's wonderfully lit all day," said designer Robert Steffy. "The sun shines in the garden in the early morning. All afternoon it's bright—I see the sunset. Then in the evening, I can see all the city lights."

When designer Robert Steffy first saw his Russian Hill house 20 years ago, it had none of the style it has today. "It was so dark inside, you could hardly see. But I did understand its quality and its possibilities. I decided to buy it and work on it," said Steffy, whose wide-ranging talents include designing Italian glass lamp bases, bamboo and *huang hua-li* (rosewood) tables, glass-topped bronze tables, and a new line of tin plates patterned after Chinese export china. "I had my architect draw up plans to remodel the whole house to give us a working scheme, even though I knew it might take years." ¶ He painted all the dark redwood walls and ceilings white and added wrought-iron balconies to the front exterior. A tiny garden was turned into an enchanting dining room, complete with french doors, a striped canvas-shade-covered skylight, and mirrors that reflect bamboo and the pretty peach-colored walls.

As the work progressed, Steffy happened to see a new marble floor in one of the galleries at the California Palace of the Legion of Honor. He searched out the same contractor and designed the bordered pattern for his own dining room. ¶ Steffy's unpretentious and inviting design includes simple natural-canvas-slipcovered chairs and sofas, red-cotton-upholstered Louis XVI chairs, and blue-and-white V'soske rugs on the new oak parquet floors. "If you think I like red, white, and blue, you're right," chuckled Steffy. ¶ Steffy, who attended Parsons School of Design in New York, prefers a crisp look with outlines that won't date.

Over the years, Steffy has added his own designs—Venetian green-glass lamps, a series of tables—but the rooms are still carefully edited and never get cluttered. "I never get bored here," he said. "It's a wonderful house to come home to."

David Peugh's apartment is in a new complex, with garden apartments on two levels, plus Trio cafe, gift stores, a dry cleaner, and other neighborhood favorites below fronting Fillmore Street.

I think of my apartment style as wacked-out classical. There's a bit of ancient Greece, a little Pompeii, but the materials and finishes are absolutely contemporary," said technical advisor David Peugh of his apartment in the Western Addition. Still, it started life as a tiny one-bedroom shell with no architectural distinction. ❡ Designer Gary Hutton brought in his special offbeat point of view, along with a canny eye for function, and installed hand-cut moldings, a travertine fireplace, and theatrical swags of metallic-painted cotton over sheer voile. ❡ Hutton's tongue-firmly-in-cheek approach spoofs classicism as it spatters new-rage Zolatone over the living room walls, the boxy tables, and even the new kitchen appliances. ❡ To show off Peugh's growing collection of paintings by contemporary California artists, including four large canvases by Joan Brown, Hutton chose a paled-out, tone-on-tone color scheme for each room. Still, there's nothing wishy-washy or still-life about these interiors. As new paintings are added to the prized foursome, the mix only gets better.

Gary Hutton's lighthearted improvisational approach created the look of large-scale rooms with this-minute freshness. The apartment is the perfect stage set for art and antiques.

Night and Day. One apartment, two moods. By day, designer Chuck Winslow's South of Market pied-à-terre is all business. Appointment books, swatches, blueprints, and plans cover his tables and desk. Clients are welcomed, telephone calls are made. Everything he needs to keep his work running smoothly is at hand. ¶ By night, as lights sparkle on the distant Bay Bridge, the efficient office becomes a romantic dining room. Drawings are rolled up and filed away, office equipment is stored. ¶ Lavish flowers and plants from the nearby flower market are set in cache pots and crystal vases, pillows plumped, and the round desk, now a suede-covered dining table, is set with colorful Italian glassware and tall candles. ¶ Lights are dimmed, candles lit, and the music turned on. Italian Consulate-style chairs are exchanged for *faux* tortoise Federal-period chairs. The door bell rings, guests arrive, and champagne corks pop. ¶ With a deft hand, a sure eye, and a generous spirit, Chuck Winslow has transformed this well-located but architecturally undistinguished apartment into a hospitable

Left: Winslow's special mix: Swedish pine chairs, bamboo stools, works by emerging artists, blooms in crystal vases. *Above:* Tall candles and fresh flowers create evening glamor.

Andy Warhol's *Howdy Doody*
strikes an irreverent
pose above the book-topped
pine dresser.

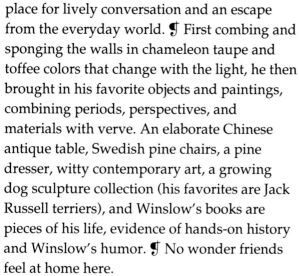

Seasonal flowers, Venetian glass plates, beeswax candles, French room fragrance, and low light set the stage for conversation and Winslow's down-home cooking.

place for lively conversation and an escape from the everyday world. ❡ First combing and sponging the walls in chameleon taupe and toffee colors that change with the light, he then brought in his favorite objects and paintings, combining periods, perspectives, and materials with verve. An elaborate Chinese antique table, Swedish pine chairs, a pine dresser, witty contemporary art, a growing dog sculpture collection (his favorites are Jack Russell terriers), and Winslow's books are pieces of his life, evidence of hands-on history and Winslow's humor. ❡ No wonder friends feel at home here.

MENDELSOHN HOUSE, RICHMOND DISTRICT

We choose furniture and art that capture our imagination. If we love a piece, we hardly bother with dates, the name of the maker, or its provenance until after we've decided to buy it. Pedigree is simply not our priority," said Barbara and Richard Mendelsohn, who brought together this clever and appealing collection in their grand 1908 shingled house. ¶ Juxtaposed in their rooms are contemporary American and European paintings, an English sideboard (ca. 1840) and a gold-inlaid French cabinet brought from the family house in Johannesburg. To this eclectic mix, they've added a fifties glass-topped table and two remarkable cowhide-upholstered chairs commissioned from California furniture designer Philip Agee, *opposite*. ¶ "We want the furniture to get an emotional reaction. Not everyone likes these pieces, but that's OK. I just don't want our house to look bland or over-designed," said Richard. ¶ In their growing art collection, too, the Mendelsohns like their funny bone tickled. "When we started collecting, we loved realism. Then we moved on to expressionism. Now we're looking for art that's on the cutting edge, more 'out there.' But it must produce an emotional charge, make you laugh, maybe even startle," he said.

The house's art-obsessed owners find their furniture, paintings, and accessories all over the world. Their grand Victorian provides endless wall space, year-round San Francisco light through bay windows, and sumptuous rooms that welcome their changing furniture and canvases.

The four-story Queen Anne-style exterior gives no clue of what's inside. While the proportions and trims of their rooms feel Victorian, the Mendelsohns say that they are really in love with art deco furnishings. Their latest finds are art deco chairs and a table discovered in Paris. "I think this unexpected mix is what San Francisco is really about," said Richard Mendelsohn. "While the exteriors of most houses seem traditional, the interiors are likely to have an edge and be highly individual."

Collections and art find their way into the Mendelsohns' paled-down bedroom, *opposite.* The couple appreciates the bathroom as it is and has no plans to update the fixtures, *right.*

Pure white walls and all-day sunshine offer a friendly California welcome to a pencil-post bed, a collection of farm stools, a chest, and framed samplers. Bare floors are very much in the Shaker spirit.

DIANE BURN NURSERY, PACIFIC HEIGHTS

Designer Diane Burn has made a highly successful international career letting her imagination roam free to create interiors of extraordinary charm and wit. In her daughter Adriana's nursery, she made a child's dream of a room, with fairytale characters on walls and heirloom laces on cradle and bed. Her fantasy was created in the high-ceilinged upstairs chamber of an imposing house she renovated, now one of the finest Victorians in the City. Diane, however, is not enamored of the period and has here filled the room with references to other eras. Which eras is a question for the enchanted visitor—and Diane's blonde daughter—to answer.

In New York, Porto Ercole, and Los Angeles, designer Diane Burn has created fantasy interiors with *boiserie,* exquisite plastering, tea-dipped silks and muslins, period furnishings, and an eye finely tuned to nuances of color. Here, for her daughter Adriana, she commissioned artist Ami Magill to paint storybook murals in the dreamy nursery.

The late afternoon sun streaks through old window shutters into designer Tom Bennett's Russian Hill sitting room. Only the occasional cheery click and clang and clatter of the cable car speeding along Hyde Street line give a clue that the room is in San Francisco. Baize-green walls, Asprey shagreen boxes, a fine Baktiari rug, garden roses, a Louis Seize chair before a Directoire architect's table, Bennett's collection of dog prints, and sculptural mounted trophies suggest an Englishman's hunting lodge—in France. ¶ To create this cozy setting, the young designer gathered together a lifetime's collection and wrote his own life story. "I like a room that tells you something about the person who lives here," said Bennett, who insists he's no longer as enthusiastic about blood sports as his collection might suggest. "As my enthusiasms change, the room will evolve within this scheme I've set up. Chairs will come, I'll see something better, and the old will go. Fabrics may change. Design is a process, not an end in itself. Rooms should never be static." Bennett happily mixes flea-market finds with family treasures to create his charming "young fogey" room.

Designer Tom Bennett mixed periods, countries, and provenance to give his Russian Hill apartment its point of view. Baize-green walls are the moody background for his relaxed style. Garden roses in an etched crystal case, a scrimshaw, and shagreen box collection are displayed on a walnut Directoire chest of drawers. Silk velvet upholstery, cashmere throws, and comfortable chairs complete the composition.

Drifts of linens, pillows, and coverlets hand-embroidered with Binche, Venise, Cluny, and Battenberg laces cover the beds—and almost everything else—in Jan Dutton's sunny Fairfax house. Clearly, white linen is the most romantic—and versatile—fabric. ❡ Inspired by her love of fine white linens, Dutton founded Paper White nine years ago to manufacture and sell her diaphanous designs. Her company has been a raging success, and these fabrics of fantasy are available (and copied) all over the world. No one, it seems, is immune to the charms of delicate lace-edged and hand-embroidered linens. ❡ In her hillside house, Dutton is most generous with her beautiful white linen. She upholsters chairs and sofas with it, swathes her four-poster with it, dresses tables with the lovely stuff, and uses it quite conventionally as curtains, pillow covers, pristine aprons, and timeless dresses.

Paper White designs have the look of heirlooms, but they're newly produced in the finest Belgian and Italian linens. Jan Dutton insists that even white-linen-upholstered chairs are practical as well as decorative. She should know. She has two young boys. Fresh flowers, the scroll of a hand-carved chair leg, lunch on the terrace, and the leafy paradise outside her windows are visions of another era against this dreamy white background.

When we first saw our house in 1974, it was pretty forlorn. It had been damaged by a storm, then stood vacant for five years until we came upon it and knew its potential," said the owner of this charming house, which was built in 1920 in the best tradition of the Northern California craftsman style. With its remarkable views of the Bay and the distant spires of the City, it's also within walking distance of the town of Tiburon and the ferry. ¶ After first repainting and replastering their hillside house, the owners—a lawyer and his wife, the editor of the local newspaper—called in a friend, architect Howard Backen. His firm's clients include the likes of filmmakers George Lucas and Robert Redford. Backen drew up a masterful plan for their 1,750 square-foot house, and supervised a remodel that eventually enlarged it to a spacious 2,850 square feet. ¶ "We wanted the floor plan of the house improved but didn't want to lose the twenties feeling," said the owners.

Interior walls were removed and windows enlarged to give a real sense of place. Clear light fills the house all day; in the afternoon, the sun seems to reach into every corner. The newly renovated rooms are superbly proportioned and thoughtfully organized. Now you can see the view—surely one of the most beautiful in the world—from all the rooms upstairs.

This Marin County house sits on a small lot, so the owners added decks off the living room and the master bedroom downstairs. Painted floor in the kitchen, *opposite,* is by Patricia Dreher. Rooms in this Tiburon house were furnished simply, comfortably, and with great charm. Pale colors form an empty canvas for patterns of changing light. Shuttered interior windows above a work counter in the remodeled kitchen invite the view, too.

Architect Howard Backen's redesign for this Tiburon house included moving the entrance from the front to the side, adding an internal staircase that gives direct access to the center of the house, and adding new floors of vertical-grain Douglas fir. ¶ The new dining area, formerly the sun porch, sits right out in front of the house with a view of Belvedere Cove, Belvedere, and the City. ¶ A square motif is reiterated on wainscotting, atop picture windows, as door trim, and along the bannisters. Pale background colors that seem to glow in the sunlight further emphasize the friendly scale of the rooms and their extraordinary natural setting.

The master bedroom, *opposite,* was created from an unfinished basement. Now it opens to a gracious lattice-shaded deck. Howard Backen updated the interiors with reverence for the original craftsman style. The owners' heirlooms fit right in.

Chuck Williams sometimes jokes that his 1906 cottage is "too tiny to spend much time in," but the likes of Julia Child and James Beard have often joined him there around the dining table. ❡ The shingled cottage, hidden away in a leafy cul-de-sac, was originally built in Golden Gate Park as shelter for 1906 Earthquake victims. San Francisco city fathers later decided that those living in the "earthquake cabins" could have them if they moved them onto their own land. This one arrived on the slopes of Nob Hill via horse-drawn dray. ❡ Williams, the founder of kitchenware purveyors Williams-Sonoma, bought the four-roomed house in the sixties. First order of business was to excavate beneath the structure to create what is now, literally, the ground floor. It's here that Williams spends much of his time, cooking in his unpretentious open kitchen and entertaining friends.

Designed so that his friends can gather around as he chops, Chuck Williams' kitchen is well-equipped with a lifetime's collection of practical cookware—but nothing flashy. His 30-year-old gas stove has more than earned its keep and is there to stay. On his eighteenth-century dresser, he has arranged vignettes of fresh fruits and vegetables, Lunéville ceramics, and Chinese porcelains.

FREDERICK HILL APARTMENT, LAFAYETTE PARK

In literary agent Frederick Hill's apartment overlooking San Francisco Bay, books are the heart and soul of the rooms. In the living room, one whole wall is covered with books neatly lined up on redwood shelves. A reflection in the gilt-framed *belle époque* cafe mirror doubles the apparent length of the floor-to-ceiling collection. An antique library table and sturdy old wooden library ladder complete the bibliophile's room. "My goal is to have all my walls covered with books by the best contemporary American writers, including many by my clients," said Hill. "The minimalist look is not for me. I like to have my favorite things around to enjoy every day." ¶ Starting with a few antique pieces, his lifetime collection of books, and the expertise of designer Chuck Winslow, Hill has given his one-bedroom apartment in a twenties building his individual stamp. One masterstroke was the choice of the rich marmalade color for the striéd walls. Painter Carole Lansdown also gave the fireplace its distinctive *faux marbre* finish. Pearl-gray, pigskin-suede-upholstered Louis XVI chairs, Knoll end tables, and an unholstered tweed screen outlined in nailheads are part of his eclectic mix. Hemp diving-board floor matting was chosen for looks and durability. Hill shares his apartment with a rambunctious Hungarian puli.

Frederick Hill's apartment, on a hill near Lafayette Park, offers grandstand views of the Bay and two bridges. The mottled marmalade-colored walls keep the north-facing apartment sunny and bright during the day and glamorous at night. With the "bones" in place, Hill will continue to see his rooms as works in progress. Still, favorite objects like the gilt-framed study by nineteenth-century American painter William Norton, Masai photographs by Carole Beckwith, and inviting down-filled sofas will always stay.

Across the Bay from San Francisco stands a bucolic Berkeley property discovered by a local artist in 1976. Formerly part of a large estate, the cow barn/granary/milking shed/hayloft was originally designed in 1908 by John Galen Howard, the campus architect for the University of California Berkeley from 1905 to 1930. ¶ With thoughtful renovation by architect Chuck Trevisan, the old barn is now the home of the artist's family. Down the hill, a horse barn eventually became their guest cottage. "I don't think Howard would recognize these buildings even though they're remodelled in the style, spirit, and symmetry of the original," said Trevisan. ¶ A shady colonnade was added and later enclosed to create a family room and bedroom. A new swimming pool and patio were built by the artist, his wife, and their three sons, using old bricks and tiles from the property. A new pergola and trelisses covered with wisteria ensure privacy. ¶ Still in the planning stages are a new dining room and a renovation of the kitchen. In the meantime, the family's glorious acre offers them the very best retreat just 20 minutes from the City.

"We repaired and updated all the old buildings on the property without changing their style or scale. They had to look as if they had always been there," said architect Chuck Trevisan, who planned the changes. Sheltered by stands of eucalyptus and a redwood grove, the property includes a new swimming pool and patio and a retro-new house, formerly a barn.

For 60 years, this is where the estate's former gardener milked the cows, tended his trees, and kept the wells working. In the spirit of Howard's rustic structure, Trevisan has guided its metamorphosis into a 2,000-square-foot cottage with light, comfort, and all modern conveniences.

GLEESON AND JEANRENAUD HOUSE, POTRERO HILL

Behind a "tough" exterior—black asbestos tile walls, perforated-metal garage doors—stands one of the most elegant contemporary interiors in San Francisco. While the simplicity and machine-made ethic may appear Early Bauhaus, the accent is on fine craftsmanship and the luxury of hands-on finishes. ¶ "The key here is the contradictions. Dan Solomon's architectural design is pure and refined, but the materials we chose were complex to install or apply," said the owner, composer Pat Gleeson. His wife, Joan Jeanrenaud, is cellist with the Kronos Quartet. ¶ Sound-softening punched-metal wall panels look to him at times like the "skin" of a 1947 DC-3, and in daylight have the subtle play of light and color of Monet's water lily paintings. A series of metal bolts attaches each panel to plywood panels on the wall surfaces. ¶ Interior designer Terry Hunziker's subtle color scheme juxtaposes warm charcoal leather and grey/beige wool serge upholstery, raw-steel table bases, and rich taupe lacquered wood. ¶ Leather-covered sculptural chairs with rakish angles by Stanley Jay Friedman are a distillation of classical forms. ¶ The inner

Preceding pages show the barrel-shaped stairwell of the Gleeson/Jeanrenaud house, with its pearl-gray hand-plastered walls. Sunlight through the front windows creates ever-changing light patterns. *Opposite:* In the living room, Seattle interior designer Terry Hunziker first planned a modular "ledge"—12-inch wide shelves and jutting tables—in steel with metallic-overlaid laquered oak. Hunziker's sofas and daybed are upholstered in handsome gray/beige serge. Articulated lamp by Artemide. Photograph, *left,* by Robert Mapplethorpe. Framed construction, *right,* by Bruce Conner. Windows give glimpses of the City skyline.

core of the house is lit by a large domed skylight. A circular stairway of painted steel-plate gives access to the master bedroom loft and an all-zinc master bathroom. ¶ Counter-tops and cabinet door fronts in the kitchen are covered with sheets of zinc. On a lower level are two practice studios. ¶ Designer Hunziker drew up furniture that is at once softly sculptural and blocky with complex interlocking shapes and surprising surfaces. "Dan Solomon provided me with wonderful spaces to work with, a blank canvas," he said. Sofas, tables, chairs, and banquettes follow a low horizontal line below sensuous perforated-metal walls. "The solid, weighty, complex patterns happen below an airy, reflective surface. The room's visual power comes from this look of 'sky' above and 'landscape' below," mused Hunziker. ¶ This is custom design at its best, and the couple's delight in living and working within this creation is very evident. ¶ "I love the paradoxes. The robust structural severity, the single-minded 'industrial' approach are very Beethoven, but the refinement, wit, and subtle shifts are move like Ravel," Gleeson said.

Victoriana

olden afternoon light shines down on San Francisco, spotlighting rows of Victorian houses that cling to the green hills and climb up impossibly steep slopes. Over in Marin County, the clear Northern California light casts its glow on a cheery yellow Victorian house surrounded by flower-covered decks and almost a century of history. ⁊ On Russian Hill, a tiny Victorian now in the shadow of tall apartment buildings casts off years of benign neglect and gains fresh all-white interiors. ⁊ In the Alexander Valley, a venerable Victorian stands amid rows of vines and looks down the valley with a certain hauteur. ⁊ In Pacific Heights, on a quiet tree-lined street, a beautifully tended shingled Victorian belonging to a painter received the John Dickinson treatment. Dickinson's plan for the upstairs bedroom—herringbone-tweed-covered walls, a steel-pipe four-poster—rocked the design world. Queen Victoria may have been amused. ⁊ A historic Victorian house in Sonoma County found an energetic new owner and designer, who dressed the old girl in new clothes and took her dancing. ⁊ No matter where the visitor wanders in San Francisco, Victorian houses stand in line, catching the eye with their powerful symmetry and rainbow-colorful detailing. ⁊ Victorians dating back as far as 1870 grace the perimeter of Alamo Square. A trio of rare Queen Anne tower houses gaze out over the Bay on Pacific Avenue, between Octavia and Laguna streets. Some Victorians are tiny gingerbread cottages, others (like the Haas-Lilienthal House) stand as tribute to the craft and art of wooden-house building. ⁊ Built at a fast clip between 1870 and 1906 of abundant coastal redwood, the house exteriors were carved, pressed, sawed, ornamented, "signed," incised, and embellished, then painted, to a fare-thee-well. ⁊ Victorians that survived the 1906 Fire range in style from the stately Italianate villa to the gable-roofed Queen Anne, quirky Gothic Revival, strictly tailored San Francisco Stick, and the rustic pretensions of the many Eastlake variations. All packed a lot of detail into typical narrow "shotgun"-shaped San Francisco lots. And almost all turned a very decorative face to the street. Once past the false parapets and five-sided bay windows, however, style stops. Sides and backs of the houses are rather mundane. ⁊ Happy in their artifice, Victorians put on a wonderful show. And to view them, all you need is a map or guide book, and a cable car or bus ticket.

Harry and Maggie Wetzel, both active in the arts and music worlds in San Francisco, can relax on the porch of their Victorian house in the Alexander Valley and enjoy the view. Over vineyards of cabernet and chardonnay grapes, they see beyond the Russian River. Their house has had many lives. The present structure was constructed around 1906 with redwood from an 1846-1848 house damaged in the 1906 Earthquake. "Gingerbread" on the porch is the 1906 original.

WETZEL HOUSE, ALEXANDER VALLEY

On a beautiful site surrounded by Alexander Valley Vineyards land, the Wetzels' refurbished house, *opposite*, is ready to face another century. The property was first settled around 1840, when the valley was a challenging two- or three-day journey north from the very young town of San Francisco.

Maggie and Harry Wetzel's Alexander Valley Victorian looks as if it has been snoozing in the Northern California sun for decades, keeping an eye on the changing seasons, watching the vineyards flourish. ¶ The picturesque house's history is rather more lively. Cyrus Alexander first settled the valley around 1840, and in 1848 (with the Gold Rush in full cry), built an adobe and timber home to house his large family. The dramatic 1906 quake split the walls asunder, so in 1906, he dispensed with the adobe and built a new house, using the same redwood timbers. The builders used plans purchased from a lumber supply company, Maggie Wetzel guesses, and added their own "gingerbread" embellishments. ¶ The Wetzels, then living in Los Angeles, purchased the 650-acre property in 1963. This house, until then owned by the Alexander family, was handsome but in need of renovation. Keeping to the original floor plan, the Wetzels opened rooms by removing walls and eliminating dark hallways. Exterior redwood timbers were removed, cleaned, replaced, and repainted. All original fireplaces, in fine functioning order, were kept in place. New wiring and a modern kitchen were added. ¶ The Wetzels did not want to disturb the fine century-old fig trees, so the exterior today looks exactly as it did in 1908.

Rooms, *above and opposite,* are
furnished in Victorian style,
with an eye for comfort and
charm rather than period
authenticity. Interior design by
Sandy Salmon.

Maggie Wetzel, who loves to garden, restored old beds of lilacs, rhododendrons, heirloom roses, ancient olives, fruiting mulberries, and figs. A large vegetable garden supplies the house with year-round fresh salads and herbs.

TOBY LEVY REDESIGN, RUSSIAN HILL

A new take on Victorian, this living room suggests formality with its precise placement of furniture and minimal details. A pair of new black-lacquered sofas was designed by New Yorker Steven Holl. An elaborate mirror was discovered in an antique store in Mexico. The owners' imposing mahogany sofa was an impulse purchase from the house's previous owner, an opera singer. *Opposite:* Not all Victorians are fussy, cluttered, and abuzz with pattern. A fine, white-marble mantelpiece set the monochromatic color scheme for this large Russian Hill living room. Afternoon light from west-facing bay windows illuminates subtle details like the rich Jacquard pattern of upholstery fabrics, quirky floor planks, and sculptural furniture shapes. Scandinavian gilt stools from Therien and Co. Collage by Joseph Raffael. Silver candlesticks by Swid-Powell from Fillamento.

Victorian houses don't have to be dark, stodgy, or uncomfortable," said young architect Toby Levy, whose crisp, focused renovation revitalized this 1896 house for its new owners. The small white house, squeezed between two apartment buildings on the crest of Russian Hill, was formerly a period piece of tiny, cluttered rooms. The living room, which now measures 17 1/2' x 27', was carved out of two small bedrooms. To fill this room with sunshine, Levy restructured and widened its bay window. Stripping away extraneous moldings, carpet, and trim, Levy opted for a monochromatic scheme, strictly edited. ¶ With its marble mantelpiece, white-upholstered sofas by New Yorker Steven Holl, stripped floors, and formal arrangement, the room celebrates the best of Victorian and modern without getting stuck in exact replication. Nor did the architect attempt to make it look like a new house. Watermarks and random planking on the hardwood floors, plus old windows and bannisters, are its endearing signs of old age.

RALPH DU CASSE HOUSE, PACIFIC HEIGHTS

Cream-colored paint ices the best features of Du Casse's shingled house. His garden, *opposite*, is a symmetrical oasis of calm.

A rtist Ralph Du Casse made the most of the terrace garden for his cedar-shingled 1882 Queen Anne house. From his sunny verandah, he looks onto a trimmed English box knot garden shaded by *Pittosporum* trees. Two iron urns stand at the corners. ❡ John Dickinson's dramatic design for Du Casse's bedroom (*overleaf*) was completed in 1968, but looks as startlingly original today. Walls upholstered with herringbone wool tweed bordered with brass strips set the stage for a 12-foot four-poster bed fabricated of industrial steel pipes and outlined with brass. The steel pipes were finished and rubbed to look like pewter. In a more Victorian mood are "antimacassar" shades of crocheted cotton. ❡ Du Casse's bedroom suite was the only part of the house Dickinson designed. Elsewhere, the painter mixes Victorian, Regency, Chinese, and Italian antiques in chic rooms of silky comfort.

The tweed bedcover is lined with summer-weight camel-colored cashmere. Bedside tables are covered with a wool Jacquard, which repeats the carpet motif in miniature. Glove-leather chairs with hand-carved "twig" legs were also designed by John Dickinson. Du Casse, an imaginative collector, has added a few pieces over the years, but the bedroom is essentially as John Dickinson designed it more than 20 years ago.

JUDY AND PETER SEVERSON HOUSE, MARIN COUNTY

In a wooded peninsula that juts out into the Bay is one of San Francisco's hidden treasures. It's also home to some of the most costly real estate in the world. With million-dollar views in all directions, mansions and estates enjoy a rare privacy, thanks to narrow, winding roads that discourage visitors. ¶ This is the quiet haven where Judy and Peter Severson, their son, Christopher, (and two Airedales) found their splendid Victorian house, *opposite*, with its close-up views of the water and vistas to Tiburon and Angel Island. ¶ The house was built as a summer cottage in 1892, but it had been cared for lovingly over the years by the six families who called it home. ¶ The Seversons live surrounded by the richness of its history. Stained-glass windows, woodwork, trims, and floors are all original.

Gracious rooms with generous doorways, *this page,* give the house its comfort and character. The family has filled terraces and decks, *opposite,* with pots of citrus, agapanthus, and flowering vines beside a flourishing hillside garden.

With great appreciation of their hillside house and the Victorian tradition, the Seversons furnished it with inherited pieces. Their special feeling for the past is everywhere evident. ¶ Oriental carpets pattern hardwood floors. An ornate Victorian table stands in the entrance hall topped with a celadon bowl of fragrant potpourri. Delicate laces on the windows enhance this nostalgic setting. ¶ It's here in her attic studio that Judy Severson creates printed "quilts" on paper, using embossing to duplicate the whitework of quilting. Her growing business now includes quilt-motif notecards, frameable prints, and a stationery collection. Traditional quilt patterns include "Rose of Sharon," "Morning Glory Wreath," "Spring Tulips," and "Birds in Flight."

Open decks and balconies of Judy and Peter Severson's house allow them to enjoy life on the water year-round. In each sun-filled room, the family has brought together English antiques and handed-down pieces to give rooms a period feel without slavish recreation of the heavy-handed Victorian style.

Blooms Judy brings in from
her garden are often fragrant
heirloom roses, and she fills
vases with cottage-garden
pansies, daisies, and pink phlox.
Her dressing table, *right,*
stands in front of a window
that looks directly over the Bay.
Judy's love of quilts is
very evident in the bedroom.
Quilting hoops hang on a
quilt rack. Quilt on the bed is
her own work.

Originally built in 1850 for the owners of the first winery in Sonoma County, this picture-perfect house was given new life by its owner, San Francisco theatre impresario Steve Silver, and interior designer Gary Hutton. ❡ "My client wanted the interiors to be casual and comfortable, with calm colors. He leads a hectic life in the City and loves to escape to his country house less than an hour from the Golden Gate Bridge," said Hutton, who grew up on his grandfather's apple ranch on the Monterey Peninsula. ❡ Overgrown trees crowded the house when its latest owner first arrived. The scene was a grim one. Landscape architect Edward Nicholas cleared trees and rampant undergrowth to reveal the charming symmetry of this early Victorian house, surely the oldest represented in this volume. ❡ "There was no view visible from the rooms, and the interiors were quite drab," said the designer, who eventually removed tacky moldings and had everything—including a knotty pine kitchen— painted white. Oak floors were bleached. ❡ All sofas and chairs were slipcovered in favorite hot-weather fabrics like blue-and-white-striped French linen, and pale-blue linen/cotton. The effect is crisp and rather tailored. ❡ The owner's growing collection of blue-and-white china is displayed in almost every room.

White wicker chairs discovered in a Sonoma antique store invite relaxation on the verandah. From the widow's walk on the roof, San Francisco is visible— on a clear day.

The bevelled glass in the front doors is original to the house. Silver's "Blue Willow" pattern collection stands on Ralph Lauren wicker tables.

Morning sun fills the office/television room with light. Crackled lacquer table by Therien and Co. Muted colors in the room are accented by a striped linen/cotton-upholstered sofa.

At one end of Silver's living
room, a grouping includes
a hand-carved wood model for
a barrel table, antique-iron
flower baskets, and an Eastlake
Victorian chair.

Designer Gary Hutton set a relaxed mood in the living room with cool cotton/linen slipcovers, fat pillows, and sisal carpet. The coffee table has a lacquered linen finish. White-lacquered tin fireplace was original to the 1850 house. A *faux* stone lamp by Randolph & Hein.

For the dining room, Hutton and Silver devised an all-white scheme. Around the table covered with painters' canvas dropcloths stand white-painted Louis XVI chairs. French doors open to the garden for summer entertaining. Terra cotta figure, Elsa Peretti terra cotta candlesticks, and potted boxwood are arranged on the summertime dining table.

A grand staircase leads to the five bedrooms upstairs. A second stair leads on up to the widow's walk on the roof.

Nine framed etchings of Spanish bullfights are mounted above the bed in the guest bedroom, *opposite*. A forties bed was painted white and striéd with blue by the owner.

In the main bedroom, the same pale color scheme provides a restful background for a handsome wicker bed with white linens, and for an odd pair of chairs previously used on a set for the cult movie *Harold and Maude*. Plaster wine jug lamps designed by John Dickinson.

SAN FRANCISCO CATALOGUE: DESIGN AND STYLE RESOURCES

By Diane Dorrans Saeks

From San Francisco to Mendocino, and in towns that are just a dot on the map, Northern California's top designers, architects, furniture designers, emerging artists, and style-store founders dream, imagine, create, inspire, and set trends. Today, creativity and originality are more than spiritual ideals—they also mean good business. Revering traditional crafts but gaining an edge using new technologies, a variety of homegrown designers dream up glazed white platters from raw clay and modernist houses from sketches and blueprints. They fashion elegant tables and curlicue gates from unpromising raw metal. The best craftspeople make classic glass goblets and bowls and for-the-ages wrought-iron stair rails by harnessing hot air, power, skill, focus, and optimism.

The following is my personal pick of the best Northern California has to offer. It's an eclectic list with large and small design stores, showrooms, galleries, antiques shops, and salvage yards. They're special, infused with the passion and vision of highly opinionated and motivated founders or knowledgeable owners. They work with power and certainty to find and develop exceptional merchandise.You will be pulled in by their generous spirit—and moved to return.

MUSEUMS AND GALLERIES

Ansel Adams Center
250 Fourth Street.
For viewing the best photography and finding new talent.

Berkeley Art Museum
2626 Bancroft Way, Berkeley.
Avant-garde and mainstream shows of contemporary arts. Provocative photography shows.

California Historical Society Museum
678 Mission Street.
Exhibits chronicling the evolution of California and its history. Artifacts, books, printed ephemera.

California Palace of the Legion of Honor
Lincoln Park.
An enduring passion of mine. Dramatic location, classical building. Dream from gallery to gallery after paying homage to graphic arts and to Rodin.

Cartoon Art Museum
814 Mission Street.
Collections of cartoon art, exploring a variety of ways to tell a story. Debut collections and classics.

M. H. de Young Memorial Museum
Golden Gate Park.
Art of the Americas, ancient glass, exhibitions for children, works in oil, and fine furniture. (Don't miss Sunday afternoon band concerts at the elegant band shell nearby.)

The Mexican Museum
Fort Mason.
Small, stimulating museum in old portside army buildings.

San Francisco Craft and Folk Art Museum
Fort Mason.
Small but charming museum showing international collections of contemporary and traditional arts and crafts. While at Fort Mason, be sure to visit Greens Restaurant, and to meander down to the old piers for fine views of San Francisco Bay.

San Francisco Museum of Modern Art
151 Third Street.
Take time to ponder new video art and challenging photography along with new acquisitions and old favorites in this new Mario Botta–designed brick building. (A personal favorite: The sunny top-floor Fisher Family Galleries.)

San Jose Museum of Modern Art
110 South Market Street, San Jose.
Worth the trip to visit this fine gallery of contemporary arts. Ongoing shows of works by leading American artists from the permanent collection of the Whitney Museum. It is also worth a detour to visit the new technology museum and the children's museum, designed by Ricardo Legoretta.

Strybing Arboretum and Botanical Gardens
Golden Gate Park.
Excellent decades-old tree collections. Take a stroll in the didactic gardens.

Yerba Buena Center for the Arts
701 Mission Street.
Excellent venue for emerging artists working in many media. Also, offbeat shows, smaller yet rewarding exhibits.

DESIGN AND STYLE STORES

Be adventurous. Tour the city's best galleries and the arboretum to catch the zeitgeist. Many of the best design and style stores are on Fillmore Street, Hayes Street, Brady Street (actually a lane off Market Street), downtown Post and Sutter Streets, the western end of Polk Street, and around Union Square. For top-notch stores, explore Fillmore Street from Jackson to Bush. Then march along outer Sacramento Street for style shopping and neighborhood flavor. And don't forget chic South Park, funky South of Market, and the edgy Mission District.

AD/50
711 Sansome Street. One of the few San Francisco furniture companies dealing in fine midcentury modern. Downtown location for classic contemporary furniture (including designs by Park Furniture and Christopher Deam).

Agraria
1050 Howard Street. (By appointment only: 415-863-7700) Very San Francisco. A fragrant favorite. Maurice Gibson and Stanford Stevenson's classic potpourri and soaps, colognes and burning sticks are tops. (Best selection is at Gump's.)

Alabaster
597 Hayes Street. Nelson and Paul have a vision—and it's entirely in white. White pottery, white chairs, clear vintage glass, plus pale and interesting prints and photographs. Chic!

Alemany Flea Market
Junction of Highway 280 and Highway 101. Free Sunday entertainment! Funky finds, furniture, books, silver, vintage photographs, Oriental art, hippie posters, excellent junk.

Anderson Harrison Books
552 Hayes Street. (Formerly called Beat Books) In this hushed setting, find rare and out-of-print books on architecture, decorative arts, antiques, social history, design, and art.

Antique & Art Exchange
3419 Sacramento Street. All the top decorators drop in for ever-changing displays of eclectic *plein air* paintings, elegant silverware, fine furniture, porcelains, silver frames, painted boxes, exceptional tramp art, Venetian glass, furnishings of impressive provenance.

Arch
407 Jackson Street. Inspire the artist in you! Susan Colliver's shop sells supplies for designers, architects, and artists—and home improvement fanatics. Excellent selection of papers.

Banana Republic
Flagship store at Grant Avenue and Sutter Street (and many other California locations, including Beverly Hills). Superbly selected home collection of linens, glassware, silverware, napkins, pillows, vases, décor—all with the classic Banana Republic sensibility.

Bauerware
3886 Seventeenth Street. Interior designer/contractor Lou Ann Bauer's new shop sells more than 1,600 pulls and knobs and other decorative delights. Traditional polished brass, vintage Bakelite, resin, wood, and rock knobs. (New customers often walk in with dresser drawers in tow.)

Bell'occhio
8 Brady Street. Charm and grace. Claudia Schwartz and Toby Hanson's whimsical little boutique offers Florentine soaps, hand-painted ribbons, French silk velvet flowers. Trips to Paris supply charming antiques, hats, posters, and retro-chic Parisian face powders.

Bloomers
2975 Washington Street. The chic people's flower and vase shop. Top people speed-dial Patric Powell, who offers the freshest cut flowers and orchids in terra-cotta pots, as well as dozens of vases, French ribbons, and baskets. Nothing overdone or fussy here—just nature's natural beauty.

Bouvardia
1977 Union Street. Compelling collection of vases that flatter flowers—and the blooms to fill them. Fragrant plants, and unusual orchids in decorative pots. (While in the Cow Hollow district, stroll along Union Street to Dosa and Workshop, then stop for coffee at Rose's Cafe and dinner at Plump Jack Cafe.)

Britex
146 Geary Street. Browse for hours. Excellent home design sections. Action central for thousands of fabrics. World-class selections of classic and unusual furnishing textiles, braids, notions.

Brown Dirt Cowboys
2406 Polk Street. Painted and refurbished furniture, housewares.

Builders Booksource
Ghirardelli Square, 900 North Point. Excellent resource for design and architecture books. In-depth selections of how-to books, plus regional style books.

Bulgari
237 Post Street.
The best diamonds, yes, but much more. Accessories, too. Browse in the elegant upstairs silver department— it's heaven. Then lavish something sparkling and elegant upon yourself.

Buu
506 Hayes Street. (Pronounced "boo!") Roxy Buu's style store offers colorful and charming accessories.

Candelier
60 Maiden Lane. Designer Wade Benson's beautifully styled candles, books, vases, home accoutrements, and updated tabletop decor.

Cartier
231 Post Street. Jewels and watches, but also clocks and other-worldly must-haves. Elegant selection of accessories, silver, crystal, vases, porcelain.

Columbine Design
1541 Grant Avenue. Kathleen Dooley displays fresh flowers and gifts, along with shells, graphic framed butterflies, bugs, and beetles.

The Cottage Table Company
550 Eighteenth Street. Fine craftsman Tony Cowan's heirloom-quality hardwood tables made to order. Shipping available.

Crate & Barrel
Grant Avenue at Maiden Lane (also in Stanford Shopping Center, Palo Alto, and other locations). Excellent basics: bed linens, glassware, silverware, picnic baskets. Great for first apartments, vacation houses, holiday entertaining.

Dandelion
55 Potrero Avenue. Old favorite. Japanese-influenced aesthetic— very versatile; antiques.

David Luke & Associate
773 Fourteenth Street. Antiques, vintage tableware, funky furniture, old garden ornaments —some of them from the estates of England. (David's boxer, Baby, is his associate.)

Decorum
1400 Vallejo Street. Collector Jack Beeler's art deco domain. Superb lighting, furniture.

De Vera
580 Sutter Street. Federico de Vera's outstanding gallery of style includes ceramics and pottery, antique and rare Venetian glass, *objets trouves*, sculpture, hand-hewn tables, *santos*, paintings, furniture. A must-visit, one-of-a-kind store. Remarkable small-scale finds, and original designs by de Vera.

De Vera Jewelry
29 Maiden Lane. One-of-a-kind jewelry with an East-West sensibility.

Earthsake
2076 Chestnut Street (also in the Embarcadero Center, as well as in Berkeley and Palo Alto). Stylish earth-friendly stores with pure and simple tableware, furniture, untreated bed linens and towels.

F. Dorian
388 Hayes Street. Cosmopolitan treasures galore at excellent prices. Contemporary accessories, folk arts, and antiques.

Fillamento
2185 Fillmore Street. Trend alert! For more than a dozen years, a "museum" for design aficionados. Owner Iris Fuller stacks three floors with style-conscious furniture, tableware, towels, mirrors, glass, toiletries, frames, lamps, linens, beds, partyware, and gifts. Iris is first with new designers and supports local talent, including Nik Weinstein, Ann Gish, Annieglass, and Cyclamen.

Fioridella
1920 Polk Street. Colorful, joyful, and fun. For more than seventeen years, this store has offered the most beautiful flowers and plants. Kelly Schrock displays a fine selection of decorative accessories and versatile vases.

Flax Art and Design
1699 Market Street. Vast collections of frames, papers, boxes, art books, furnishings, lighting, and tabletop accessories. One-stop shopping for art supplies. Catalogue.

Forrest Jones
3274 Sacramento Street. Look at the baskets piled on the sidewalk, then poke about among the housewares, porcelain, excellent lamps inside.

Forza
1742 Polk Street. Subtle colorations. Handcrafted furniture, candles, accessories with an urbane elegance. Great aesthetic.

Fraenkel Gallery
49 Geary Boulevard. Tip-top photography gallery.

George
2411 California Street. Pet paradise. Style for dogs and cats, including Todd Oldham– and Tom Bonauro–designed charms, toys, cedar pillows, bowls, and accessories. Best dog treats: handmade whole grain biscuits.

Gordon Bennett
2102 Union Street (also at Ghirardelli Square and in Burlingame). This growing business offers fresh garden style throughout the seasons. Vases, plants, books, candles, decoupage plates, and tools. (Ask the owner to explain the name—and to introduce his standard poodles.)

Green World Mercantile

2340 Polk Street.
Herbs, flowering plants, and gardening equipment. Earth-friendly housewares, clothing, gardening equipment, books, and unpretentious decorative accessories.

Gump's

135 Post Street.
A must-visit! This new, chic Gump's has superbly selected fine crafts, art, and Orient-inspired accessories, plus tip-top names in silver, crystal. Cushy and very elegant bed linens. Treasures large and small. Be sure to visit the Treillage garden antiques shop and the decorative glass department. Catalogue.

Gypsy Honeymoon

Twenty-fourth Street at Guerrero Street.
Magical and romantic decor. Art glass, refurbished furniture, beds, old mirrors, trunks, framed vintage prints.

Hermes

212 Stockton Street.
Head upstairs, up the limestone steps. Silk scarves here are the ultimate in timeless style, but pass them (for the moment) to find tableware, blankets, cashmere throws, picnicware, silver, glassware, chic decor.

House of Mann

2727 Mariposa Street, No. 104.
Great California style. Located in a former mayonnaise factory, this striking interior design studio is far from white bread! Ron Mann's muscular Douglas fir and steel furniture. Louise Mann's handpainted fabrics. Fresh and modern.

In My Dreams

1300 Pacific Avenue.
Hard to find but worth taking the time. Jewelry designer Harry Fireside's dreamy shop offers soaps, antiques, and Chinese lanterns.

Intérieur Perdu

340 Bryant Street.
It's a little hard to spot. Hint: look in the loading dock. Fresh-off-the-boat French antiques of the funky, charming, hard-to-find kind. Fritzi, Coco, and Fred's excellent adventure!

Japonesque

824 Montgomery Street.
Serene gallery. Passionate Koichi Hara demonstrates his lifelong devotion to refinement, tradition, harmony, simplicity, and natural materials. Japanese sculpture, glass, furniture.

Jefferson Mack Metals

2094 Oakdale Avenue.
Jefferson Mack handcrafts iron gates, fences, balustrades, and furniture the old-fashioned way—with his hands, handmade tools, and his fired-up forge. Blacksmiths in San Francisco? Visit Jefferson and see the white-hot metal, and then the one-of-a-kind, heirloom-quality gazebos, tools, tables.

Juicy News

2453 Fillmore Street.
This neighborhood favorite is a jumping joint for every possible international fashion, design, architecture, and style magazine—and fresh fruit refreshments.

Kozo Arts

1967A Union Street.
Handcrafted papers in traditional Japanese style. Unusual textures and colors. Custom-crafted albums, address books, boxes, invitations, and photo frames.

Limn

290 Townsend Street.
Dan Friedlander's empire! The place to be on Saturday afternoons after the Farmers' Market at Ferry Plaza. One of only a few Northern California stores selling top-of-the-line contemporary furniture, accessories, and lighting by more than three hundred international manufacturers. Well-priced, to-go collections along with to-order Philippe Starck, B & B Italia, Andree Putman, and Mathieu & Ray, plus top Northern California talent. Visit the new gallery behind the store.

MAC

1543 Grant Avenue.
Chris Ospital's trend-setting salon sells style inspiration, accessories. Stop and chat: Talent-spotter Chris knows who's new. Take a detour to MAC at Claude Lane, between Bush and Sutter Streets, to visit Ben Ospital and see USDA's selection of handsome modernist furniture.

Macy's

Union Square.
The jam-packed Cellar has an impressive and thorough selection of kitchen equipment, tools, dinnerware, glasses, tableware. Furniture and accessories floors and the interior design department are now in the old Emporium building on Market Street.

Maison d'Etre

92 South Park.
In a Toby Levy-designed building, changing collections of vintage garden furniture (for indoors), lighting, handblown glass bowls by local artists, candlesticks, metal vases, and candles are presented with spirit. (While at South Park, shop at Isda & Co.'s outlet, then sip an espresso at South Park Cafe.)

Mike Furniture

Fillmore Street at Sacramento Street.
Directed by Mike Moore and partner Mike Thakar and their energetic crew, this friendly, sunny store offers updated furniture classics-with-a-twist by Mike Studio, Beverly, and other manufacturers. Custom and bespoke design here is very accessible. One-stop shopping for fast-delivery sofas, blankets, fabrics, lamps, tables, fabrics, accessories.

Modernism
685 Market Street.
This outstanding international contemporary art gallery represents a broad range of top artists.

Naomi's Antiques to Go
1817 Polk Street.
Hard-to-find American art pottery! Lots of Bauer, of course, plus historic studio pottery. American railroad, hotel, luxury liner, navy, dude ranch, and bus depot china.

Nest
2300 Fillmore Street.
In a dreamy old Victorian building where a neighborhood pharmacy operated for decades, Marcella Madsen and Judith Gilman have feathered their new Nest. Seductive treasures include books, silk flowers, antique beds, rustic French antiques, lavender sachets, sofas, Shabby Chic bed linens, and Bravura lampshades and pillows.

Paint Effects
2426 Fillmore Street.
Colorful! Inspiring. Sheila Rauch and partner Patricia Orlando have a fanatical following for their innovative paints and tools. Hands-on paint technique classes by talented artist Lesley Ruda, along with everything for French washes, gilding, liming, crackle glazing, decoupage, stenciling, and other fine finishes.

The Painters Place
355 Hayes Street.
Extraordinary frames—all handcrafted and hand-finished with water gilding, gessoing, and other traditional methods. Beautifully crafted simple and elaborate frames in a multitude of styles.

Paxton Gate
1204 Stevenson Street.
It's a bit out of the way, but Peter Kline and Sean Quigley's gardening store offers uncommon plants (such as sweetly scented Buddha's Hand citron trees), vases, and hand-forged tools.

Polanco
393 Hayes Street.
This colorful gallery offers superbly presented Mexican fine arts, photography, and crafts. Museum curator Elsa Cameron says you can't find better quality anywhere, even in Mexico.

Polo Ralph Lauren
Crocker Galleria, corner of Post and Kearny Streets.
Ralph Lauren's handsome emporium purveys the complete Home collection. Great beds, best-quality furniture, towels, and linens, and the trappings of fine rooms and country houses.

Pomp and Circumstance
561 Hayes Street.
Gunther's great little shop sells quirky, individual decor. Fun to visit.

Pottery Barn
Stores throughout California.
This San Francisco–based company has stores all over the country, including New York. Action central for contemporary furniture, rugs, well-priced draperies, special orders. Practical, easy-to-live-with home style. Excellent bedroom basics; classic, accessible design. Catalogue.

Rayon Vert
3187 Sixteenth Street.
Brave the (sometimes) gritty Mission streets and discover brilliant floral designer Kelly Kornegay's garden of earthly delights—which just got bigger and better. Vintage furniture, Oriental porcelains, flowers, artifacts, glasses, architectural fragments in a full-tilt, humble-chic setting.

RH
2506 Sacramento Street.
This well-edited garden and tableware store has beeswax candles, vases, goblets. Inspiring selection of cachepots. Lavender topiaries, too.

Richard Hilkert Books
333 Hayes Street.
Designers and book addicts telephone Richard to order out-of-print style books and the newest design books. Browse here, buy, then stroll to the Opera or the Symphony.

Rizzoli Books
117 Post Street.
Library-like, well-located near Gap, Polo, Diesel, TSE, Gump's. Book-lovers' paradise. Outstanding collection of design, architecture, and photography books.

SAN FRANCISCO DESIGN CENTER
Henry Adams Street (near Fifteenth Street). Come to this South of Market design destination with your decorator or architect. Selections and temptations are extraordinary. Showplace West, the Vermont Center, Baker Knapp & Tubbs, and other nearby showrooms offer top-of-the-line furniture, fabrics, and furnishings. Randolph & Hein, Kneedler-Fauchere, Baker, Sloan Miyasato, Shears & Window, Clarence House, Jack Lenor Larsen, Palacek, Brunschwig & Fils, Schumacher, Milieux, McRae Hinckley, Donghia, Summit Furniture, Enid Ford Atelier, McGuire, and Houles are among my personal style favorites. (Purchases may be made through a buying service.) Explore the neighborhood and find Therien & Co (Scandinavian, Continental, and English antiques), Therien Studio Workshops, Robert Hering Interiors, John Drum Antiques, and the handsome Palladian outpost of Ed Hardy San Francisco (finest eclectic antiques, garden antiques).

San Francisco Museum of Modern Art MuseumStore

151 Third Street.
Very thorough selections of design and art books, modernist accessories, framed posters, handcrafted designs by local artists. Browse, then surge upstairs to the galleries.

Satin Moon Fabrics

32 Clement Street.
Twenty-seven-year-old store sells a superb collection of decorating linens, trims, chintzes, and other well-priced fabrics.

Scheuer Linens

340 Sutter Street.
Old San Francisco favorite for fine-quality bed linens, blankets. Staff facilitates custom orders particularly well.

Shabby Chic

3075 Sacramento Street (also in Santa Monica). Specializes in fat and slimmed-down chairs and cozy sofas with comfortable airs and loose-fitting slipcovers.

Slips

1534 Grant Avenue.
Sami Rosenzweig's spirit lives on! Custom-made slipcovers for chairs, headboards, and sofas, plus draperies, ottomans.

Smedley Herrera

511 Laguna Street.
Friendly flower shop; handsome, natural flower arrangements.

Stanlee R. Gatti Flowers

Fairmont Hotel
(on Nob Hill).
Visit for fresh flowers, Agraria potpourri, vases, and candles.

Sue Fisher King

3067 Sacramento Street.
Cosmopolitan style for beds and tables. Sue King's Italian, French, and English bed linens, cashmere throws, and tableware are the prettiest and most chic. Luxurious blankets, hand-dyed Himalayan cashmere-fringed throws, accessories, books, soaps, furniture and Diptyque candles.

Sue Fisher King Home at Wilkes Bashford

375 Sutter Street.
Luscious luxuries. Sue's obsessive perfectionism is evident in her fine and thorough selections of Ann Gish linens, Florentine cashmere throws, beds, hand-blown glass, Venetian pillows, and *objets d'art* from Italy, France, London. Books.

Surprise Party

1900A Fillmore Street.
Conchological heaven! Susan Vanasco Howell's sweet side-by-side boutiques sell shells, prints, beads, coral. Specimen seashells.

Swallowtail

2217 Polk Street (also at 1429 Haight Street). Chic antiques—with bracing flea-market charm. Glamorous, all-white, sunny studio setting for furniture, glassware, paintings. Visit weekly for best finds (especially Sunday).

Thomas E. Cara

517 Pacific Avenue.
Old San Francisco with new steam. Espresso machines and hardware—from an authoritative family-owned company.

Tiffany & Co

350 Post Street.
Lust for a sapphire ring or a Paloma Picasso necklace, then step upstairs to the venerated crystal, china, and silver departments. Order Elsa Peretti's classic glasses, bowls, and silver.

Virginia Breier

3091 Sacramento Street.
A gallery for contemporary and traditional American crafts.

Williams-Sonoma

150 Post Street.
Flagship for the Williams-Sonoma cookware empire. Everything for cooks and kitchens. Delicacies, quality lifetime basics for both serious and dilettante cooks. Excellent catalogues.

William Stout Architectural Books

804 Montgomery Street.
Worth a detour. The best! Architect Bill Stout's chock-a-block bookstore specializes in old and new, basic and wonderfully obscure twentieth-century architecture publications, along with new and out-of-print interior design and garden books. Catalogues.

Worldware

336 Hayes Street.
Shari Sant's eco-store sells cozy sheets and blankets and such delights as patchwork pillows and aromatherapy candles. Interiors crafted by Dan Plummer from salvaged materials.

Zinc Details

1905 Fillmore Street.
Modernism rules! The store has a cult following. Well-priced contemporary furniture, lighting. Handblown glass vases and lampshades by California artists. Domain of Wendy Nishimura and Vasilios Kiniris. (No, they don't sell anything made of zinc.)

Zonal

2139 Polk Street.
Scott Kalmbach and Russell Pritchard set out for fresh fields and pastures new. Upholstery, bed linens—plus lots of friendly painted furniture.

Zonal Home Interiors

568 Hayes Street.
Russell Pritchard's pioneering store presents rustic furniture and decorative objects. He made rust and old paint textured with loving use fashionable. Old Americana at its most whimsical.

BERKELEY, ELMWOOD

Head over the Bay Bridge for design store action focused on wonderfully revived Fourth Street. We recommend, too, a detour to Cafe Fanny, the Acme Bread bakery, Chez Panisse, and the Elmwood.

Berkeley Mills
2830 Seventh Street. Handcrafted Japanese- and Mission-influenced furniture. Blends the best of old-world craftsmanship and high-tech methods. Catalogue.

Builders Booksource
1817 Fourth Street (also in San Francisco). Definitive selection of essential design books. Well-considered design, architecture, gardening, and building tomes.

Camps and Cottages
2109 Virginia Street. Visit the cafe at Chez Panisse or the great Cheese Board, then pop in for a visit. This little shop/garden sells charming homey furniture and low-key accessories. Owner Molly Hyde English has perfect pitch for Adirondack styles.

Elica's Papers
1801 Fourth Street. Japanese handmade papers. Custom-made stationery, albums, frames, paper wall hangings, decorative boxes, sketchbooks (some from mulberry bark). Papers can be used for making lampshades, window shades, screens, even wallpaper.

Erica Tanov
1627 San Pablo Avenue (also on Claremont Avenue, Berkeley). The place for linen pajamas and romantic bed accessories. Erica's lace-edged sheets and shams and linen duvet covers are quietly luxurious. (While in the Cedar Street neighborhood, drop into Kermit Lynch Wine Merchants, Acme Bread, and Cafe Fanny.)

The Gardener
1836 Fourth Street (also, a new country store in Healdsburg). Pioneer Alta Tingle's brilliant, bustling garden-style store sells vases, books, tables, chairs, paintings, clothing and tools for nature-lovers—whether they have a garden or are just dreaming. Asian antiques, terracotta pots. Consistently original, classic style.

Lighting Studio
1808 Fourth Street. Lighting design services. Cheery and chic contemporary lamps.

The Magazine
1823 Eastshore Highway (also, a new store near the Embarcadero in San Francisco). Brian and Rainer's excellent idea! Six-year-old store sells contemporary American and European designs. Artemide, Flos, Flexform, Aero and Cappellini, and many others.

Omega Too
2204 San Pablo Avenue. Founded by a hippie collective and still thriving. Gold—from salvaged houses in the area: building materials, fixtures, lighting, plus treasures. Some aficionados mine this store and sibling Ohmega Salvage, at 2407 San Pablo Avenue, weekly.

Sur la Table
1806 Fourth Street (also in San Francisco). Outpost of the twenty-four-year-old Seattle cookware company, but feels entirely original to Berkeley. In a five-thousand-square-foot "warehouse," the shop stocks every goodie, gadget, tool, utensil, plate, machine, and kitchen decoration for serious and dilettante cooks. Catalogue.

Tail of the Yak
2632 Ashby Avenue. Gracious Alice Hoffman Erb and Lauren Adams Allard have created a magical mystery store that is always worth a trip—across the bay or across the Atlantic. Whimsical accessories, wedding gifts, Mexican furniture, fabrics, ribbons, notecards, linens, antique jewelry, and Lauren's books.

Trout Farm
2179 Bancroft Way. Smart modernists (and their chic friends) have been finding mid-century furniture, glass, and paintings here for years. (Visit Designs for Living, Market Street, in San Francisco, too.)

Urban Ore
1333 Sixth Street. Recycled style! One city block of salvaged architecture and house throwaways. Doors, window frames, shutters, lighting, furniture, and vintage fixtures. An adventure!

Zia Houseworks
1310 Tenth Street. Colin Smith's sun-filled gallery store offers a vivid variety of hand-crafted furniture designs and art. Maine Cottage and Mike Furniture Studio collections. Smith, who is also an artist, often has shows of his collages and compositions. (When in the neighborhood, hop over to Solano Avenue for book bargains.)

BIG SUR

The Phoenix
Highway 1. An enticing store where you can linger for hours to the sound of windchimes. Handcrafted decorative objects, candles, glass, books, sculpture, woven throws, hand-knit sweaters by Kaffe Fassett (who grew up in Big Sur), and soaps. Coast views from all windows. Crystals and handmade objects on all sides. Visit Nepenthe restaurant up the hill. The sixties spirit lives on in Big Sur.

BURLINGAME

Anugrah
220 California Drive (at Burlingame Avenue). The Sanskrit name means "divine blessings are a gift." You get the drift. Tranquil setting for Indonesian teak furniture, ceramics from Borneo, sea grass chairs, Chinese chests, aluminum vases, Anglo-Indian chairs.

CARMEL

Carmel Bay Company
Corner of Ocean and Lincoln Streets. Tableware, books, glassware, furniture, prints.

Francesca Victoria
250 Crossroads Boulevard. Decorative accessories for garden and home. Fresh style.

Luciano Antiques
San Carlos and Fifth Streets. Cosmopolitan antiques. Wander through the vast rooms to view furniture, lighting, sculpture, and handsome reproductions.

CARMEL VALLEY

Tancredi & Morgen
7174 Carmel Valley Road. Easygoing country style with painted furniture, old-fashioned fabrics in handsome colors, painted flower vases, candles, furniture. (Just across the road from Quail Lodge, site of the annual spring Carmel Garden and Flower Show.)

EMERYVILLE

Cyclamen Collections
1311 67th Street. (Information: 510-597-3640) Ceramics designer Julie Sanders is beloved for her colorful Neo Traditions dinnerware. Occasionally she has popular seconds sales.

FORT BRAGG

Studio Z Mendocino
711 North Main Street. (Phone 707-964-2522 for an appointment) Trend-setting interior designers like Michael Berman and Barbara

Barry of Los Angeles love Zida Borcich, one of the last letterpress printers. Glamorous Zida hand-sets old letterpress ornaments on fine papers and prints on antique presses. Her gold foil and black logos—flowers, teapots, bees, dragonflies, a chef, a watering can—are chic and smart for modern correspondence, and letter writing in bed.

GLEN ELLEN

The Olive Press
Jack London Village, 14301 Arnold Drive. Everything pertaining to olives, including handblown martini glasses. Extra-virgin olive oils, cooking equipment, tableware, linens.

HEALDSBURG

The Gardener
516 Dry Creek Road (off Highway 1). (Thursday, Friday, Saturday) Alta Tingle's The Gardener goes country. Citrus trees in terra-cotta pots, Indian pleasure tents, bamboo trellises, tools, outdoor furniture—and the Gardener

Club chair (it's reminiscent of a wheelbarrow) designed by Ted Boerner.

Jimtown Store
6706 State Highway 128. Cycle on country roads to J. Carrie Brown and John Werner's friendly store in the Alexander Valley. The Mercantile & Exchange vintage Americana is cheerful and very well-priced. Taste superb new preserves.

Sotoyome Tobacco Company
119 Plaza Street. Myra and Wade Hoefer's chic cigar store is in a Greek Revival building, originally a Bank of America. The name is that of the original Spanish Land Grant upon which Healdsburg was founded. Humidors, French silver cutters, cigar posters, and cigars.

MENDOCINO

When in Mendocino, be sure to walk along the coast on the headlands, and visit the Mendocino Arts Center.

Fittings for Home and Garden
45050 Main Street. Furniture, lighting,

hardware, accessories. Large selection of garden tools and lamps.

The Golden Goose
45094 Main Street. Superb, pristine classic linens and antiques, overlooking the headlands and the ocean. Baby linens, cashmere and merino throws. The most stylish store in Mendocino.

Lark In The Morning
10460 Kasten Street. Handcrafted musical instruments to display and play. Traditional harps, guitars, violins, as well as ethnic instruments from around the world: ouds, bagpipes, pennywhistles, flutes, and even CDs. (You can also find them on the Web.)

Sticks
45085 Albion Street. The utterly charming "twigs and branches" store of Bob Keller. Rustic furniture, decor and accessories—without the cliches. Great chairs, willow headboards.

WilkesSport
10466 Lansing Street. Wilkes Bashford, a Mendocino resident, showcases Northern

California talent plus antiques and fine paintings.

MENLO PARK

Artefact Design and Salvage
966 Willow Road. (By appointment: 650-321-0907) David Allen is a finder of objects. Architectural and garden antiques.

Millstreet
1131 Chestnut Street. Objects of desire: Continental antiques, Ann Gish bed linens and silks, Tuscan pottery, tapestries, orchids, mirrors, botanical prints, silk and cashmere throws.

MILL VALLEY

Capricorn Antiques & Cookware
100 Throckmorton Avenue. This quiet, reliable store seems to have been here forever. Basic cookware, antique tables, dressers, and cupboards.

Mill Valley Sculpture Gardens
219 Shoreline Highway. A fine collection of outdoor sculpture curated by the talented Schwartzes—Isis Spinola Schwartz, her husband, David, and his parents, Howard and Leah. Sculptors Barton Rubenstein and Lucia Eames of Design Demetrios are standouts among the forty-five artists. Fountains, kinetic works, furniture.

Prairie Garden
14 Miller Avenue. Seasonal garden style for indoors or out. Furniture, plants, great color palette.

Pullman & Co
108 Throckmorton Avenue. Style inspiration. Luxurious bed linens (the standouts are those by Ann Gish) along with furniture, lamps, tableware, and accessories.

Smith & Hawken
35 Corte Madera (also in Berkeley, Los Gatos, Palo Alto, San Francisco, Santa Rosa, and points beyond). The original garden style store . . . now much copied. Nursery (begun under horticulturist Sarah Ham-

mond's superb direction) and store. Everything for gardens. Catalogues.

Summer House Gallery
21 Throckmorton Avenue. Fragrant with aromatherapy candles and handcrafted soaps. Impossible to leave empty-handed. Artist-crafted accessories and (to order) comfortable sofas and chairs. Witty handcrafted frames, glassware, candlesticks, slipcovered loveseats, vases, tables, and gifts.

OAKLAND

Maison d'Etre
5330 College Avenue. Indoor/outdoor style. Eccentric and whimsical decorative objects and furniture for rooms and gardens. (Be sure to stroll down College Avenue to Paul Bertolli's restaurant, Oliveto, and the Market Hall with it's fruit, pasta, and Peaberry's coffee.)

OAKVILLE

Oakville Grocery
7856 St. Helena Highway.

No visit to the Napa Valley would be complete without a stop here. Extraordinary wine selection, prepared foods, local olive oils, herbs, international cheeses, organic coffees, and locally baked artisan breads. Everything for picnics, parties. Catalogue. (Check out Dean & DeLuca in St. Helena, too.)

PALO ALTO

Bell's Books
536 Emerson Street. Walls of fine and scholarly selections of new, vintage, and rare books on every aspect of interior design, gardens, and gardening. Also literature, decorative arts, photography, cooking.

Hillary Thatz
Stanford Shopping Center. Reliable. A dreamy view of the interiors of England as seen by Cheryl Driver. Traditional accessories, furniture, frames, decorative objects, and garden furnishings.

Polo Ralph Lauren
Stanford Shopping Center. Just gets better and better—great versatile decor, linens, blankets. A

spacious, gracious store that shows the expanding world imagined through Ralph Lauren's eyes. Outstanding selection of furniture, imaginary-heritage accessories. Catalogue.

RUTHERFORD

Olive Grove Sculpture Garden
Auberge du Soleil, 180 Rutherford Hill Road. Superb outdoor setting for seventy-five fine contemporary works by California sculptors. Curated by Ira Wolk.

ST. HELENA

Bale Mill Design
3431 North St. Helena Highway. Decorative and practical updated classic furniture in a wide range of styles. A favorite with decorators. Ira Yaeger paintings.

Calla Lily
1222 Main Street. Elegant European luxury bed linens, accessories, frames.

Ira Wolk Gallery
1235 Main Street.
Ira Wolk presents an uncommon selection of contemporary painters and sculptors.

St. Helena St. Helena Antiques
1231 Main Street.
Rustic furniture, vintage wine paraphernalia, vintage accessories. (Yes, the name is intentionally repetitious.)

Showplace North St. Helena
1350 Main Street (also in Carmel).
Interior design, fabrics, custom furniture.

Tantau
1220 Adams Street.
Charming atmosphere. Decorative accessories, furniture, handpainted furniture, gifts.

Tesoro
649 Main Street.
Stylish. Fresh-flower heaven. Topiaries, wreaths, vases, too. Weddings.

Tivoli
1432 Main Street.
Tom Scheibal and partners have created a sunny indoor/outdoor garden furniture and accessories store. Tables and chairs and occa-

sional pieces in iron, aluminum, concrete, and recycled redwood. Antique garden ornaments.

Vanderbilt & Co
1429 Main Street (also in the Stanford Shopping Center, Palo Alto).
The best! Extensive collections of luxury bed linens, books, glassware, Italian ceramics, accessories. A year-round favorite in the wine country.

SAN ANSELMO

Take a detour to this sleepy town to find a trove of antiques shops, antiques collectives, rare book galleries, excellent used book shops.

Modern i 1950
500 Red Hill Avenue.
Steven Cabella is passionate about modernism and time-warp midcentury (1935–65) furnishings. Vintage furnishings, Eames chairs, furniture by architects, objects, and artwork. Located in a restored modernist architect's office building.

SAN MATEO

Restoration Hardware
113 Hillsdale Mall (also located throughout California).
Excellent resource for traditional-style hardware and lighting, easygoing furniture, garden accessories. Always a thorough collection of design and style books.

SANTA ROSA

Randolph Johnson Studio
608 Fifth Street.
Master craftsman/ designer Randy Johnson makes dreamy furniture and accessories with superb detail in a wide range of styles. Draperies, painted finishes. Finest custom artistry.

SONOMA

Sloan and Jones
First Street West on the Square.
Friendly Ann Jones and Sheelagh Sloan run and stock this splendid antiques store. Set in a fine old corner building, it's the place for country porcelains,

silverware, Asian vintage furniture, photography, linens, and table accessories.

Studio Sonoma
380 First Street West.
Designer Robin Nelson offers beautifully selected home furnishings, paintings, slipcovers, lighting. Seasonal delights include hammocks for summer, quilts for winter.

TIBURON

Ruth Livingston Design
72 Main Street.
Interior designer Ruth Livingston's studio offers elegant art, furniture, crafts.

FLEA MARKETS
Any serious style watcher will tell you, watch newspaper listings for auctions, antiques sales, estate sales, weekend flea markets, and seasonal vintage and antique furniture shows. Catch flea market fever in San Francisco, but don't forget to adventure to old, small towns in California's hinterlands. In dusty, cobwebbed shops you may find heirloom linens and laces, old brass beds, Edwardian chairs, Venetian vases, faded prints and hand-bound books, old tools, rusty tins, and quirky signs. These eccentricities give new rooms history and individuality.

INDEX

Allen, Jeanne **106-113**

Backen, Howard **144-149**

Belfield, Jois and Irving **62-63**

Bennett, Thomas **60-61, 107, 140-141**

Bourn, Mr. and Mrs. William Bowers II **26**

Burn, Diane **138-139**

Caen, Herb **6-7**

Cameron, Elsa **108, 114-117**

Church, Thomas **44**

Cowan, Tony **60**

Cyckevic, Michael **115**

Dickinson, John **16, 17, 48-55, 79, 84, 96-97, 165, 172-175**

Dreher, Patricia **146**

Du Casse, Ralph **16, 49, 172-175**

Dutton, Jan **142-143**

Eckbo, Garrett **44**

Filoli **20-29**

Ford, Eleanor **84**

Gleeson, Pat **158-163**

Grant, Marc **106-113**

Hail, Anthony **23, 36-41**

Hill, Frederick **152-153**

Howard, John Galen **155**

Hunziker, Terry **158-163**

Hutchinson, Robert **82-91**

Hutton, Gary **58-59, 122-123, 182-193**

Jeanrenaud, Joan **158-163**

Keesling, Mary **96-97**

Lamb, Scott **76-77**

Lansdown, Carole **53**

Leavitt, Craig **74-75**

Levy, Toby **Cover, 170-171**

MacMasters, Russell **1**

MacSweeny, Angus **43**

Magill, Ami **138-139**

Mann, Ron **18, 19, 49, 70-73, 83**

McCredie, Darwin **14**

McKeon, Elaine **42-47**

Mendelsohn, Barbara and Richard **128-133**

Meyer, Byron **83, 92-95**

Michael, Eileen **98-101**

Morgan, Julia **37**

Nicholas, Edward **183**

Peugh, David **107, 122-123**

Pfister, Charles **56-57**

Platner, Warren **65**

Polk, Willis **25-26, 31, 69**

Porter, Bruce **26**

Posey, Charles **36-41**

Putman, Andree **16**

Rosekrans, John and Dodie **12-13, 30-35**

Rosequist, Ivy **19, 71**

Roth, Lurline **23**

Salmon, Sandy **165-169**

Schaeffer, Rudolph **83**

Severson, Peter and Judy **176-181**

Silver, Steve **182-193**

Smith, Glen **102-105**

Solomon, Daniel **158-163**

Steffy, Robert **118-121**

Strauss, Joseph **25**

Swig, Charlotte **10-11**

Taylor, Michael **12-13, 30-35, 42-47, 84, 92-95**

Tedrick, Michael **60-61**

Trevisan, Chuck **154-157**

Walker, Jeffrey **78-81**

Walker, Sandy **98-101**

Warren, Whitney **2**

Weaver, Stephen **74-75**

Welch, Mr. and Mrs. Andrew **31**

Wetzel, Harry and Maggie **165-169**

Whiteside, William **68-69**

Williams, Chuck **150-151**

Winslow, Chuck **64-67, 84, 124-127, 152-153**

Worn, Isabella **26**

Wright, Frank Lloyd **106-112**

Wurster, William **60**

Yazzolino, Sam **79**

COMPOSED IN VELJOVIC MEDIUM

BY CREATIVE GRAPHICS, INC.,
ALLENTOWN, PENNSYLVANIA

PRINTED AND BOUND BY
DAI NIPPON PRINTING CO., LTD.,
TOKYO, JAPAN